Operational Policy Making for Professional Security

Operational Policy Making for Professional Security

Practical Policy Skills for the Public and Private Sector

Allen R. Sondej, J.D., D.Sc. CSLMP (ABD)

AMSTERDAM • BOSTON • HEIDELBERG • LONDON
NEW YORK • OXFORD • PARIS • SAN DIEGO
SAN FRANCISCO • SINGAPORE • SYDNEY • TOKYO

Butterworth-Heinemann is an imprint of Elsevier

Acquiring Editor: Tom Stover
Editorial Project Manager: Hilary Carr
Project Manager: Punithavathy Govindaradjane
Designer: Mark Rogers

Butterworth-Heinemann is an imprint of Elsevier
The Boulevard, Langford Lane, Kidlington, Oxford OX5 1GB, UK
225 Wyman Street, Waltham, MA 02451, USA

ISBN: 978-0-12-801628-2

British Library Cataloguing-in-Publication Data
A catalogue record for this book is available from the British Library

Library of Congress Cataloging-in-Publication Data
A catalog record for this book is available from the Library of Congress

For Information on all Butterworth-Heinemann publications
visit our website at http://store.elsevier.com/

Working together
to grow libraries in
developing countries

www.elsevier.com • www.bookaid.org

Contents

Preface

POLICY

This book gives organizational leaders a one stop reference and resource for producing effective and defensible policies. The chapters are designed to be useful to the smallest organization yet provide building blocks to work with even the largest organizations.

Each chapter will include real life case studies that illustrate the concepts covered and will include real life professional practice pointers. As a collateral function, this book contains information that is suitable for use as a university textbook. Each chapter has theoretical content that is broken down from source materials cited at the end of each chapter. This source material is supported by a case study suitable for class discussion and analysis. The book content relies heavily on my personal experiences and training in policy making in a high risk zero sum environment as well as my experiences as an advocate for best practices and accreditation. This approach comes from years of trying to find a singular practical answer to operational policy making. The focus of the book is professional security but the concepts are applicable to any organization from law enforcement to fooded service. Policy is policy and people are people.

We start the process by exploring selected theories of policy making and organization seeking to provide just enough academic context for practical use. We follow by asking the question "why bother?" which at face value may seem a bit flippant, yet I honestly believe that if more people and organizations asked this questions before undertaking tasks, life for them might be a lot easier.

Given the expansive nature of policy study this book is not intended to be a substitute for policy theory, organizational theory, or legal theory. It is not intended to be the basis for any legal advice, and any actions that involve organizational liability must be review by legal counsel. It is my sincere hope that readers of this book will take it as a starting point and research and publish additional new information or perspectives thereby expanding our field of knowledge.

About the Author

Allen R. Sondej served as a police officer for twenty-five years starting with the Trenton Police Department. He recently retired as a Captain with the South Brunswick Police Department in New Jersey. During his tenure the department he commanded the Support Services Division. As part of that assignment he was in charge of the contracting of police officers to private companies and individuals for security and traffic control services. This included client relations, post orders, payroll, and scheduling. This role complemented his private sector security experience. He was the agency accreditation manager bringing the department successfully through state and national accreditation. As part of that role he created the policy system for the department and routinely researched, developed, and implemented agency directives. He also was instrumental in developing homeland security initiatives for the Township of South Brunswick after the attacks of 9-11. He helped developed and oversee the police/school district security program to include response to active shooters and incident command. Additional support services responsibilities included administration, budget, logistic, training, communications and building maintenance and security. Each requiring distinct and effective policy. When the South Brunswick Police Department implemented a strategic policy of community policing he was instrumental in its growth. He developed and implemented programs such as the citizen's police academy, the police explorer post, and the police honor guard. He was also an experienced crime prevention officer who has planned and implemented many security-based loss prevention programs. While assigned to the community relations bureau he was assigned as the deputy public information officer. As a member and later commander of the training unit he authored many training programs such as liability mitigation, constitutional law updates, policy development, as well as training devoted to all aspects of policing. He is the co-founder of the PEEL Institute, an organization devoted to cultural change in American policing.

Prior to his law enforcement career he served in the United States Marine Corps and was called back to active service in support of Operations Desert Shield and Desert Storm as a Military Police Officer. He is currently the President of the New Jersey Public Safety Accreditation Coalition and is a frequent lecturer at the coalition's annual conference. He is also an Adjunct Professor at a State University and teaches all aspects of professional security, including risk mitigation. He is a graduate of both the FBI Law Enforcement Executive Development Seminar and the New Jersey State Association of Chiefs of Police Command and Leadership Academy, winning the Chief Harry Wilde Award for Academic Excellence. He received his Associates Degree in Criminal Justice from Mercer County Community College. He earned his Bachelor's Degree from New Jersey City University in Criminal Justice and was one of the very few to do it with a concentration in Security. As part of his undergraduate internship he co-authored a security customer service and training program and manual for Wackenhut Security Service and Bristol-Myers Squibb security. He earned his Juris Doctor from Seton Hall University School of Law. He is a current doctoral student and expects to achieve his Doctor of Science in Civil Security, Leadership, Management and Policy in 2016.

Al is an attorney admitted to the New Jersey Bar and the Bar of the Federal District Court of New Jersey. He is currently a part time attorney with an Edison N.J. law firm. Also prior to becoming a police officer, he was a security site manager, and a security account executive, responsible for providing all facets of security services to a Fortune 500 (#114 in 2010) company.

Leading up to his management positions he served as a security line supervisor and line officer. He holds certifications as a certified security officer and certified security supervisor. He was also selected as California Plant Protection, CPP Security Service National Officer of The Year. As a security consultant he has worked for companies such as E.R. Squibb and Sons, Michael Stevens Ltd., and Independent Pharmacy Alliance. This is the first book he has attempted to author. In each of his capacities he has been a recognized leader in policy development, accountability and training.

Allen R. Sondej, Esq.
Adjunct Professor, New Jersey City University

Acknowledgments

I would like to thank my wife Laura for all of the support and encouragement to pursue writing this book. I would not have been able to finish the manuscript without your proofreading and grammatical help. To my son Nick who helped with my research, I love you and you make me proud every day. To my peers who taught me many things about being a professional, there are too many to list, but you know who you are. To my editor, Hilary, thank you for your understanding and guidance. To my parents, thank you for teaching me never to quit. To my brother Gary and sister Jenn, family is everything. Finally, to everyone who stands between citizens like myself and all the dangerous things in the world, the U.S. military, law enforcement, security professionals and other first responders, thank you.

Theory and Organization

There are many books available that cover policy and practically all of them deal with either public policy or foreign policy. Most books deal with theory; this book is not one of them. This book is designed to be functional through a focus on internal regulation and direction of organizations through strategic and functional policy. This book is about the practice. The intent is to provide a resource that assists leaders in positively impacting their own organizational effectiveness.

To simplify matters, in this book the elements of policy are bifurcated into two types, strategic and operational. The practical goal of this book is to provide a resource that focuses on operational policy. Organizational leaders must have a skill set that allows them to transfer the goals and missions of organizations to action. The action occurs at the grassroots level; it does not occur in the board room or in executive staff meetings. The goals are carried out by the operational staff and this is where a policy system has the greatest impact. I hope practitioners of all levels will be able to apply the information in this book regardless of their experience or skill level.

This book is written largely from my background as a policy executive in law enforcement and from my experiences as a leader in best practices and accountability in law enforcement. I combine this with my legal education and experience as an attorney, which gives me a unique perspective on the drafting of directives and liability issues. My experiences as a university professor, teaching policy at all levels, has also been an opportunity to perform academic research. The degree program I teach in is intended for professionals, which gives me access to practitioners in the security field. As the president of a law enforcement accreditation organization devoted to best practices and accountability, I have significant policy-making experience.

Although this book is not one that is steeped in policy theory, there are many theories and resources that are applicable. It is not my intention to detail every applicable theory, only those that I feel are supportive to the goal of the book. It is my experience that policy writers are less concerned with the underlying theory and more concerned with the application. But in any endeavor, a strong foundation is needed, therefore it is important to provide some theoretical background to the policy process. This chapter will examine some foundational theories and tenets of policy.

POLICY DEVELOPMENT

The practice of policy making and drafting policy instruments calls into play a great many disciplines. One has to have a working knowledge of strategy, tactics, and the law and an understanding of human and organizational behavior, as well as the concepts of sensing and communicating. It takes years to amass these skill sets and it is often accomplished through trial and error. It is often time consuming and requires a certain level of understanding of the operation, the organization itself, and the threats and opportunities facing the organization. It is not uncommon for organizations to simply buy boilerplate policy manuals that are produced by reputable organizations, including law firms. Why bother learning a whole new skill set when one can just buy canned policies off the Internet? The first reason is the lack of flexibility. Using canned policies only works for your organization as it is; Boilerplate policies do not self-adjust to changes in the organization. This means that unless someone in the organization has a policy skill set, any changes to the directives may not be effective. The second reason is that using canned policies is a limited choice in that they may not be viewed as due diligence. A fixed set of policies can meet the needs of most organizations most of the time. But no organization is exactly like another and the world is not static. Even if you buy canned policies, someone in the organization has to be able to adapt these to fit individual organizational requirements. This requires a policy skill set. When it comes to operational policies, the adage "there is no need to reinvent the wheel" is a slippery slope. Each organization is different and their operational policies require tailoring. This is called *due diligence* in the legal world, which means you did the reasonable level of investigation and work to produce the product – you *do* have to reinvent the wheel. Think of it this way: Which looks better – an off-the-rack suit or a personally tailored one?

Policy is often driven by the industry or background of the writer. Lawyers, managers, subject matter experts, and employees all write policy. For example, many attorneys are involved in drafting policy implements, but these tend to be very legalistic. They also tend to be wordy and highly risk adverse. Lawyers tend to write in a highly technical manner, but effective operational policy must be simple and concise. Having lawyers as the primary authors of directives can be problematic as the writers often lack a true operational understanding of the nuts and bolts of the processes of the organization. Operational policies designed primarily to be legally defensible tend to be one dimensional. While great for the legal defense of policy, they can serve to undermine the necessary day-to-day actions of an organization.

There are other groups that can be stakeholders in the development of operational policy. Having subject matter experts design operational policy allows for the inclusion of the subtle everyday aspects of accomplishing the organizational mission. The drawback is that these employees tend to be mission focused and can create directives that are geared to effectiveness in accomplishing the mission but lack controls that mitigate liability. Organizational managers are often the point people for drafting organizational policy and can be competent at doing so. They understand the operation and have a vested interest in limiting liability as they share in it. The drawback is that managers are focused on efficiency and sometimes are influenced by performance and output imperatives. This can undermine both the legal concerns, such as negligence, and the operational effectiveness concerns. Aside from lawyers, managers, and subject matter experts, employees are sometimes involved in the process through committees or labor unions. Employees tend to have an interest in workplace safety and employee benefits. This role can be perceived as self-serving but looking out for yourself is not necessarily a bad thing. The downside to employees driving operational policy is that sometimes efficiency and legal aspects can suffer. In addition, an employee centric policy system can undermine management.

As you can see, each group brings strengths and weaknesses to the policy development table. No one group is the best choice for producing operational policy; the goal is to engage all parties. If each group has a seat at the table, then all of the positive aspects that they possess can be leveraged. A healthy policy system encompasses the concerns of efficiency, operational effectiveness, legal defense and liability mitigation, and employee welfare and morale. The formation of organizational policy must be inclusive.

THEORETICAL POLICY FOUNDATIONS
Public Policy

Although public policy studies are not directly on point, they do provide context for the understanding of internal organizational policy. A discussion on how and why public policy is made will shed some light on how internal organization policy is made. Public policy decisions are broad and made at high levels of government that affect the nation and can trickle down to the average person or organization. A good example of a public policy is the tax exempt status of religious institutions.

Tax Exemption as a Public Policy

It is because religious organizations are considered charitable and thus a benefit to society that they are given tax exempt status. Identifying a religious organization for special tax treatment brings up one of the issues with public policy as opposed to what I call operational policy. It is not unreasonable to say that religious-based tax exemption is controversial and has borne examples of abuse. This is because a public policy is the execution of a grand strategy. Grand strategy at the national or state level is the prioritizing of resources and efforts to achieve a political goal. Much as the name implies, grand strategy paints in broad brush strokes, with finer policy adjustments left to agencies in government to develop. For example, the Internal Revenue Service produces the fine-point rules dealing with religious group tax exemptions. Although it is important to recognize that public policy decisions are massive in context and implementation, there are parallels for the private sector. Examining public policy can be instructive as the policy-making process for smaller nonpublic organizations is much the same. Unlike public policy, whose success can often be a matter of public perception, functional policy success is easily quantifiable through lawsuits, physical harm, and bankruptcy.

Policy as a Colloquialism

The study of policy is confusing and sometimes contradictory and it is practically always discussed in terms of public policy. The characteristics and theories of public policy can be extrapolated to provide data and processes that work in the organizational context of this book. Given that most work on the topic is done in the academic discipline, it is important to recognize that policy, as a unique field of study simply, does not exist. That lion share of policy study is in the public policy area. Even in academia, this study is fragmented and dispersed among the various academic disciplines. Furthermore, it has been noted by policy researchers that in its study, there is no central question or problem guiding research (Smith & Larimer, 2013). There are arguments that policy study, public policy or otherwise, is a not science at all. Some researchers have dismissed policy making as an art form, even simply describing it as a "persuasion." In other works, policy making has been categorized as a mood more than a science. It has been identified as a loosely organized body of precepts and positions rather than a tightly integrated body of systematic knowledge – more art and craft than genuine "science" (Moran, Rein, & Goodin, 2010). The academic research community struggles to agree on exactly what policy is. Does it mean strictly public policy? Does it mean policy as it relates to politics and governance? Is it just foreign policy? Or is policy a tool for management? Based on the evidence and the many different disciplines of policy, the answer has to be yes; policy encompasses all of these. The disagreement is more fundamental than theoretical disagreements; it goes right to the very word itself. No one can even agree on what the word *policy* means. It would seem that the use of the word *policy* has the same functional impact as the word *aloha*. It means many things and is used in the vocabulary accordingly.

The word policy itself has multiple definitions as well as multiple interpretations of those definitions. It is also commonly used in an exceedingly broad manner. It is just one of those words that is used to the point of defying the common definitions. The problem with this is that without a clear understanding of exactly what the term policy means, the resulting work product cannot be uniform. It can be complicated when using the term in an organizational setting. How does an employee distinguish between policy as an organizational goal and policy as the way things must be done? The simple fact is that words mean things and using words has consequences. Incorrect interpretation of the meaning of policy can affect efficiency or effectiveness. What's worse is that they carry a disproportionate weight in legal proceedings. In a trial, the words used will be thoroughly scrutinized and can result in adverse outcomes for an organization.

An effective organizational leader must know not only how to work in policy but how to employ words effectively. To that end and to simplify the task of making the policy skills readily applicable, I have coined terms to describe the elements of policy. These terms are used to bring a basic level of clarity and identification to the language of policy. These terms are not accepted by anyone in academia or otherwise as universal definitions. I have coined them from the standpoint of common sense out of necessity to have at least workable definitions for the target audience of this book. They may not be perfect, but we have to start somewhere. This concept and the following terms will be repeated throughout the book.

Directive: A directive is the formal written document that is used to carry out the strategic policy, also known as the goals of the organization. Directives come in various forms, depending on the level of discretion permitted. They include rules, orders, procedures, and protocols.

Operational policy: Operational policy is the term I employ to compensate for the colloquial use of the term *policy* when people really mean *directives*. Directives are rules, procedures, plans, budgets, and so forth. Operational policy is focused on the day-to-day, tasks involved in reaching the strategic policy. In the public sector, this means the delivery of services on behalf of the public; in the private sector, it means organizational profitability. Operational policy is essential to accomplishing the strategic policy without lawsuits.

Policy system: A policy system is a set of principles or procedures that lead to the accomplishment of a goal. It includes both strategic policy and operational policy. Supporting functions include training, supervision, and discipline.

Policy making: Policy making pertains to the determination of organization goals and ideals. The end product is the setting of strategic policy or an organizational goal. For example, the chief executive officer, in consultation with the board of directors, has introduced a strategic policy of selling 1 million mallets in China this year. In this example the goal of selling 1 million mallets is clear. The specific sales goal is what the organizational decision maker has set as the strategic policy. Aside from strategic policy, policy making also involves deciding on how the organization plans on meeting their goals. This is known as operational policy. Operational policy includes: rules, orders, procedures, and other sources of organizational direction.

Policy drafting: Policy drafting pertains to the development and committing to writing the formal organizational directives that are used to carry out organizational goals. This is operational policy making.

Strategic policy: Strategic policy involves those policy decisions and tools that are end results oriented. This is operating in the context of the big picture. A strategic policy is defining the goals of an organization; it is not concerned with the processes of reaching the goals. Strategic policy in a police department would be to protect and serve.

Policy Confusion

If you surveyed the public on what policy is, you would likely get any number of responses. This is understandable as the academic discipline of policy study is full of contradiction and competing theories. Most people think they know what policy is and believe it is straightforward, dry, and dull. It is no wonder; if one were to search Google, it would return several choices. For example, Merriam-Webster.com (http://www.merriam-webster.com/dictionary/policy) defines policy as:

- Prudence or wisdom in the management of affairs
- Management or procedure based primarily on material interest
- A definite course or method of action selected from among alternatives and in light of given conditions to guide and determine present and future decisions
- A high-level overall plan embracing the general goals and acceptable procedures especially of a governmental body

Whereas Dictionary.com (http://dictionary.reference.com/browse/policy) defines policy as:

- Definite course of action adopted for the sake of expediency, facility, etc.: *We have a new company policy.*
- A course of action adopted and pursued by a government, ruler, political party, etc.: *our nation's foreign policy.*
- Action or procedure conforming to or considered with reference to prudence or expediency: *It was good policy to consent.*
- Sagacity; shrewdness: *Showing great policy, he pitted his enemies against one another.*
- Rare. government; polity.

Business Dictionary.com (http://www.businessdictionary.com/definition/policies-and-procedures.html#ixzz3VJv3ResT) defines policy as:

- A set of policies are principles, rules, and guidelines formulated or adopted by an organization to reach its long-term goals and typically published in a booklet or other form that is widely accessible.
- Policies and procedures are designed to influence and determine all major decisions and actions, and all activities take place within the boundaries set by them. Procedures are the specific methods employed to express policies in action in day-to-day operations of the organization. Together, policies and procedures ensure that a point of view held by the governing body of an organization is translated into steps that result in an outcome compatible with that view.

These examples are simply the first three I found using "definition policy" in a Google search. The fact is that policy means different things to different people. Policy is abstract and individually defined. You cannot define it with a singular definition, but you know it when you see it. In fact, policy is all around us from the public policy decisions that affect all Americans to the policy decisions that determine if you can return the sweater you bought at the store last week. The most common impact of strategic and operation policy is the effect on how we perform our jobs. The concept of policy causes so much trouble because it is both vague and ubiquitous. Because it always seems to be there, it is often taken for granted. Because it is vague and confusing, the uninitiated do not like to think about it, so it becomes just more background noise.

When I start to discuss policy in social circles, people get that glazed-over look and some even run away. Policy is not a topic that engenders passionate discussion or acute interest. It has even been enshrined in the lexicon of America. The term *policy wonk* is recognized as a pejorative. A *wonk* is defined by Merriam-Webster.com as someone who knows a lot about the details of a particular field and often talks a lot about that subject. To make matter worse, the synonyms for the term are *nerd* and *dork*. This underscores the general level of discomfort people have with policy. Most people see operational policies as something to work around or a way for management to exploit the little guy or worse, a mysterious thing that results in just another thing to complicate our lives. In all too many situations, this can cause people to ignore or undermine the directives, which is sadly against the self-interest of the employee and the organization. It is a situation that keeps the plaintiffs' attorneys in business.

Notwithstanding popular beliefs about policy and viewing the issue from my background, as a lawyer, social scientist, and police officer, I know policy to be a foundational element of all well-run and productive organizations. I know what you are thinking; I am just another egghead policy wonk trying to sell a book. Well, part of that is true, but I am mainly writing this book to provide practical information and strategies for demystifying the policy process. I do this because I have seen how effective a sound process can be to the health of an organization. Law enforcement is a zero-defect game. Every time a cop makes a mistake, it can result in death, serious bodily injury, lawsuits, criminal charges, or job loss. Cops tend to take policy pretty seriously and with good reason. I have also seen what happens when lawyers get hold of an organization that has not paid proper attention to policy development or has opted to wing it without a formal policy system. As you can imagine, the results are not usually happy ones. Organizations need polices, and to do it correctly, one has to apply a common sense and thorough process that gets intended results. This book will put you in a position to do just that.

Policy and Organization

As a starting premise, policy is important as it is the link between the goals of the organization and the people who are tasked with carrying them out. Any organization requires several things to exist; first it must have human capital, also known as people. Second it requires a product, which can be a service or good. And finally, it needs a means to deliver that service or good. To make all of these things work in concert, several techniques are used. The first is some sort of supervisory scheme, which means there has to be a defined leader. A defined and singular leader is crucial to any successful endeavor. There has to be a plan to accomplish and provide direction, and there has to be communication. To tie all of these things together, there has to be a defined process telling the human capital how to deliver the product. This process is the *policy system*.

Policy Systems

A policy system is the combining of multiple elements to ensure that the employees or people in the organization can accomplish the organizational mission. There are three system parts:

1. A decision maker
2. A process to make decisions, also known as *policy making*
3. A means to communicate decisions, roles of individual people, instructions on how to carry out the organizational mission, and limits on discretion, also known as *operational policy*

If you are reading this book, then you are probably a person who has a leadership responsibility and is on the hook to produce results. To get results, you have to have a plan, a strategy. There are volumes written on this topic and it has been academic fodder since the start of the industrial age. But this is where the concept can become confusing because the policy model is pretty much a chicken-and-egg proposition. To have a plan, you must have a policy. The term *policy* in this case means a description of the goal. Once the goal is determined, it is necessary to determine how it will be accomplished, which requires planning and strategy development. Having a plan is not enough, there needs to be some nexus between the plan and the execution. Once a plan is developed, more detailed task-related instructions have to be designed to carry out the plan. These operational instructions are commonly called *policies*. Using the term *policy* is commonplace, but it can be problematic as policy means different things to different people. So for the moment we should think of policy as a system and not a descriptive term.

Informal and Formal Policy

The policy system has two components: *strategic policy*, which deals with the desired end result, and *operational policy*, which deals with operational instructions to employees. In practice, the operational policy is the manner in which plans are implemented. These two elements of policy can exist either formally or informally. Formal policy is clearly defined and documented and there is minimal room for individual interpretation. Informal policy is word of mouth and because of this, it is subject to individual interpretation and unguided evolution. In effect, the existing staff teach the new staff the way things are done. This creates a system where the goals and processes of the organization mutate. No clear formal policy system equals failure. But given that oftentimes policy is abstract and exists in the background in the hectic world of running a company, the nuances of operational policy are easy to overlook. Yet policy has a nasty way of happening whether you want it to or not. Those that do not have formal policy, either strategic or operational, do business by consensus of the workers, which is not exactly an organized method. This is bottom-up control of the organization, which has the potential to create havoc for organizations, particularly in times of crisis.

As a matter of fact, this type of disorganized process leads to inefficiency, lack of control, and can lead to something worse. This type of informal process can lead to adverse impacts in the courts, as the judicial system recognizes this as a *pattern or practice* system. A pattern or practice is an organization operating under informal policy; in the legal context, it is used to show intent or negligence. In some cases, it is used to prove discrimination or organizational culpability in harming a plaintiff. Simply put, the lawyers use informal policy to show that the organization and its leaders intended the harm or negligently allowed it. In a more self-serving context, you, as an organizational leader could find yourself on the hook for allowing informal policy.

Having formal policy is the more effective course, but it also comes with its own set of drawbacks and dangers. One drawback is the false sense of security that might result by simply having something written. The simple act of possessing something tangible is reassuring; it is just human nature. It is why we buy alarm systems and cameras. The simple existence of written policy falls short. Strategic and operational policy have a definite qualitative element. Good policy is much like computer programming that way. I am sure you have heard the term *garbage in, garbage out*. This maxim is just as true for policy. If you have ineffective or poorly drafted policy and directives, then the organization will have adverse outcomes. Taking a cue from computer programming, think of it this way: *bad policy, bad outcomes*.

This idea of garbage in–garbage out results in what I call a *policy failure*. The failure is a result of a flaw in the policy-making process. It is often hard to distinguish until something bad happens. In other words, when bad outcomes occur, people could be doing exactly what the organization told them to, and it is just that the organization was wrong. For example, think of the public policy of segregation, which in its day was the law of the land. This policy was carried out strategically as *separate but equal* accommodations depending on race – a policy scrutinized not only by legislatures but the courts as well. The analysis was incomplete because it was confined to a narrow view; it lacked a qualitative aspect. It was a policy decision that too readily accepted the status quo and did not factor in the good of society as a whole. In other words, it was a clearly unsustainable path and against the strategic policy of the nation found in the Constitution and the Bill of Rights. Still, society at large and those charged with carrying out the policy were legally correct by the standards of the day and were effective. History teaches us that it was, nonetheless, harmful and immoral. The end result was that many people did immoral things without malice or harmful intent; the policy itself was a failure.

SENSEMAKING

Sensemaking is described as the process of structuring the unknown so we are able to act accordingly. According to Karl Weick, sensemaking consists of formulating a plausible understanding of an ever changing environment otherwise known as a *map* (Weick, Sutcliffe, & Obstfeld, 2005). The map is then tested through data collection, action, and conversation. The map is then refined or abandoned, depending on how credible it is (Snook, Nohria, & Khurana, 2012). Sensemaking effectively means coming to terms with the unknown through the collection and assessment of known information. Once we have sufficient reasonably reliable information, we can act or not act, based on our goals. The better the sensemaking of a person or organization, the more likely the goal or mission will be accomplished. In cases where organizational sensemaking is corrupted or skewed, the outcomes can be negative, even fatal.

CASE STUDY: MANN GULCH

The story of Mann Gulch is the retelling of a tragedy that affected the U.S. Forest Service firefighting community. It contains examples of organizational structure, rational choice theory, and sensemaking. It highlights that when sensemaking breaks down, it can lead to the breakdown of the organization itself. In this case, the organization was a group of smoke jumpers, elite firefighters who parachute into remote areas to fight fires. As you might imagine, it is a very hazardous mission and one that requires exceptional situational awareness.

On August 5, 1949, a group of 12 forest service smoke jumpers and one Forest Service ranger were killed when a wildfire overtook them in the Helena National Forest in Montana at a location known as Mann Gulch. The deaths were a terrible tragedy and a shock to the U.S. Forest Service who had not had a loss of a single smoke jumper since the inception of the unit. The fire was reported that day prior to the dispatch of a smoke jumper crew. The crew that day was hastily assembled and had not previously worked together, consisting of a mix of veteran smoke jumpers with their leader "Wag" Wagner Dodge, who was the foreman, and squad leader William Hellman. The crew who jumped that day were significantly inexperienced.

Smoke jumpers Diettert, Piper, Sherman, Thol, Rumsey, and Sallee were on their very first jump. Smoke jumpers Navon and Newton Thompson were in their first year in the service and smoke jumpers Reba and Silas Thompson were in their second season.

The fire was reported to be at the top of a ridge and Dodge believed it would be contained there. Before they departed, the foreman Dodge did not believe there was anything out of the ordinary about this fire. The smoke jumpers had dealt with uncounted similar wildfires over the past decade. Upon landing, the two-way radio for the group was destroyed, cutting off communication with the outside and higher command and control. Despite this, Dodge left the rest of the crew and scouted the fire and decided the ridge where the fire was burning was not the safest place to attack it. Dodge sent crew second-in-command Hellman and the crew down the gulch away from the ridge toward the Missouri River. The smoke jumpers were going to attack the fire in a safer location that would be on the upwind side of the fire, near the river. Dodge, however, remained away from the crew and had a clear view of the fire, which was rapidly spreading because of high winds. As the crew advanced toward the river, they were not aware of the danger they were in. At this point, understanding the danger, Dodge returned to the group and told them to drop their tools and started to lead them away from the safety of the river. Dodge knew that the way to the river was blocked and led them toward a grassy area without explanation. At the grassy area he began to start an escape fire to create a safe area in the advance of the fire by removing the fuel. As he was doing this, members of the crew stopped to see what he was doing. Dodge was making an intuitive last ditch effort to prevent disaster. It was intuitive because the tactic of an escape fire had not been adopted by the Forest Service and no one had been trained in the tactic. Despite his pleas to follow him into the escape fire, the rest of the crew left him there alone, instead fleeing on foot from the advancing wildfire. Two members ran directly up the gulch back toward the ridge where the initial fire started. The remainder of the crew broke into two groups trying to outrun the wildfire. Dodge and the two smoke jumpers who fled up the ridge survived. The remainder perished.

It might seem a stretch that a group of 18 firefighters can serve as an example for other more formal organizations. The group was small and a part of a larger organization, but it was its own organization nonetheless. From a structural perspective, an organization clearly existed. There was a formal decision maker –Wagner Dodge. There were clear roles – the firefighters and a supervisor Hellman. There were procedures in place as well, although many were informal. The smoke jumpers had a set of routines, parachuting into the area and extinguishing the fire using contemporary techniques. More than half of the jumpers that day were rookies with the majority of the group having fewer than two seasons. This inexperience was compounded by the fact that the smoke jumpers were seasonal employees;

most of them were college students doing this during their summer breaks, and with this intermittent employment, the sense of role seems weak at best. The group itself appears to have been ad hoc in nature and was deployed piecemeal. The relationships of a more defined and established group were not present, and thus the trust in the decision maker was limited. In the alternative, the routines used by the smoke jumpers were a common experience. These factors would prove lethal to many in the group.

The investigation of the incident suggests that the most effective sensing of the group was limited to Dodge, and sadly, the inexperience of the group affected their beliefs. When faced with the overwhelming threat to life, they acted in a manner consistent with their makeup, a group of individuals. At the moment of truth for the highly inexperienced jumpers, the concept of willingly walking into an intentionally set fire was not conceivable; they had no information, training, or directives to the contrary. It was not a prevailing tactic at the time, and Dodge did not communicate the reason why, nor did they know enough about him to trust him blindly. The common experience of the group in employing routines time and again successfully worked against them. This fire was unlike any the smoke jumpers had ever faced, and the routines were not applicable here. Thus when placed in a critical situation, the crew made what they thought was a rational choice, which was to run. They simply could not make sense of what they were observing and made a fatal decision (Rothermel, 1993).

This story illustrates an ad hoc organization that existed inside a larger organization, the U.S. Forest Service. It also shows the impact of sensemaking on organizational and individual rational choice. The crew that jumped into Mann Gulch also had limited formal operational policy.

ACADEMIC POLICY THEORIES

Much in the way there is little agreement on the definition of the word *policy*, there is little in the way of a singular academic theory of policy. The fact is that it is not uncommon for multiple theories to be at work at the same time in a given situation. In addition, elements of certain policy theories can also be at play. The importance of having a basic understanding of these academic theories is to understand that policy choices do not just happen – there are processes involved. An organizational leader must be able to identify the process involved and to ensure that it is relevant and leading to a worthy outcome. The research and absorbing of these theories can be time consuming and intellectually challenging. While I truly believe that the readers of this book are more than capable of researching and absorbing policy theories, I also believe you probably do not have the luxury of time to do so.

There are many policy theories as well as derivative theories, and I have attempted to select the ones I believe to be most relevant to the essence of this book. In that spirit, I have summarized those select policy theories and attempted to paraphrase them in practical terms that can be readily applied to most organizations. Please keep in mind that a single chapter cannot do justice to these theories; they have been distilled to their basics.

Rational Choice Theory

When public policy is studied, it is examined in the construct of the organization. Policy is seen as being made by organizations and issued under the organizational authority. But an organization is not actually a being at all. Organizations take on the impression of a being because all organizations are made up of people. These people interact and are either decision makers or have the potential to influence them. Because of this, all policy theory must take into account the human factor and individual choice. Rational choice theory is a theory that advances the idea that choices are made by individuals in an attempt to maximize benefits and minimize costs. This theory articulates that people make choices about their actions through a cost-benefit analysis of sorts by comparing the costs or benefits of different courses of action. The theory of rational choice effectively looks to two different driving forces, which are beliefs and desires. Desire is an internal manifestation and is made without factoring in the external circumstances. Beliefs are the result of the sensing process and situational awareness of the options that are available.

This theory can also be applied to organizations; in fact, it is a cornerstone of business and investing. There is a theory of institutional rational choice that accounts for organizations acting according to rational choice. People and organizations have a genuine focus for return on investment and rightfully so. The goals or desires of the organization are driving forces for the actions that occur. Successful organizations place a significant priority on the assessment of the environment through sensing in order to develop situational awareness. When effective due diligence is performed, the beliefs or available choices are accurate, and informed decision making can occur. In an organizational environment, policy decisions are driven by rational choice. For example, a company might make the choice to sell a product with a known defect because the benefit of doing so outweighs the cost of lawsuits.

It is important to note that even unstructured organizations, for example, those that are not formally organized still exhibit traits of rational choice theory. For our purposes, this accentuates the idea that even without formal goals, members of the organization will still engage in an unbounded rational choice process. The drawback of this is that each person may have very different beliefs and desires.

Multiple Streams Theory

The multiple streams policy theory grew out of dissatisfaction with the traditional policy-making model. The main criticism was that the traditional model and its processes did not take into account the realities facing policy makers, such as limited choice and political considerations. The multiple streams model theory identifies three separate and distinct streams: the problem stream, the policy or solutions stream, and the political stream. These streams are always engaged simultaneously. There may be times when there are multiple policy streams that are in play as a result of the problem stream. This is just like in real life when there may be competing solutions to a problem. The opportunity for the streams to converge occurs when the political stream supports the solution stream. In other words, there may be many solution streams, but only one solution stream will achieve political support. When the three streams do actually converge – a problem stream, a solution stream, and political stream – the situation is ripe for the emergence of a new policy. Take, for example, the days following the tragedy that occurred on September 11, 2001. There were many policy changes brought about by the attacks. At the federal government level, one problem identified was the vulnerability of the screening process (the problem). A solution was advanced by the Bush administration to create an entirely new organization, the Transportation Safety Administration (TSA), to deal with it (the policy). Despite the enormity of the endeavor and the costs, there was clear political support. All of the streams converged and a window opened for the creation of the TSA. If this solution stream had been proposed before the events of September 11, it is unlikely that it would have had the political support, even in light of the known vulnerability of the private airport screening process. Let's take a closer look at the streams.

The Problem Stream

The problem stream is based on the belief or perceptions of those inside and outside the organization. The observations of both internal and external stakeholders can prompt a policy maker to address a particular problem. The driving force is the realization that a problem exists that requires a policy to address. This realization is driven by the sensing and situational awareness of stakeholders. The sensing encompasses incoming data, the level of focus on the issue, a triggering event, and communication between stakeholders and policy makers. A significant part of the equation is the classification of the issue and how it affects the strategic policy of the organization. For example, will ignoring the problem be hazardous to the continuation or effectiveness of the organization? How serious is it?

The Political Stream

The political stream is engaged when the policy makers of an organization begin to set an agenda. The agenda is effectively the list of problems that must be solved by the organization. The agenda is influenced by political factors, such as stakeholders. These include interest groups (internal and external), public and employee opinion, and the dynamics of the organization. If a consensus can be achieved, then the policy stream is viable. In other words, if there is political will to deal with the problem, then a policy can emerge.

The Solution Stream

The solution stream, otherwise known as the *policy stream*, is engaged when all of the options are weighed and are presented. This is the domain of the policy makers, and before a decision is made the options may be beta tested to gauge acceptance by the various stakeholders. The solution stream can be affected by stakeholder influence and persuasion as well as business concerns, such as budgetary limitations and technical limitations. The solution must also comport with the strategic policy of the organization to include the core values and mission statement. Once each these criteria are met, then a viable solution emerges and activates the stream.

Multiple stream theory states that in order for a new policy to be implemented, a policy window must be engaged. A policy window can only occur if the three streams are activated at the same time. The multiple stream theory is significant because it highlights the role politics plays in policy making. The study is focused on the U.S. political process, but politics are politics be they national, local, corporate, or office. The multiple streams theory compensates for the lack of the political dimension in the rational choice theory. The political aspect has to be considered as there are many decisions that occur because of political reasons contrary to desires and contrary to beliefs about the situation. We can all appreciate the persuasions that occur at the highest levels of government and corporations, but they also occur every day at all levels of organizations. A good example of this is the salesperson's expense account. These accounts are used to wine and dine key organizational players in the course of business. The key is to recognize the role politics can play in strategic and operational policy.

ORGANIZATIONAL STRUCTURE

From an intuitive sense, every organization has a defined structure. These can range from a partnership to a highly diverse corporation. Each of these organizations have individual people as the most basic building blocks. When two people agree to undertake an endeavor, they are organized into a simple partnership. When additional functions or employees are taken on, the structure evolves. The more employees or functions, the greater the structure of the organization.

Organizational structures are taught in university organization and administration courses all over the country. This is particularly true in degrees devoted to the protective services. A student in a criminal justice, fire science, or security program is likely to see examples of horizontal and vertical structures in their classes. They are a thumbnail generic description of how organizations are structured. These are often shown in graphics or flow charts, and they are characterized by relative positions of functions in the chart or graphic. A vertical organization also known as *tall* is defined as a structure with power centralized at the top of the organization. This structure also has a specific chain of command that works from the top down, thus its designation as a *vertical organization*. The decision maker resides at the top of the organization. Intermediaries (managers) exist between the decision makers and the employees and link them together. Employees are grouped by function or unit, and each function or unit reports to a singular manager. Large or complex organizations tend to be vertical.

A horizontal or flat organizational structure is characterized by a decentralized power structure. As the name implies, the functions and units are essentially equal and there are little or no intermediaries between the decision maker and the workers. This structure is good for start-up companies and smaller organizations that are not complex. Now that you have a visualization of these basic structures, we will examine organizational structure in more detail.

According to Henry Mintzberg, a renowned organizational theorist, organizations come in many different configurations although they all have some common dimensions. This applies, as Mintzberg puts it, "… from the making of pottery to the placing of a man on the moon…" (Mintzberg, 1989). Regardless of size and makeup, organizational goals are accomplished because the organization defines employee roles through division of labor and coordination of work through operational policy. The common dimensions of any organization are the executive decision-making (key) part of the organization, the primary coordinating mechanism, and the type of decentralization or employee discretion employed. The manner in which these dimensions are employed determines the type of organization. Given the different forms an organization can take, it is important to understand the characteristics of each. Organizations can move between the different types based on the circumstances. Mintzberg illustrated this using an allegory about the growth of an organization in the story of Ceramico.

STORY: CERAMICO

This story is about a woman, Ms. Raku, who made pottery in her basement. She was quite good and very ambitious and soon her orders outstripped her ability to keep up with them. To compensate, she hired another woman, Miss Bisque, with no pottery experience, who she trained to perform basic preparatory tasks, thereby dividing the labor. This arrangement worked well for a while because it still allowed Ms. Raku to actually make the pottery. The communication between the two was effective because it was direct. The arrangement was informal and the supervision was one to one with Miss Bisque having full discretion in carrying out her assigned function and Ms. Raku making all of the decisions regarding overall production. Fortunately (or unfortunately), the demand for the pottery expanded even more, outstripping capacity. This time Ms. Raku hired three graduates from the local pottery school. This time she did not have to train them and they could actually make the pottery. Even with people working in the basement, coordination was not a problem as the span of control was still workable. (A span of control is the number of people a leader can effectively manage.)

The growth of the organization continued and an additional two assistants were hired. This is when the problems started: Pottery was painted incorrectly and breakage began to occur out of confusion. It was at this point that Ms. Raku realized that the informal communication was no longer working. With seven people in the basement with an informal organization, the span of control became ineffective. To make matters worse Ms. Raku began calling herself president of Ceramics Limited, and more and more of her time was spent dealing with customers. To compensate, Ms. Raku assigned Miss Bisque to be the pottery studio manager and left the supervision and coordination of the other five employees to her. This division of labor and the added layer of supervision allowed for a more detailed division of labor and a more detailed coordination of efforts. As you might imagine, demand grew even higher and to address the issue, Ms. Raku hired an efficiency expert. The expert recommended a fully integrated division of labor in which each step of the process was performed individually, allowing less skilled workers to be hired on an assembly line process. Moving to a larger facility, the workers on the assembly line carried out their work based on clear operational policies that ensured that their work was coordinated. Because of the impact of the division of labor and formal rules and policies, the company expanded beyond selling small batches to craft shops. Ceramic Limited was now selling in bulk to chain and discount stores. Because of Ms. Raku's ambition, the company expanded into producing other products, including ceramic tiles, bathroom fixtures, and bricks. This diversification resulted in the company to again redivide the labor. To this end, Ceramics Limited was broken down into three divisions: consumer products, building products, and industrial products. The company grew again and the physical plant expanded both in size and geographic location. Now situated in an office on the fifty-fifth floor of the Pottery Tower, Ms. Raku now performed executive decision making. She led the three divisions by reviewing their performance each quarter and acting if profit and growth figures exceeded or fell short of the budget. "It was while sitting at her desk one day going over these budgets that Ms. Raku gazed out at the surrounding skyscrapers and decided to rename her company 'Ceramico'" (Mintzberg, 1979).

The story illustrates the movement of Ms. Raku's company through various organizational structures. It starts out with Ms. Raku simply selling the pottery she made without organization and moved to a sole proprietorship when she hired Miss Bisque. Once she hired additional employees, it was clear that she needed to evolve into a formal company as Ceramics Limited. But as happens with many companies with in-demand products, her small business had to expand and so it did from small company, to medium sized, to large and finally ending up as a corporation, Ceramico. During the transition, the organization took on various structures each with its own traits, each with its own advantages and disadvantages. In reading about Ms. Raku and her organization's journey through structures, we see an example of a process that can apply to any organization.

Organizations can be broken down to the following structure types:

- Simple structure
- Machine bureaucracy
- Professional bureaucracy
- Divisionalized form
- Adhocracy

Simple Structure

A simple structure is just as its name implies – a simple, flat structure. It is a singular unit with typically one manager. The organization is informal and unstructured and lacks standardization. This simple structure has the benefit of being focused yet flexible. A good example of this structure is a start-up company. In a start-up, the owner exercises very strong control and communication lines are short. This structure is very lean, which ironically is considered an asset in contemporary management theories such as lean manufacturing. As indicated by our pottery story, once the organization begins to grow, this structure is difficult to maintain.

Machine Bureaucracy

The machine bureaucracy is distinguished by its standardization. Much like government bureaucracies, the decision making is centralized and the division of labor is strict. The hallmark of this structure is formality and an overriding mission of efficiency. This type of organization is tall; in other words, there is a precisely defined chain of command and communication channel that is vertical from top to bottom. An example of this kind of organization is a federal government agency or military contractor organization. Any organization that must meet exact specifications and perform in a high regulatory environment is a good candidate for this structure. One of the drawbacks to this kind of organization is that workers become specialized in their jobs and meeting specific regulations so that they can come to see their narrow functions and compliance with regulations as more important than the goals of the organization.

Professional Bureaucracy

The professional bureaucracy, like the machine bureaucracy, is very bureaucratic. The main difference between the two is that the division of labor is not to the point of having individual workers perform singular functions. In this case, professionals are employed who are capable of producing the product and in doing so require control of their own work. The specialization is more holistic in the professional bureaucracy, whereas in the machine bureaucracy, the process is broken down to its most basic functions, allowing unskilled workers to perform insular functions. An example would be the difference between an automobile assembly plant and a hospital. The assembly plant division of labor may include people who just put rivets in sheet metal, which is a singular function that does not require a significant skill set. The hospital division of labor has many professionals who perform individual functions but with a high degree of skill and autonomy, such as doctors, nurses, pharmacy technicians, and laboratory technicians. The professional bureaucracy has decentralized decision making, but it is guided discretion with lots of operational policies in place. In the case of a hospital, there is also a machine bureaucracy in play that includes the non-highly skilled support staff such as janitors, food service, and administrative support. An obvious disadvantage to allowing workers, regardless of how professional, high degrees of discretion is the lack of control by organizational executives. This type of organization is also very resistant to change and can be inflexible.

Divisionalized Form

The divisionalized structure applies to organizations that, as the name implies, involves different divisions. This structure is most appropriate when there is a lack of commonality between the various products or units of the company. This structure is distinguished by a mother organization that has suborganizations attached. These suborganizations, like children, may have their own individual structure with varying degrees of autonomy. The major advantage of this structure is that those managers who are closest to the action can make decisions that ensure the health of the subsidiary company. In this structure, the mother company provides support to the subsidiaries and focuses on the strategic goals of the overall organization. This structure is appropriate when the size of the organization is large and diverse enough to limit the effect of centralized decision making. An example of this type of organization is Proctor and Gamble, known for soaps, whose subsidiaries include Crest toothpaste, Eukanuba dog food, Pampers diapers, and Vicks cough syrup, among many others. The subsidiaries are not only diverse in product line but are also geographically different. The weakness of this kind of structure is that there is significant duplication of efforts and resources. There is also a tendency for different divisions to compete for resources and for lines of communication between the subsidiaries and the mother organization to be strained. This kind of structure is also unwieldy and inflexible.

Adhocracy

The adhocracy is a structure unlike the others. As its name suggests, it is based on being ad hoc. According to Merriam-Webster the term *ad hoc* means "for the particular end or case at hand without consideration of wider application" ("Ad Hoc," n.d.). In other words, organizations like this are suited to singular tasks. An example of an adhocracy is a construction job. In construction, the contractor subcontracts out each individual part of the job to specialists. These specialists have an insular skill set and once they are done with the job, they move onto the next job. Framers, roofers, masons, plumbers, and electricians move from project to project and once their work is done, they are no longer part of the organization. This type of organization can also be seen in technology companies where purpose-built work groups are assigned to a singular project and function independent of the mother organization. The advantage of an adhocracy is the ability to critically mass skilled people to deal with a problem or a rapidly evolving opportunity. These people are given broad discretion to solve problems. This structure is decentralized and highly flexible as it can generally expand and contract as needed. The downside of an adhocracy is that because of its itinerant and decentralized nature, it can be difficult to maintain talented people and can present control issues for executive leadership.

An organization can be any one of these structures or can contain multiple examples of each. This is particularly true in this age of a global economy where geographic boundaries are blurred. As evidenced by the pottery parable, an organization from inception to end will likely move through any number of these structures.

There are some significant commonalities that any organizational structures possess from the most basic to the most complex. Each one of these structures share essential organizational elements:

- A leadership or a decision-making element
- A designation of functional roles
- Formal rules and policies

There will always be someone who makes the decisions. We see this all around us; in every group, there will always be someone leading. The role can be identified clearly, leaving no questions with titles such as owner, president, or chief executive officer. There can be other decision-making elements, such as a partnership, a board of directors, or some other format of individuals. Even in the social experiment of communism, the organization evolved into having one singular decision maker. The communist ideal held out that everyone was equal and everyone owned the means of production. Further, this was to be accomplished in a stateless organization. Yet in short order, a singular leader emerged. I am hard pressed to cite a leader who exercised more control of a people than Joseph Stalin. Regardless of the configuration, there will always be an entity which makes the final decision for the organization.

The use of the term *structure* is indicative of the fact that it is made up of parts and each part has a function. This is true for engineered physical structures as well as organizational structures. The reason for the designation of functional roles is to ensure that each necessary function in the structure is performed. Think of it this way: Because organizations are made up of people, when new people are brought into the organization, they need to know what part they will play. Even if they are simply told to "clean up," they have still been given a functional designation. In the overwhelming majority of situations, new people are brought into organizations to fill a specific function.

RULES AND STRUCTURE

The presence of formal rules and policies is an essential part of any organization. As we have observed in the various organizational structures, the larger the organization, the more significant the need for rules. These rules and policies are the link between the decision-making element and the workers carrying out their designated functions. The larger the organization and more complex the structure, the more pressing the need to control discretion by employees. Employee discretion is controlled through the employment of operational policies, otherwise known as *directives*. Directives create what is called *bounded discretion*. Bounded discretion is often employed in organizations that are too large or complex to allow for a high degree of centralized control. Bounded discretion is discretion permitted within certain criteria. For example, a discretion boundary could be a strict limit on expenditures for an ad hoc work team detailed to a specific project. The discretion to innovate is not limited, but the discretion to spend money is. This permits the work group freedom in one aspect – problem solving – but provides a degree of control in the fiscal aspect. In most cases, even groups who have a high degree of autonomy and discretion still have to abide by a budget. In Chapter 3, we will explore how discretion is guided. This type of discretion is not to be confused with unbounded discretion where the choice of action is completely left up to the individual.

In discussing organizational and policy-making theories, it is important to note that we have just touched the surface and that there are many other theories that may be relevant. Mintzberg's work encompasses the most basic tenets of organizational structure theory and is a solid foundation. That said, I would encourage you to explore the topic in greater detail. It is as simple as typing "policy theories" or "organizational theories" into your preferred search engine. You can even do it on your smart phone while waiting in line at the store. It will make you a better leader, I promise.

This chapter was a lot of information to absorb, but it represents the foundation from which virtually all policy making will flow. The primary area of policy study is in the field of public policy, which shares many traits and theories that are applicable to the scope of this book. Observing how public policy works can be instructional for our purposes. We looked at the drawbacks of simply buying canned policy manuals and saw that they lack flexibility and can be seen as failing to perform due diligence. We highlighted the confusion that affects not only the word *policy* but the entire discipline of policy making. We established that policy exists in the context of an organization. We also noted that organizations can only exist if they are made up of people. Organizations exist in different structures and these structures evolve, depending on the complexity, size, and mission. The person is the most basic unit in an organization. We examined the theoretical basis for policy making, exploring the rational choice theory and the multiple streams theory. The rational choice theory accounts for the human aspect of policy making. People make decisions based on desires and beliefs. Because people are the most basic units in an organization, policy making involves choices made by people. The multiple streams theory builds on older policy-making theories but accounts for the political aspects, which exist in all organizations. The concept of sensemaking was covered in the chapter – an organization must have situational awareness to adapt and survive. Sensemaking allows for the organization, through its people, to analyze information from the environment and make sound choices. A case study on the Mann Gulch fire and its demonstrated organizational structure was presented showing how rational choice theory affects strategic policy making and demonstrating the impact of faulty sensemaking. Henry Mintzberg's structure of organizations was examined and five organizational structures were looked at in detail. The structures examined were simple structure, machine bureaucracy, professional bureaucracy, divisionalized form, and adhocracy. We read about Ms. Raku and saw how an organization can move through Mintzberg's different organizational structures. Finally, we detailed the common elements in every organization. They are a leadership or a decision-making element, a designation of functional roles, and formal rules and policies.

PRACTICE POINTERS

- Identify the structure that currently exists in your organization and ensure that it is appropriate.
- Recognize that there is a human factor in every organization and that policy comes from choices that people make.
- Policy makers must employ a complete rational choice process that includes the assessment of all outcomes.
- The multiple stream theory presents an opportunity to be a change agent for those who recognize when it is in play.
- Be aware that aside from the human factor, there is a political factor in policy making.
- Organizational sensemaking plays a critical part in making sound policy choices.
- Sensemaking can be influenced by deficiencies in or lack of operational policy, supervision, or training.

Chapter Recap

- This chapter is the foundation for all following chapters.
- Policy exists in the context of an organization.
- People are the most basic unit in an organization.
- The policy-making theories of rational choice and multiple streams account for the human factor and the political factor.
- Sensemaking is essential to the adaptability of an organization; it is the process that allows for the interpretation of external information.
- Organizations can come in different structures; each has its form driven by factors such as size, complexity, and mission.
- The amount of employee discretion required plays a key role in organizational structure.
- There are some common elements in all organizations, which are a decision-making element, designated roles, and policy.

BIBLIOGRAPHY

Ad Hoc. [Def. 1]. (n.d.). In: Merriam Webster Online. Retrieved November 27, 2014, from <http:// www.merriam-webster.com/dictionary/adhoc>.

Aguiar, F., & de Francisco, A. (2009). Rational choice, social identity, and beliefs about oneself. *Philosophy of the social sciences*, *39*(4), 547–571.

Al-Habil, W. I. (2011). Rationality and Irrationality of Max Weber's Bureaucracies. *International Journal of Management and Business Studies*, (4), 106–110.

Burstein, P. (1991). Policy domains: Organization, culture, and policy outcomes. *Annual Review of Sociology*, *17*, 327–350.

Cairney, P. (2013). Standing on the shoulders of giants: How do we combine the insights of multiple theories in public policy studies? *Policy Studies Journal*, *41*(1), 1–21.

Cairney, P., & Heikkila, T. (2014). A comparison of theories of the policy process. *Theories of the Policy Process*, 363–366.

Cohen, M. D., March, J. G., & Olsen, J. P. (1972). A garbage can model of organizational choice. *Administrative Science Quarterly*, 1–25.

Dalton, D. R., Todor, W. D., Spendolini, M. J., Fielding, G. J., & Porter, L. W. (1980). Organization structure and performance: A critical review. *Academy of Management Review*, *5*(1), 49–64.

Jones, B. D., Boushey, G., & Workman, S. (2006). Behavioral rationality and the policy processes: Toward a new model of organizational information processing. In G. Peters & J. Pierre (Eds.), *Handbook of public policy* (pp. 49–74). SAGE Publications.

Kingdon, J. W., & Thurber, J. A. (1984). In *Agendas, alternatives, and public policies* (Vol. 45). Boston, MA: Little, Brown.

Keeton, P., & Prosser, W. L. (1984). *Prosser and Keeton on the law of torts*. St. Paul, MN: West Pub. Co.

Lafley, A. (2015, January 9). *P&G 2014 annual report*. Retrieved from: <http://www. pginvestor.com/interactive/lookandfeel/4004124/PG_Annual_Report_2014.pdf>.

Leunens, G., Verstraete, J., Van den Bogaert, W., Van Dam, J., Dutreix, A., & Van der Schueren, E. (1992). Human errors in data transfer during the preparation and delivery of radiation treatment affecting the final result: Garbage in, garbage out. *Radiotherapy and Oncology*, *23*(4), 217–222.

Levin, J., & Milgrom, P. (2004). Introduction to choice theory. Retrieved from: <http:// web.stanford.edu/~jdlevin/Econ%20202/Choice%20Theory.pdf>.

Matland, R. (1995). Synthesizing the implementation literature: The ambiguity-conflict model of policy implementation. *Journal of Public Administration Research and Theory*, *5*(2), 145–174.

Mead, L. M. (1995). Public policy: Vision, potential, limits. *Policy Currents*, *5*, 1–4.

Mintzberg, H. (1979). *The structuring of organizations: A synthesis of the research*. Englewood Cliffs, NJ: Prentice-Hall.

Mintzberg, H. (1989). *Mintzberg on management: Inside our strange world of organizations*. New York: Simon and Schuster.

Mintzberg, H. (1993). *Structure in fives: Designing effective organizations*. Englewood Cliffs, NJ: Prentice Hall.

Moran, M., Rein, M., & Goodin, R. E. (2010). *The Oxford handbook of public policy*. Oxford: Oxford University Press.

Nave, D. (2002). How to compare six sigma, lean and the theory of constraints. *Quality Progress*, *35*(3), 73–80.

Nowlin, M. C. (2011). Theories of the policy process: State of the research and emerging trends. *Policy Studies Journal*, *39*(s1), 41–60.

Rothermel, R. C., & Intermountain Research Station (Ogden, Utah). (1993). Mann Gulch fire: A race that couldn't be won. Ogden, UT (324 25th St., Ogden 84401): U.S. Dept. of Agriculture, Forest Service, Intermountain Research Station.

Sabatier, P. A., & Weible, C. M. (2014). *Theories of the policy process*. Boulder, CO: Westview Press.

Shepsle, K. A. (2006). Rational choice institutionalism: *The Oxford handbook of political institutions* (pp. 23–38). Oxford: Oxford University Press.

Smith, K. B., & Larimer, C. W. (2013). *The public policy theory primer*. Boulder, CO: Westview Press.

Snook, S. A., Nohria, N., & Khurana, R. (2012). *The handbook for teaching leadership: Knowing, doing, and being*. Thousand Oaks, CA: SAGE Publications.

Suddaby, R. (2010). Challenges for institutional theory. *Journal of Management Inquiry*, *19*(1), 14–20.

Teodorović, J. (2008). Why education policies fail: Multiple streams model of policy-making. *Zbornik Instituta za pedagoska istrazivanja*, *40*(1), 22–36.

Van Meter, D. S., & Van Horn, C. E. (1975). The policy implementation process: A conceptual framework. *Administration & Society*, *6*(4), 445–487.

Weick, K. E. (1993). The collapse of sensemaking in organizations: The Mann Gulch disaster. *Administrative Science Quarterly*, *38*(4), 628–652.

Weick, K. E., Sutcliffe, K. M., & Obstfeld, D. (2005). Organizing and the process of sensemaking. *Organization Science*, *16*(4), 409–421.

Werts, A. B., & Brewer, C. A. (2015). Reframing the study of policy implementation: Lived experience as politics. *Educational Policy*, *29*(1), 206–229.

Chapter 2

Why Bother?

OVERVIEW

The goal of this chapter is to present a compelling argument about the need to implement an effective and comprehensive policy system. To accomplish this, we will also explore the significant risk to industry and organizations from lawsuits. The potential for worst-case impacts will also be examined by looking at policy decisions that contributed to incidents as true cause factors. The case studies include situations with bad outcomes and lawsuits and are employed not only to capture the reader's interest but to provide the personal incentive to be sound policy makers (strategic policy) and effective drafters of directives (operational policy).

In civil suits, there are two elements in a legal cause of action against an organization. They are classified as either purposeful or negligent actions. If you take the time to read enough case law, you will find that regardless of the intent, being brought into court for either is a bad thing. The goal is to have a policy system that mitigates the underlying factors that allow both purposeful and negligent actions to occur. We now examine these two causes of action in detail.

PURPOSEFUL INTENT

Purposeful intent is exactly what it sounds like: The organization or person took an action on purpose knowing full well that a harm would result. This can and does happen, but it is very difficult to prove. Conversely, it is not particularly difficult to allege purposeful intent. The lack of a formal policy system creates a vulnerability to this charge in that it allows attorneys to manipulate fact to support their cases. Remember that informal policy is a pattern or practice and is subject to interpretation. The most effective way to counter this is to engage in analysis to recognize adverse outcomes of strategic policy decisions and to develop operational policy to mitigate them. A collateral benefit to having a strong policy system is that if an individual member of your organization does something harmful on purpose, a strong policy system will limit the impact of respondeat superior, or *vicarious liability*. This is not simply about cutting losses and hanging out individual employees, it is a strategy to reduce the attractiveness of the target. An organization that can be enjoined in a suit on the basis of vicarious liability encourages actions as they present deeper pockets than just a single plaintiff. If the organization can be removed from the equation, then the opportunity for financial reward from the suit diminishes considerably. Simply put, suing an individual employee is not a reasonable return on investment.

NEGLIGENCE

Adverse outcomes that do not involve purposeful acts are usually the result of negligence. Negligence occurs when a person or organization has a duty to act a particular way and fails to do so. Intent to cause harm is exactly what the name intends, a state of mind where a person or organization acts on purpose to hurt a person or organization. Obviously, proving intent to harm is extremely difficult in the civil context, so most lawsuits occur because of negligence. To have negligence, a person or organization must have a duty to the injured party. A duty implies a relationship in some way. This will be covered in depth in Chapter 7 when we look at the role of stakeholders.

Stakeholders in any endeavor are normally owed a duty by the person or organization charged with fault. For example, a fast-food restaurant counts their customers among stakeholders. When a customer of a fast-food place suffers an injury from the restaurant's act or product liability occurs, the restaurant has a duty to its customers.

If your organization deals with other people or organizations to do business, then there are many potential stakeholders and duties. Breaching a duty does not have to be purposeful; the only thing that needs to exist for liability to exist is that the danger was foreseeable. This means as an organizational leader, you have the responsibility to assess all the foreseeable dangers that can happen from organizational products or actions. In other words, if you do business in the global economy, you will have many stakeholders and thus must deal with any foreseeable dangers. Dealing with foreseeable dangers has been called risk management.

Risk management is an integral part of many industries and drives a significant amount of policy. Some industries place a much higher premium on risk management than others – one such industry is civil aviation. You would be hard-pressed to find another that has more regulation and redundancy in operation policy than the airline industry, particularly when it comes to safety. But this is not a guarantee, and bad things do happen when directives are not in place or not followed properly as demonstrated in the following case study.

CASE STUDY: MASKING TAPE

What would you do if I told you that a single piece of adhesive tape could kill 70 people? You might be surprised; I know I was. In 1996 a Boeing 757-23A crashed in the South Pacific Ocean 48 miles away from the airport of departure. This tragedy is well known as the Aeroperú Flight 603 incident. This incident is studied in many risk courses as an example of how a simple mistake can be catastrophic. The mistake Flight 603 made was that the ground crew failed to remove masking tape that was covering instrument ports on the left side of the aircraft. The tape was placed there as part of a routine process to protect the instruments during the washing and polishing process. The impeded instruments caused conflicting readings in the cockpit shortly after takeoff that led to the pilots flying with erroneous readings on altitude and airspeed. They believed they were flying at 9500 feet when the wing hit the ocean, killing all on board.

Many risk managers see this as a cautionary tale about things such as complex systems or cognitive lock-in. From my perspective, this begins and ends with a policy issue. Covering the instrument inlets during cleaning and polishing was standard policy. There were also requirements for checklist inspection of the aircraft by the maintenance crew chief, the line chief, and finally the pilot. Several quality control requirements were ignored or ineffectively performed. The aircraft wreckage was recovered with the tape still on the instruments. This is an abject lesson on the role of policy formulation and implementation. There were measures in place to prevent this type of disaster, but they were ineffective. The lesson, for our purposes, is that it takes more than just having a system of how we do things or even just having written directives. Policies must be viewed as an integral part of day-to-day business and implemented as a system. As a starting premise, recognize that it is not enough to simply have policies. An effective leader, manager, or executive understands that a policy system promotes efficiency and provides accountability. A policy system involves many aspects, including organizational sensing, risk assessment, analysis of policy options, effective drafting, training, supervision, and ongoing review and revision. Employing a policy system can make an organization highly effective and in worst-case scenarios, prevent disaster.

There are many ways that liability can accrue. Aside from policy failure and lack of formal policy, simply not addressing issues that should have policy consideration and representation in the policy system can also be dangerous. If you are unlucky enough to have an injury occur because of a lack of policy or a policy failure, it can have very real consequences. These include lawsuits and injuries and can even lead to the death of the organization. Even when the effects are not as dire as the death of the organization, they can cause lingering effects. Organizations big and small are vulnerable to this. If you will not believe me, maybe the following case study will change your mind.

CASE STUDY: HOT COFFEE

Sometimes well-thought-out sound business motivations lead to poor policy decisions. Take for example, the day Stella Liebeck decided to get herself a nice hot cup of coffee. She asked her grandson, who was driving, to go to the local McDonald's restaurant drive-up to get a cup of coffee. In an action that was repeated millions of times a day across the United States, Stella received her coffee and her grandson pulled forward and stopped so Stella could put some sugar into the coffee. Holding the cup between her legs, she took the lid off and promptly spilled the contents into her crotch. Unfortunately for Stella, the coffee at McDonald's on February 27, 1992, was being kept at a temperature between 180 and 190 degrees Fahrenheit. Considering the coffee was at a scalding temperature, it is not surprising that Stella suffered third-degree burns that required skin grafts and a lengthy hospital stay. The case made national headlines as the poster child for frivolous lawsuits, but incorrectly so. The transcripts from the trial clearly indicate that this type of accident was not only foreseeable but was a clear-cut policy decision that was strictly enforced by the company.

It was the McDonald's company policy, as indicated by the company policy manual, to keep the coffee at a scalding temperature. This was the policy because the company believed incorrectly that most people did not start drinking the beverage until they reached their destinations.

Any person who has ever had to commute to work in the morning can tell you that he or she buys the coffee to drink it immediately. McDonald's was so convinced of the reasonableness of their policy that they refused to pay Stella's medical bill of about $80,000, instead offering her $800. The offer is comical when you consider that the average daily income that McDonald's receives from coffee sales is approximately $1.35 million. Incensed by the insulting offer, Stella hired a lawyer and sued.

It is important to know a little about the lawsuit process. An integral part of a lawsuit is the discovery process. Once a complaint is filed, the plaintiff can ask for discovery. This means that the organization sued must turn over any information that is relevant to the case or any information that can lead to relevant information. Discovery is a broad investigative tool. The discovery process quite simply gives the plaintiffs' attorney access to all of your organization's dirt. I want to take a moment here to underscore this fact. If you get sued, you will not be able to hide because your organization was operating without policies, had a policy system but nothing covering the cause of action, or that the policy was defective. As an organizational leader, you exist one civil complaint away from your whole professional life changing. I say this from experience, having been deposed many times by plaintiffs' attorneys.

During the discovery phase, the facts did not paint a good picture for the company. As it turns out, they were keenly aware of the danger of their scalding coffee policy, having 700 claims of burns from scalding coffee brought against them from 1982 until the incident. In addition, it appears that the corporate policy of serving 190-degree beverages was driven by market research and sales motivations. The research indicated that customers wanted hot coffee and sales reinforced this. Customer desires and company profitability arguments did not help McDonald's in the trial. The McDonald's quality assurance manager was compelled (under oath) to admit that the coffee served at this temperature was not fit for immediate human consumption and that scalding burns would likely result. He also admitted that the policy of keeping the coffee at that scalding temperature was regularly enforced by the company.

The policy was driven by profit motivation, which in itself not a bad thing, given the purpose of a business is to make money. But making money at the cost of harming people does not play well with juries. At the end of the day, a jury awarded a verdict of guilty against McDonald's and assessed $160,000 in compensatory damages and $2.7 million in punitive damages. The award sent shock waves through any company selling coffee and caused them to scramble to protect themselves from this type of event. I am sure we have all seen coffee cups with the hot liquid warning on them. Later, the award was appealed and in a remitter action, the award was reduced to $640,000 and settled for an amount assumed to be $500,000. To a corporation such as McDonald's, this type of award is nothing more than a bump in the road. But a half million dollars in an award to a plaintiff and the hundreds of thousands of dollars to litigate the suit would be significant to most organizations. How would it affect your organization, especially if you do not have an army of lawyers like McDonald's?

The Liebeck–McDonald's saga is a good case study on policy. There are some obvious strategic and operational policy issues here. McDonald's had two opportunities to prevent injury to customers at both the strategic and operational levels. The McDonald's strategic policy was to sell lots of coffee, when it should have been sell lots of coffee safely. At the operational policy stage, injury could have been prevented by lowering the holding temperature. It seems clear that security and safety concerns were investigated and considered but were ignored in the face of profit motives. In this case, it will probably work out for them as they make a half a billion dollars selling scalding hot coffee. But it seems that smart money would say that eventually a jury will punish them for this type of policy and there are a number of similar lawsuits currently pending.

From a policy theory perspective, this incident is a good example of the rational choice theory. The beliefs and desires of the company played an important part. The company believed that most customers actually wanted scalding hot coffee, or more specifically, wanted to believe it. The second element of rational choice theory is that desire clearly played a part. The desire for profit was admitted in court. Understanding the theoretical process used to reach decisions can give you a foundation for testing organizational decisions. The sensing was incomplete in that the obvious danger of serving scalding hot liquids was not recognized. Especially in light of the fact it was being served to people who McDonald's knew were driving cars.

CASE STUDY: EXPLODING CARS

For huge a company such as McDonald's, the Liebeck award was just a cost of doing business, but juries can take steps to punish huge corporations and really make it hurt. This is exactly what happened to U.S. automaker General Motors (GM) in 1999. A jury awarded a $4.9 billion verdict against the manufacturer. That's right, I said billion. In 1999, a jury in California awarded $4.9 billion to six plaintiffs who were horribly burned as a result of a rear end collision. The mechanism of injury was the placement of the gas tank in their 1979 Chevrolet Malibu, which was only 11 inches away from the rear of the car. The placement of the gas tank made the vehicle vulnerable to fires caused by rear end impacts. Evidence presented at trial showed that the cost to remedy that vulnerability was only $8.59 per vehicle. GM policy makers made the decision that it would be cheaper to pay for lawsuits involving the gas tank explosions.

This case has similarities to the McDonald's scalding case. The policy makers employed the rational choice policy theory in giving priority to the desire to avoid paying the $8.59 to remedy the defect and thus make more profit. The belief was based on the information that paying the average lawsuit settlement for lawsuits would result in a net profit. The belief was faulty as it failed to recognize facts that were unrelated to profit and loss. For example, the concept of knowingly allowing a defect to remain that results in burning passengers horribly leads to other threats to profit. At trial it was discovered that a policy decision was made to not change the design of the car despite evidence that there was a defect. Much like the case of scalding hot coffee, the jury saw that the organization acted because it was cheaper to pay damages in lawsuits than to make things safer. But in this case, the jury did not get the joke and awarded damages in the billions because they saw GM as callous and indifferent. The discovery process uncovered that both strategic and operational policy documents existed that were then introduced as evidence. The award was later reduced to $1.2 billion and later settled. One thing that is clear is that there is a trend of juries awarding massive awards in cases such as this. Organizations are being handed huge verdicts against them in order to make an impact and to signal that making choices based purely on profit motives can be extremely costly. The organizational sensing in this case was incomplete and failed to consider the effect that horribly burned people would have on a jury. It also failed to consider the damage to GM's reputation, which can affect profits in its own right.

Assuming risk is a viable practice in business, it is becoming clear that it must now be done after careful policy analysis. It is important to note that both McDonald's and GM had a defined and considered policy. They made a decision based on a cost-benefits analysis. Even this is better than not having policies or defective ones and hoping for the best. Few organizations deal with the volume McDonald's does. Your organization can be painted in a trial as callous and indifferent if you have faulty policies, and it is practically certain it will happen if you have no policy. Having a formal policy system is not just about avoiding lawsuits; it is about accomplishing the mission. Good things and bad things rarely happen by accident. We see instances of these wins and losses on a daily basis in the news. If you take a moment to dig deep enough, you will find that at the heart of every exhilarating success and every heartbreaking failure, a policy issue is present. For example, I wonder how many of us would have predicted the policy decisions behind the "stand-your-ground" law in Florida as the cause of a racially polarizing event that paralyzed the nation. The legacy of this decision is still reverberating in the United States and will for years to come. If I mention the names George Zimmerman or Trayvon Martin, it is still likely to trigger a visceral response. In this case, the state of Florida enacted a public policy that citizens could stand their ground and did not have to retreat, effectively expanding the castle doctrine to all self-defense situations. It ended up becoming a flashpoint on the disparity between the wealthy and the poor and other social ills. But a policy decision put the wheels in motion for that deadly encounter. One thing for certain is that local events can quickly become global and take on a life of their own. Or in other words, local policy decisions can have national and international impacts as shown in the following case study.

CASE STUDY: CHANGING AMERICA FOREVER

Not all adverse effects from policy decisions are local or financial; some policy decisions can have horrifyingly tragic results. An abject lesson in the effect of strategic and operational policy is the September 11, 2001, hijackings. Although each airline had their own security procedures, federal regulations did not bar box cutters from flights. Box cutters were used by the hijackers to kill the pilots and carry out their attack on the Pentagon and the World Trade Center. The Federal Aviation Administration (FAA) regulations of the day allowed knives with blades measuring less than four inches. Before the horrible events on September 11, the FAA policy on edged implements was that those under 4 inches were not prohibited. This policy decision did not effectively take into account a foreseeable risk. We now recognize that these box cutters, which by the pre-September 11 policy were deemed as a non-threat, played a critical part in the death and destruction on that terrible day. While we would like to be able to blame some faceless bureaucrat for failing to see the obvious, it is not that simple. This policy was made in good faith based on a belief that a knife short of four inches did not constitute a deadly weapon.

Government was not solely to blame. There was a nongovernmental dimension to the attacks on September 11, one that rested solely on the backs of the airline companies. The individual airline companies were responsible for passenger screening. To support the effective screening of passengers, the Air Transport Association, a cooperative industry organization of major air carriers published a *Checkpoint Operations Guide*. This guide was a manual that directed security checkpoints at airports. This compendium of operational policy clearly directed security staff to screen out all knives, including box cutters. Because checkpoint security was the responsibility of the airlines, they, not the FAA, had the ultimate responsibility to secure flights. In this case the strategic policy of the airlines was to prevent knives and other dangerous edged weapons aboard their aircraft. To this end, it had a formal operational policy, that is, seize the items as contraband. The attacks occurred anyway.

This was a policy failure of a different type, it was a nonfeasance: the failure of a company through its personnel to perform a required act. It is reported that airline security personnel of the time were poorly paid, poorly supervised, and poorly trained. In this case, the company policy was stricter than the law, it just was not followed. Airlines have also been sued over this failure to ensure that the policy was enforced. The attacks of September 11 and the policy consequences are an example of acceptance of a status quo and a failure to predict unintended consequences.

Predicting the consequences of a policy decision requires a formal process during the development phase of strategic and operational policy making. Without a defined policy-making process, things tend to get missed; September 11 is a tragic example of what can happen when policies are developed in a vacuum. Prior to September 11, we just were not thinking of a takeover of a jet as a threat. Government policy writers were focused on bombings, and their institutional history, for the most part, indicated that a plane takeover would result in a hostage standoff and demands. The private airline screeners were not properly trained or supervised and, as a result, were lax. The point here is that we must learn from our mistakes and implement real-world basic processes that give us the best chance at avoiding negative foreseeable consequences and, more importantly, unintended ones.

CASE STUDY: FLAMING GAS CANS

If you are still not convinced that a policy decision can affect you, here is another case study. If you have ever driven an automobile, I am sure you have had occasion to see or even use a red plastic gas container. If you did, in all likelihood, it was a container manufactured by a company called Blitz USA. This company started by selling metal gas cans to the U.S. government, and up until a short time ago, it sold approximately 75% of all red gasoline containers in the United States. Recently this company had to file for bankruptcy because of dozens of lawsuits over people, including children, being burned while using their containers near open flames. The cost of the litigation, which is stated to be in the tens of millions of dollars, has presumptively ruined the company. Much like the McDonald's scalding coffee lawsuit, it has become a poster child for runaway frivolous lawsuits. The company maintains that it should not be responsible for misuse of their product in what seems to be a painfully obvious danger. The fallout from this is the loss of a respected U.S. company and irreparable damage to the town of Miami, Oklahoma. If you read the resources that detail this case, you will be greeted by the overwhelming belief that this is just an outcome of a runaway problem of frivolous and unscrupulous lawyers and plaintiffs, and maybe it is. But for our purposes, we have to dig a bit and try to identify a policy issue. In this case, testimony was presented that a device called a *flame arrestor*, costing approximately 4 cents, could have prevented the types of injuries claimed in the lawsuits against Blitz USA. A flame arrestor is a device that prevents a fire by keeping flames from entering the fuel storage device. Flame arrestors have been around for decades and are a proven technology. Why didn't Blitz USA simply install this device? Perhaps it was a decision similar to McDonald's, which was based on its huge market share. Perhaps it was profit motivations and the company felt it was able to absorb the losses in litigation as a cost of doing business. Perhaps they honestly believed that it was not necessary based on a lack of guidance from the U.S. Consumer Product Safety Commission. In any event, they made a policy decision not to include a device that cost approximately $1.

It appears that someone in the organization failed to perform an effective policy analysis that took into account foreseeable consequences and unintended ones as well. I qualify my discussion about the decisions made by Blitz USA because no one will know what really happened as the company engaged in the destruction of documents and evidence. Accounts regarding the case are mainly testimonial and Blitz USA was subjected to verdicts of more than $250,000 for failing to provide discovery. My intention is not to hold out Blitz USA as a callous organization that made a poor policy decision for selfish reasons. My intent is to highlight the very real consequences of policy decisions and underscore the need to have a process that allows key organizational players to make informed decisions. In this case, it was again an example of incomplete rational choice making and the importance of organizational sensemaking. It only takes one leader to be the catalyst for this type of change to a policy process. Perhaps if those in executive positions at the company had bothered to fully assess the policy implications, none of this might have happened.

CASE STUDY: FACEBOOK UPDATES

The only thing constant in life is change. Technology has a nasty way of forcing policy decisions whether you are ready or not. Take, for example, the phenomenon of social media. Facebook alone is now a mega organization and it is a pretty safe bet they have a very robust policy system. But even in nontechnology organizations, social media affects them just the same. With almost two-thirds of all adults on social media, it is a real issue. Many companies adopted reasonable social media policies and found them to be vulnerable to challenges based on foreseeable issues. In one such case, a company in New England fired an employee for making a derogatory statement about a supervisor on Facebook. The company had a policy that prohibited making negative comments about coworkers. On its face, the policy seemed reasonable, but the National Labor Relations Board ruled this kind of speech was protected. In a more recent case, a company was sued because of a Facebook page post by an employee. In the case of *Shoun v. Best Formed Plastics, Inc.*, employee George Shoun was out of work, recovering from a workers' compensation–covered shoulder injury. A human resources employee, Jane Stewart, made a post on her personal Facebook page that called Shoun out for the length of his absence and because of his filing a lawsuit against the company. The comment was:

Isn't [it] amazing how Jimmy experienced a 5 way heart bypass just one month ago and is back to work, especially when you consider George Shoun's shoulder injury kept him away from work for 11 months and now he is trying to sue us. (Shoun v. Best Formed Plastics, Inc., Cause No. 3: 14-CV-463 RLM (N.D. Ind. Aug. 26, 2014)).

The post by employee Jane Stewart is problematic for several reasons. First, it disclosed the medical information of not one but two employees. The second is that Stewart discussed an obvious private matter on a public forum. The post stayed up on her Facebook page for 76 days and was accessible to peers and businesses in northeastern Indiana and southern Michigan. The company attempted to get the case dismissed because Mr. Shoun disclosed his medical condition in his lawsuit filing prior to Stewart's Facebook post. The court rejected this on first view and on appeal, citing that the company had an obligation to keep employee medical data confidential. The end result is that the company is now liable for the action taken by its employee and the case will see a trial. The case information is unclear if the company had a social media policy and directives. This is irrelevant as even if policies did exist they were not enforced. How effective and well thought out are your social media policies?

These examples are proof that issues involving social media continue to unfold almost daily. The social media problem is an example of the impact of new technology. These issues are central to the Internet as a disruptive technology and new issues continue to emerge, including electronic discovery, intellectual property, privacy, and more. When organizations are met with novel issues, they cannot just buy and adopt canned policies. A sound policy system requires that organizational leaders develop them specifically to the disposition of company. Without the proper skill set or tools, this can be almost impossible.

POLICY AND PEOPLE

Good policy is the cornerstone of getting people to perform effectively. When I started my career in law enforcement, I was taught that if people know why they are being told to do something, it makes it easier to get them to go along with the mission. In more than 25 years of leadership, I have found that axiom to be true. A great reason to understand the fundamentals of policy is that it allows you to communicate to your people the way things need to be done and provide a uniform manner of stating the underlying reasons. As a leader, if you can accomplish just this one thing, you will have increased efficiency and improved morale in one fell swoop. When I was a police commanding officer, our sound policy system also allowed the organization to spell out exactly when our staff had to do things a specific way without question. It also told our staff when they could do things and at what level of discretion. This also allowed the supervisors to have a concrete answer to questions about why things had to be done a certain way. This universal understanding came in very handy in crisis situations as everyone knew what to do and to do so without question. On the flip side, it also helped encourage dialogue and fostered improvements in cases where staff knew they could provide input.

Aside from the leadership function, there are many other very practical and self-serving reasons to engage in the process of writing and employing sound policies. The most selfish of all is that it frees you up as a leader to do things other than continually directing and engaging in close supervision. It makes your job a little easier, people know exactly what is expected of them and sound policies normally only require supervisory follow-up. In reality this is not selfish, it is supervisory efficiency. With the additional time gained from this efficiency, a leader can focus on employee job enrichment. Job enrichment is a management tool that provides different sources of job satisfaction through increased job responsibility or different job tasks for the employee.

Although on the surface the function of drafting and implementing policy seems as if it is mostly ministerial and mundane, it often provides the opportunity to be a change agent. The person who writes the policy has a significant say on how things are done. It puts you in the driver's seat for organizational change.

Typically, organizational managers employ transactional leadership. A transactional leader focuses on the implementation of policies and the operational aspects of the organization. But having the opportunity to strongly influence policy making allows a manager to employ transformational leadership. A transformational leader is one who causes change in individuals and social systems. A transformational leader motivates followers, naturally encouraging them to function as a collective to achieve a common aim based on shared values. Transformational leadership is embodied by getting all of your staff involved to develop policies that reflect how things are actually being done in the organization. The merger of transformational and transactional leadership has the benefit of greater organizational efficiency and buy-in by the staff. When done right, it can make organizations nimble and responsive. This book strives to give you the tools to do just that.

Nobody likes to write policy, but if you can perfect the skill set, you will become invaluable to your organization. In the field of law enforcement, officers with a policy skill set often advance quickly through the ranks as they become critical to the management of the department. In the private sector, you can also become a player in the management of the organization and if you effectively implement policy, any successes that derive from it will be irrefutably tied to you. If the idea of being in a position to have your solid work recognized and not worry about someone else taking credit does not appeal to you, then maybe a more altruistic approach does. Developing and implementing good policy is just the right thing to do. As a professional, constantly seeking improvement should be a priority. This is at the heart of a sound policy system.

If none of the above reasons are sufficient to answer the question, "Why bother?" I saved the most self-serving for last. It is not just the company that can get sued; your assets could easily be on the hook too. Well-thought-out policy can protect you from those ever-present lawyers who want to haul you into court and take your house. Yes, lawsuits are a very real danger, and if you botch up bad enough, your home and stuff can be taken from you. This alone is a compelling reason to work to build a policy system and this book can help.

PRACTICE POINTERS

- As an organizational leader, you have a responsibility to ensure that the organization is run correctly and does not cause harm purposely or negligently.
- As an organizational leader, you and the organization can be sued for policy failures.
- Policy decisions must be made with a broad assessment of the environment and circumstances.
- Policy decisions made for singular reasons, such as profit, can result in adverse outcomes such as large awards against the organization.
- Organizations are made up of people, and the human factor must always be a consideration in policy making.
- Policy making is a never-ending team process.
- Policy making is a discrete skill set and those who possess it are invaluable to their organization.

Chapter Recap

- The consequences of poor or no policy can be civil liability, fiscal harm, or even physical harm.
- There are two types of civil liability: purposeful intent and negligence.
- Purposeful intent is difficult to prove but having only an informal policy system leaves the organization vulnerable to plaintiff's interpretation of intent.
- Negligence requires that the organization have a duty to the injured and that the injury was foreseeable.
- Being sued under either theory of fault is still being sued.
- In cases where organizations have made policy decisions that favored profit over safety, the outcomes were poor. These include huge jury verdicts and even the death of the organization.
- Emerging technology can present distinct problems as existing policies may not suffice in the face of new innovations.
- As an organizational leader you have an obligation to yourself and the company to ensure that a good policy system exists.
- By becoming a subject matter expert on policy making, the opportunity exists to be a transformational leader.

BIBLIOGRAPHY

Alexander, R., & Hawes, A. (*2008, March 26*). Gas tank fires: The $4.9 billion verdict against general motors for the explosion of 1979 Chevrolet Malibu. *FindLaw.com.* Retrieved from: <http://corporate.findlaw.com/finance/gas-tank-fires-the-4-9-billion-verdict-against-general-motors.html>.

Anderson v. General Motors, 817 F. Supp. 467 (1993).

Birkland, T. A. (2009). Disasters, catastrophes, and policy failure in the homeland security era. *Review of Policy Research*, 26(4), 423–438. http://dx.doi.org/10.1111/j.1541-1338.2009.00393.x

Brannen, F. P., Jr. (2013). Product liability. *Mercer Law Review*, 65, 221.

Cain, K. G. (2007). And now, the rest of the story… the McDonald's coffee lawsuit. *Journal of Consumer and Commercial Law*, 11, 14–17.

Diamond, S. S. (2003). Truth, justice, and the jury. *Harvard Journal of Law and Public Policy*, 26, 143.

Directorate General of Air Transport. Report of the Peruvian Ministry of Transport and Communications, December 1996. Retrieved from: <http://www.skybrary.aero/bookshelf/books/1719.pdf>.

Fleischer-Black, M. (2004, June 1). One lump or two? *The American Lawyer*. Retrieved from: <http://www.americanlawyer.com/id=900005408902/One-Lump-Or-Two>.

Goodnow, E. J., & Wayman, J. C. (2009, November). The intersection between transformational leadership and data use in schools. Paper presented at the 2009 Annual Convention of the University Council for Educational Administration, Anaheim, CA.

Green v. Blitz U.S.A., Inc., 2011 WL 806011 (E.D. Tex. Mar. 1, 2011).

Hanberger, A. (2001). What is the policy problem? Methodological challenges in policy evaluation. *Evaluation*, *7*(1), 45–62.

Hickey, C. R. (2013). Comparative fault and strict products liability: are they compatible? *Pepperdine Law Review*, *5*(2), 8.

Higginbotham, F. M. (2010). *Race law: Cases, commentary, and questions*. Durham, NC: Carolina Academic Press.

Internal Revenue Service. (2013). *Tax guide for churches and religious organizations*. Washington, DC: U.S. Department of the Treasury.

Kurtz, H. E. (2013). *Trayvon Martin and the dystopian turn in U.S. self-defense doctrine*. *Antipode*, *45*(2), 248–251. http://dx.doi.org/10.1111/j.1467-8330.2012.01057.x

Miller-Merrell, J. (2013). History of terminations & firings because of employee social media. *Blogging4Jobs doi: #SMApkfxkgtidDBTQ.97.*

National Commission on Terrorist Attacks upon the United States, Kean, T. H., & Hamilton, L. (2004). *The 9/11 Commission report: Final report of the National commission on terrorist attacks upon the united states*. Washington, DC: National Commission on Terrorist Attacks upon the United States. Retrieved from: <http://www.9-11commission.gov/report/911Report.pdf>.

Pan, W. S. Y., & Werblow, J. (2012). Does good job enrichment policy and practices impact employee's job satisfaction? *Journal of Global Business Issues*, *6*(1), 1–5. Retrieved from: <http://search.proquest.com/docview/1461910383?accountid=12793>.

Plessy v. Ferguson, 163 U.S. 537 (*1896*).

Pollack, A. (*1999, July 10*). $4.9 billion jury verdict in G.M. fuel tank case. *The New York Times*. Retrieved from: <http://www.nytimes.com/1999/07/10/us/4.9-billion-jury-verdict-in-gm-fuel-tank-case.html>.

Reinsch, R. W., & Goltz, S. (2014). You can't get there from here: Implications of the Walmart v. Dukes decision for addressing second generation discrimination. *Northwestern Journal of Law and Social Policy*, *9*, 264–390.

Rothman, K. J., & Poole, C. (1985, April). Science and policy making. *American Journal of Public Health*, *75*, 340–341.

Rubin, P. H. (2011). Markets, tort law, and regulation to achieve safety. *CATO Journal*, *31*(2), 217–236.

Rutherford, D. G. (1998). Lessons from Liebeck: QSRS cool the coffee. *The Cornell Hotel and Restaurant Administration Quarterly*, *39*(3), 72–75.

Selmi, M. (2002). Price of discrimination: The nature of class action employment discrimination litigation and its effects. *Texas Law Review*, *81*, 1249.

Shoun v. Best Formed Plastics, Inc., Cause No. 3: 14-CV-463 RLM (N.D. Ind. Aug. 26, 2014).

Twerski, A. D. (2006). Chasing the illusory pot of gold at the end of the rainbow: Negligence and strict liability in design defect litigation. *Marquette Law Review*, *90*(1), 7–20.

Vries, L. (2002, November 12). Boxcutters weren't allowed pre-9/11. *CBS News*. Retrieved from: <http://www.cbsnews.com/news/boxcutters-werent-allowed-pre-9-11/>.

Walters, J. M., & Sumwalt, R. L. (2000). *Aircraft accident analysis: Final reports.* New York: *McGraw-Hill.*

Weiser, B. (2011, September 16). Court filing details shortcomings of airport screeners on 9/11. The New York Times. Retrieved from: <http://www.nytimes.com/2011/09/17/nyregion/court-filing-details-shortcomings-of-911-airport-screeners.html?_r=0>.

"What is a flame arrester?" (n.d.). Retrieved from: <http://gascansafety.org/gas-can-safety-and-you/what-flame-arrester>.

Ybarra, S., & Poole, R. W., Jr. (2013). Overhauling US airport security screening. *Reason Foundation*, 1–5.

Basic Training

At the heart of sound policy making is the understanding that it is, in fact, a system. The system consists of two distinct parts: the policy elements and the supporting elements. The policy elements are those that go into the making of the policies. Policy elements are the analytical and policy communication tools. The second part are the mechanisms that support the policies. These are communication, training, supervision, and discipline. The purpose of this chapter is to cover the basics of operational policy tools, including the various types and the pros and cons of each. We will discuss the different ways operational policy tools are drafted and explore why one size does not fit all. The necessity for a strong foundation and the correct use of terminology will be examined. The value of doing everything for a reason will also be examined.

Many years ago I found myself standing on yellow footprints with 60 other young men on a very muggy South Carolina island. I didn't know it then, but this very strange act was the foundational step in my becoming a member of the United States Marine Corps. I learned a valuable lesson on Parris Island, aside from not swatting sand fleas. I learned that to become proficient at a task, every action you take in that direction has to be for a purpose. As a first-phase boot recruit, it was often difficult to understand why the heck I was doing some of the things I did there. Looking back, it becomes clear why things were done the way they were. The drill instructors worked from a specifically designed plan that focused on doing the little things right. In addition to the focus on detail, each action taught was designed to support a larger goal. For example, sitting on the floor in boot camp was done a very particular way, that is, cross-legged with the left foot over the right. It was difficult to understand why we had to sit cross-legged, as it was not comfortable, and the choice of left over right was a mystery. The reason became crystal clear when my platoon went to the rifle range and had to qualify from the sitting position, which requires all of your weight be on the ankles and buttocks. The daily act of sitting cross-legged was training us to shoot from that position. Sitting a particular way could never be described as a mission-critical skill for a U.S. Marine, but shooting effectively from the proper sitting position certainly is. The moral of my story is that little things matter and that effective outcomes require effective and well-thought-out foundations. If you find yourself doing something in the policy-making process and you aren't sure why, then you need to analyze exactly why you are doing it. If you can establish exactly why, then you can proceed, but if you cannot, the action or element should be abandoned.

The act of developing policy and drafting directives is no different. In Chapter 2, we identified two elements in a policy system: strategic policy and operational policy. Strategic policy is the setting of organizational goals or desired outcomes. Operational policy is the process of producing formal materials to support and accomplish the strategic policy. In both, a well-thought-out foundation is essential to getting results. You may have noticed I have introduced the word *directives*. A directive is the proper term for the written documents that are the products of the operational policy part of our policy system. Directives can be laws, rules, orders, procedures, protocols, memorandums, and any other number of formal documents that are used to carry out the operational policy. Most people call everything policy, but it is critical to begin to understand and adopt the accurate terminology. The use of accurate terminology may seem unimportant, but much the same way sitting a particular way helped me shoot effectively in boot camp, proper terminology will yield dividends later. As a leader, you will have to be the change agent for this adoption of correct lexicon. I assure you it will not be easy, but it will be worth it.

Coworkers, superiors, and subordinates will not initially recognize the importance of an effective policy system, let alone the need to be precise in vocabulary. Resistance to organizational change is normal and is part of the natural human response of moving from the known to the unknown. By its very nature, the act of effectively determining strategic policy and then writing the supporting directives is often a mystery to those who are not tasked with doing so. If an organization or person undertakes strategic or operational policy making without having a distinct purpose, they will be left with a vague jumble of words on paper in the best case and at the genesis of an adverse event in the worst case.

The goal of any directive is set by the chief executive and is the starting point. In other words, the chief executive lays out the intended outcome he or she desires. Once this is determined, it must be communicated to all members of the organization. The person responsible for drafting the communication must determine the best directive drafting tool to use. The key to understanding when to employ the different types of directives will be driven by the level of employee discretion desired or appropriate. Employee discretion is normally relative to the risk or reward involved in the outcome. The greater the risk or reward, the more restrictive or permissive the employee discretion. A thorough cost-benefits analysis will guide the extent of discretion.

Once the appropriate directive is determined, the process of drafting of the document will commence. The process will require the drafter to have some basic information. The first piece of information required will be to identify and understand the strategic policy or outcome desired as set by the chief executive of the organization. The second piece of information will be to determine why the directive is being issued or what the purpose is for creating a formal document. The final piece of information to determine is the target audience for the directive.

The initial process can be reduced to these short questions:

What? = The policy or outcome desired
Why? = The purpose of issuing the directive
How or Who? = The actual organization members targeted by the written directive

To demonstrate how this might work in practice, consider this vignette: If you have seen the TV show *Storage Wars*, you have undoubtedly observed employees cutting locks off storage lockers. Imagine you are the head of operations of a storage company and you are called into the company president's office. He advises you that one of the managers was injured by flying debris while cutting a lock off a locker; he demands that "you do something about it." This is an indicator to begin the policy process basic steps. The first thing you need to do is answer the "What?" question. In this case, we know the president wants to prevent injury during lock cutting. This is the strategic policy or goal determined by the chief executive officer of the organization. Next is the "Why?" question, and it requires a bit more analysis. Based on the business, you know that stopping the practice of removing locks is not an option. It is a necessary and reasonable step in the reclamation of the locker space and authorized by the contract. Under different circumstances, prohibiting the action could be appropriate. In this case, cutting the locks is an essential function, so a way to make it safer is required. The *why* equates to doing it without injury and the answer is that it is an essential part of the business to recoup losses for nonpaying clients and to free up the space to rent.

A cost-benefit analysis indicates that the cost of not performing this action is to lose revenue and the benefit is to procure revenue. It is essential to the fiscal survival of the company. A risk assessment indicates that forcibly removing the locks carries with it inherent dangers from application of physical force or cutting. Because it is a critical function, the risk assessment will also examine risk mitigation tools and tactics and will provide solutions to accomplish the task safely. The final basic analysis is to ask "How or who?" This is where you determine the specific action desired to deal with the answers to the first two questions. The operations manager must pick the mitigation process, for example, adding safety equipment, such as eye protection and gloves. The tactics employed to enhance safety could be to provide training and direction on how to safely cut a lock and how to prevent third parties from sustaining injury. The eye protection, gloves, and formal direction (operational policy) on how to safely perform the task would be how the organization will meet the policy set by the president. The *how* also will include the exact circumstances the eye protection will be worn and will dictate the level of discretion. In this case I would require any employee cutting locks to wear eye protection without discretion and would completely restrict discretion on the process.

The case study of our fictional storage company manager is rooted in reality. The insurance group Deland, Gibson Insurance Associates, Inc. of Massachusetts published an assessment of the actions of storage company employees cutting off locks as seen on the popular show on their company web page. Insurance companies certainly have a vested interest in preventing accidents, and operational policy is a tried and true mitigation tool. Granted, this is a simple example of the first steps employed in formulating and drafting directives. Yet the steps will be the same regardless of how complex the issue. We will go into much greater detail in Chapter 9.

Once the analysis is completed and the basic questions are answered, the proper directive format must be selected to communicate the policy. The second level of implementing the process is understanding the tools available. This is where using the proper terminology, identifying the operational policy directives, is critical. To accomplish this successfully, an organizational leader and policy expert must embrace the language of the policy system. A law professor once said to me, "Words mean things." In response I chuckled and left with what I thought would be a great catch phrase. Yet after thoughtful reflection and some maturing, I realize that this is no joke. Words really do mean things and they can have very real consequences. Allow me to introduce you to the lexicon of effective policy makers.

The policy part of the policy system is a hierarchy with a highly specific top and a general base. When thinking of the policy aspects of the system, think of an Egyptian pyramid. These are structures of four triangular sides with very wide bases and an apex at the top. For our purposes, the pyramid represents the discretionary policy-making structure of our policy system. The base of the pyramid represents the strategic policy of the organization. It is the goal or end result desired by the organization and represents the general direction that the organization is intended to pursue. It allows for the broadest amount of discretion. If you look closer, you will also recognize that the base is the critical first building block of the pyramid, and in the construction of the structure, the starting point. Thus the strategic policy is the foundational building block of the policy system. As the pyramid moves up toward the apex, it begins to narrow. This is how a policy system works, the higher up the structure, the more narrow the focus of the directive and the less discretion allowed the employee. At the top of the pyramid is the rule. The rule is also the apex of operation policy and the directive that allows virtually no discretion. From apex to foundation, the order of directives is: rule, order, special order, procedure, and strategic policy (Figure 3.1).

The foundation of the pyramid is built on something that is not actually part of the pyramid; it already existed. I am, of course, referring to terra firma, also known as the ground. In the same way the ground supports a physical pyramid structure, the policy structure is also supported. The support in this case is through the functions of training, supervision, communication, and discipline. Without an acceptable foundation, the pyramids in Egypt would not have survived. Keeping with the building construction example, consider the Leaning Tower of Pisa in Italy. The construction commenced in August 1173 for a beautifully ornate bell tower in the City of Pisa. The construction of the tower was gradual and was eventually completed in 1370. Obviously an incredible amount of work went into the

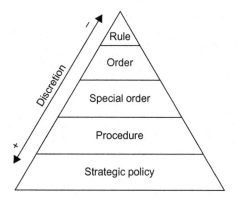

■ **FIGURE 3.1** Graphic by Matthew Bremer.

creation of this bell tower and the design of the structure itself is sound. Nevertheless the bell tower got the moniker "leaning" for a reason. The tower was built on an insufficient foundation and the only reason that it did not topple over was because of the gradual and interrupted building process. The tower is reported to have moved 1.55 millimeters every year until the 1990s, when efforts began to shore it up. Even though the structure itself was well thought out and perfectly constructed, the supporting element was weak. In the same way a physical building is a system, policy can only exist as part of an effective system. If you make exceptional policy-making choices and draft well-thought-out directives, the end result may still be a failure if the supporting elements are not in place. Without communicating the directives to your staff and then training them, your foundation is weak. If the directives are not thoroughly enforced by supervisors, the foundation is even weaker. If there are no consequences or remedial actions for violating directives, then the foundation fails.

The key to understanding how policy works in this system is to recognize the role discretion plays in the process. Directives should manage human freedom of choice by effectively communicating the limitations. Discretion clearly defined by directive helps both staff and supervisors understand their role clearly. For example, a procedure allows employees discretion and they can depart from the procedure for a practical reason. In contrast, an employee cannot deviate from a rule. Aside from communicating the level of discretion employees have in carrying out their duties, the different types of directives also indicate how much justification is required for departing from the directive. This is particularly important when the directive is an order. An order allows for discretion but only when justifiable and necessary. This can be a valuable tool in post–action reporting and can also be used as a diagnostic tool for the appropriateness of the discretionary level in the directive, or even the effectiveness and the applicability itself. For example, if employees routinely depart from the requirements of an order, this could signal that the environment has changed and the employee can no longer perform the task as directed. It also may signal that if this was undetected, the sensemaking and situational awareness of the organization may be suffering.

POLICY TOOLS
Policy

Policy can mean to organize, order, or regulate (a state, country, etc.). This term has its origins in the word *police*, which refers to the power of a state to regulate in their jurisdiction. As we have previously examined, the word *policy* has many different meanings and there is no universally accepted definition. Since the intent of this book is to make policy making as efficient as possible, working definitions will be employed. Therefore to achieve that goal, the definition of policy is *a flexible set of broad guidelines used to communicate the intended direction of the organization or an intended result*. The leader of the organization uses a policy statement to communicate the end result he or she desires. The policy should be clear and concise. I remember by heart the unambiguous mission (strategic policy) of the United States Marine Corps rifle squad: to locate, close with, and destroy the enemy by fire and maneuver, or repel the enemy assault by fire and close combat. Otherwise taught to us as, Find 'em, fix 'em, kill 'em. But between the stated mission and the execution were various levels of directives and training on exactly how to do it. Cutting loose heavily armed U.S. Marines without those supporting directives and training would lead to a very bad outcome.

To demonstrate this point another way, I will use a less violent example in the following case study depicting global commerce.

CASE STUDY: MALLETS FOR CHINA

The chief executive officer of the XYZ Company determines that it will be beneficial to have a policy of selling one million rubber mallets to China. The strategic policy is communicated: "It is the policy of the XYZ Mallet Company to expand our global market share by selling at least one million units of the Rubber Hawk mallet in the nation of China."

This policy statement provides a guiding principle to everyone in the organization in everything they do. Everyone knows that the company wants to sell one million mallets, specifically the Rubber Hawk model to China. The goal or strategic policy is unambiguous. Note that this is a general expectation that leaves the *how* to each subordinate person or group. This works well because it can effectively be applied to each work unit. The sales force knows that whatever they do must support this result as does the accounting department, and perhaps less obviously, the chief security officer or security director should take note. The term *policy* tends to be used as the blanket term for any type of written direction and can in itself, be a formal directive. Using only the strategic policy statement as the company directive, absent any operational policy directives, indicates to the organizational members that they have a high degree of discretion in achieving the result communicated by the policy.

Although relying on the formal communication of the strategic policy can produce the desired results, it also can produce many undesired results.

Without the issuance of formal directives to support the strategic policy, each employee can accomplish the goal in the manner that he or she sees fit. Employees could mistake the full intent of the CEO, as there could be many interpretations of just how the goal could be accomplished. Even though the number of units to be sold and the model and market have been identified, the statement is still a general, rather than specific, direction. For example, does China mean the People's Republic of China or the Republic of China, otherwise known as Taiwan? What is the price point desired for the sale of the Rubber Hawk mallet? The methods employed may also be up for interpretation. Would it be acceptable to use bribes to get the product sold? Are there any situations where the company would not want to sell the product? Perhaps an intended use of the mallet in China is to beat prisoners or dissidents.

This is why it is important to perform a risk analysis and to be sure that the goal is achieved in a manner that is not detrimental to the organization. In this case study, the strategic policy communicated a high level of discretion permitted to the members of the organization, which could have resulted in potential adverse consequences. It is rare to have a formal policy issued without supporting directives. It must be noted that an effectively written directive will contain a clear and concise *policy statement* to indicate the overall result desired. A policy statement serves an important function of providing strategic policy context to operational policy documents.

Procedure

A procedure is the most common type of directive. It can go by various names such as *standard operating procedure*, *process*, or *modus operandi*. Regardless of its title, a procedure sets out the recommended steps in carrying out the intended action. Whereas a policy answers the *what* of an analysis, the procedure is the *how*. For example, what are we trying to accomplish and how will we accomplish it? A procedure authorizes less discretion than a policy grants but still provides latitude for the member to deviate in the furtherance of accomplishing the organizational objective. In some cases, organizations are tempted to limit the discretion in a procedure by adding limiting terms such as *shall* or *must*. This is a bad practice and should be avoided. We will discuss policy construction in much greater detail in Chapter 8. A procedure should be used when discretion and creativity are acceptable.

Order

An order is as direct as it sounds. It is simply a command to do something specific. There are several types of orders and each has its place.

General Order

For our system, a general order is used to direct personnel in situations where discretion is least desired. For example, if you were in a food service organization, the food prep area cleaning directives should be general orders. The need for very specific actions in food preparation are great as they can cause serious health issues and/or be grounds for regulatory violations. In the security profession, any discussion of the use of force would be guided by a general order. In any situation where health and safety are involved, tight control is indicated. There is an accommodation for deviation from a general order, but deviation from a general order can only be for just cause. Some organizations use general orders as a singular medium for directives. In this case, they differentiate discretion through the use of words such as *shall* or *may*. This can be highly confusing and leaves much room for interpretation. It also relies on single words hidden within the directive to establish the level of discretion permitted.

Special Order

A special order is a type of order that is used in circumstances that deviate from the norm, are preplanned yet are short in duration. This order is useful in situations where the current orders or procedures would be ineffective or impractical during the event. These orders are specific to the incident or event and are normally self-cancelling. These orders are particularly useful for events that bring multiple units or departments together to accomplish an event. An example of this type of event would be a shareholder meeting. A special order would be all encompassing and would cover the desired actions in one document.

Personnel Order

A personnel order is used to assign a member of an organization to a unit, department, or function. It is a critical yet seldom-used directive in small to mid-sized organizations. The value of this order is that is specifies the job responsibility of the member and sets the supervisory responsibility for the member. It is a foundational document that clearly communicates a person's place and function. It can be extremely useful for training and discipline.

Rule or Regulation

A rule or regulation is at the opposite end of the spectrum of the policy. A rule or regulation leaves no room for discretion. Think of it as the organization's law, much like laws in society, they are absolutes. Rules and regulations are the foundation of a sound directive system. Many organizations include these as part of their employee manuals. This type of directive is best used to delineate actions that are completely forbidden or actions that must be performed.

Divisional, Departmental, or Unit Order

A divisional, departmental, or unit order is a limited authority order that is used by the senior leader of a division or a department. This allows the leader to communicate expectations or direction to members of a singular department, division, or unit. These orders are used in very narrow circumstances that apply to a select group of people. This type of order must be used with caution, as it cannot be used in a manner that supplants directives issued in general or that contradict. An example of its use would be a unit that is working in an area of the organization that may be required to work weekends to complete a project and the division leader wishes to allow for relaxed attire but still wants to maintain a corporate casual look.

Management Memorandum

A management memorandum is an effective tool that can be used to communicate in a less formal manner yet it ensures accountability. This can be issued by executive management to remind staff of organizational intent or to make a correction that is preventive in nature. This type of memorandum could be used to remind staff members that they are not permitted to leave their work stations for the purpose of a smoking break, or to direct staff members not to park in certain areas during construction or during peak public access hours. Much like the divisional order, this type of directive should only be used sparingly.

Although this might all seem a bit basic, ensuring that everyone understands the difference between each type of directive plays a critical part in the organization's effectiveness. As you have seen, the trick with this system is that the type of directive signals the amount of discretion that the member can employ when carrying out the mission of the organization. This makes supervision more effective as there is no question about what is expected. It also protects the individual member and the organization because everyone understands that when their actions deviate from the stated direction the more justification is required. For example, if a member deviates from a general order that requires specific action, the member knows that the underlying reason for the departure must be documented and for good cause. When a member has to deviate from a general order, it presents two opportunities. First it allows for others to learn from the experience, and second, it may uncover an innovative way to perform a task that was not envisioned when the order was developed and drafted.

The key to a successful directive system is that all the members in the organization know what is expected, how it is expected to be carried out, and the consequences for failing to follow the directive. These considerations are controlled by the policy supporting elements of training, supervision, communication, and discipline. Policy making is also supported by the planning process. Every organization should engage in regular planning and testing of plans. Directives can contain planning provisions, but the actual planning documents should be separate and referenced in the directive. A planning document should be separate because a plan should be a robust document that deals with many contingencies and as such, are large and contain too much data to be effective as a directive.

Plan

A plan is a document designed to prepare an organization for a future event. The plans can cover a wide range of situations or contingencies. Plans are the written product of preparation and are essential to organizational resiliency. Planning is most often called for to deal with events that are low frequency and high risk. The value of a plan is that it provides a process to deal with situations that are outside the normal scope of the organization. Additionally, plans can be tested through drills or exercises to ensure that they are relevant and effective.

BUY-IN, CAUSE AND EFFECT, AND COMMUNICATION

Central to the success of your directive system are the concepts of buy-in, cause and effect, and communication. Even if an organization has a formal directive system that uses the correct language and format, the job is not done. Equally important to format and syntax is the content of the directive. When drafting a directive, the content has to create an environment that communicates to members the benefits and consequences of their actions relative to the directive. This concept is not new and has been effectively employed throughout history. A dramatic example of this comes from antiquity. No one can argue that the Roman Empire was one of the most organized and efficient in history. The leaders were able to achieve this because they were able to impress a workable directive system into their military. That is to say, they set a mission and a penalty for failure and communicated it in an unmistakable way. As the military was a major part of the success of the empire, the mission was typically to perform during combat. A compelling example of this is the policy of decimation. Central to the effectiveness of the Roman legion was the discipline of each cohort. Each member was expected to perform as directed. This level of meeting expectation allowed battlefield commanders to maneuver with confidence. How could the commander be sure that this discipline would hold? Because each soldier knew what was expected and he also knew what would happen if he failed. A disgraced soldier faced several types of discipline, from removal from the legion without pension to corporal punishment and worse. The policy of decimation was imposed when a unit failed to perform or showed cowardice in the face of the enemy. One man out of every 10 men were chosen by drawing lots. The unlucky man who drew the lot was executed by the remaining nine members. The punishment was random in that every member of the unit could suffer regardless of guilt. The effect of this was that each member of the unit had a personal stake in the successful outcome of the organizational mission. It is very likely that each man made sure that the man next to him stood his ground and performed his duty. In addition, it allowed for rehabilitation of the offending unit. By taking 10% of the group, the remaining members were still viable and were unlikely to repeat the offense. This visceral directive was allegedly employed beyond the era of the Roman Empire with incidents being reported in World War I by the Italian army and in World War II by the Soviet army. While I do not advocate this type of generalized and extreme punishment, there is no arguing its impact. Taken in the context of hand-to-hand combat where the stakes are extremely high, the use of decimation as a policy is arguably acceptable in a utilitarian way.

The lessons of decimation are that it contains key features that make a directive system successful:

- The intended goal is clear and unambiguous.
- The consequences of failure to perform are clear.
- The use of the directive supports the overall policy.
- While extreme, it provides training to the remaining members.

Decimation demonstrates the element of cause and effect that is required for each directive. The cause and effect were communicated in simple terms and this resulted in buy-in by every member of the army. The basic lesson presented here is know what the boss wants, know why you are doing it, and select who will do it and how it will be done. Once you have made these determinations, select the proper policy tool and then produce content that effectively communicates the expected outcome, highlight the cause-and-effect relationship relative to performance, and foster buy-in by personnel. Effective communication in a directive must be accomplished by keeping the information clear and concise. Directives should be constructed so as to avoid extraneous or overly technical information. Asking

"Why is this in here?" is a test that can prevent unnecessary information and/or overly technical information. This follows the "everything for a purpose" techniques discussed earlier in the chapter.

The use of decimation is obviously an extreme way to achieve buy-in to a policy. How do we achieve buy-in today? Buy-in can be achieved by soliciting meaningful input from staff, particularly when developing operational policies. In fact it is a good idea to assign the task of developing the directive to the very staff that performs the task on a daily basis. It is essential to honestly assess input from staff members and where possible, include it in the directive. This policy-making approach has two distinct benefits. First, it can expand internal situational awareness for upper management who are not exposed to the operational aspects of the organization on a daily basis. The second benefit is that the more members of an organization that can get *their* fingerprints on a directive, the more likely there will be buy-in. This employee ownership of the policy-making process and outcome engenders policy advocates. These advocates help ensure that directives are followed and also ensure that they remain effective. This is simply a matter of empowering employees and is a central tenant of many management efficiency strategies.

■ SUMMARY

Policy making is at its heart a system with two parts: policy elements and supporting elements. In developing policy, everything is done for a reason, and if you do not know why, then reevaluate.

In this chapter, the term *directive* was introduced. A directive is the written document that conveys operational policy. The goals of these directives are set by the chief executive, and the use of proper process and terminology is critical to success. When drafting directives, it is essential to determine the amount of discretion allowed and then draft accordingly. The higher the risk, the lower the discretion. To draft directives, a basic analysis should be performed that identifies what, why, and who or how. Once policy analysis supported by risk and cost-benefits analysis is complete, the selection of the proper directive format must be undertaken. These formats or tools are policy, procedure, special order, order, and rule. Policy provides for the greatest discretion and rule the least discretion. These can be thought of as a pyramid structure with the rule being the apex and the policy being base. Supporting this policy structure are training, supervision, communication, and discipline. Critical to the success of even a well-built policy structure is the buy-in from the employees. This can be accomplished by soliciting active and meaningful participation by employees. In doing so, employees can take ownership of the process and outcomes. An effectively drafted directive will also include clear rewards and penalties and a cause-and-effect statement. Effective communication in a directive must be accomplished by keeping the information clear and concise. Directives should be constructed so as to avoid extraneous or overly technical information.

PRACTICE POINTERS

- Every action or element included in policy should be done for a purpose that can be exactly identified and quantified.
- When engaged in policy making, always test your actions and directive content by asking, "Why is this being included or performed?"
- When drafting directives, the key is to effectively identify the level of discretion permitted and then draft accordingly.
- When engaging in the creation of directives, it is critical to encourage employee ownership of the policies through meaningful solicitation of input. This creates employee ownership of directives and the outcomes.
- When drafting directives, avoid unclear or overly technical information.

Chapter Recap

- Policy making is at its heart a system with two parts: policy elements and supporting elements.
- In developing policy, everything is done for a reason, and if you do not know why, reevaluate.
- When drafting directives, it is essential to determine the amount of discretion allowed and then draft accordingly.
- The policy tools are policy, procedure, special order, order, and rule.
- The policy structure can be thought of as a pyramid.
- The policy structure is supported by training, supervision, communication, and discipline.
- A well-built policy structure includes buy-in from the employees based on meaningful employee input.
- Directives should be clear and concise and free of extraneous or overly technical information.

BIBLIOGRAPHY

Amos, J. (2007). *Marine corps combat marksmanship programs* (MCO 3574.2K). Department of the Navy, United States Marine Corps. Retrieved from: <http://www.marines.mil/Portals/59/MCO 3574.2K.pdf>.

Bovey, W. H., & Hede, A. (2001). Resistance to organizational change: the role of cognitive and affective processes. *Leadership & Organization Development Journal, 22*(8), 372–382.

Burland, J. B., Jamiolkowski, M. B., & Viggiani, C. (2009). Leaning Tower of Pisa: Behaviour after stabilization operations. *International Journal of Geoengineering Case Histories, 1*(3), 156–169.

Cameron, E., & Green, M. (2004). *Making sense of change management: A complete guide to the models, tools & techniques of organizational change.* London: Kogan Page.

Canadian Trade Commissioner Service. (2015). *Doing business in China – the dangers of engaging in corrupt practices.* Retrieved from: <http://www.tradecommissioner.gc.ca/eng/document.jsp?did=153381>.

Coulston, J. (2013). Courage and cowardice in the Roman Imperial Army. *War in History, 20*(1), 7–31. http://dx.doi.org/10.1177/0968344512454518

Cross, H., Hardee, K., & Jewell, N. (2001). Reforming operational policies: A pathway to improving reproductive health programs. POLICY Occasional Paper Series, No. 7. Washington, DC: Futures Group, POLICY Project.

Dowd, E. T., & Wallbrown, F. (1994). Psychological reactance and its relationship to normal personality variables. *Cognitive Therapy and Research, 18*(6), 601–612.

Filson, L. E., & Strokoff, S. L. (2008). *Legislative drafter's desk reference.* Washington, DC: CQ Press.

Fitzgerald, G. A., & Desjardins, N. M. (2004). Organizational values and their relation to organizational performance outcomes. *Atlantic Journal of Communication, 12*(3), 121–145.

Green, L. R. (2008). Behavioral science and food safety. *Journal of Environmental Health, 71*(2), 47–49.

Haynes, D. (2015, March 23). *Storage wars.* Retrieved from: <http://www.delandgibson.com/blog/business-insurance/storage-wars/>.

Jacobs, J. A. (1999). Drafting proper governance documents. *Association Management, 51*(4), 111–112.

Kanji, G. K., & Asher, M. (1996). *100 Methods for total quality management.* London: Sage.

Mowles, C. (2011). *Rethinking management: Radical insights from complexity sciences.* Farnham: Gower.

Neves, P., & Eisenberger, R. (2012). Management communication and employee performance: The contribution of perceived organizational support. *Human Performance, 25*(5), 452–464. http://dx.doi.org/10.1080/08959285.2012.721834

Ortega, J. (2009). Employee discretion and performance pay. *The Accounting Review, 84*(2), 589–612.

Peacock, L. (2008). Employee buy-in delivers productivity gains. *Personnel Today,* 51.

Pendleton, A. (2001). *Employee ownership, participation, and governance: A study of ESOPs in the UK.* London: Routledge.

Simmons, T. (2015, March 23). Locate, close with and destroy. Retrieved from: <http://www.marines.mil/News/NewsDisplay/tabid/3258/Article/560453/locate-close-with-and-destroy.aspx>.

Whitty, M. (1996). Co-management for workplace democracy. *Journal of Organizational Change Management, 9*(6), 7–11.

Chapter 4

Incoming!

This chapter examines the triggering events, both internal and external that signal an organization to make strategic or operational policy changes. To recognize a triggering event, the organization and its members must engage in the process of sensing. A series of small sensemaking errors can result in large-scale damage. This is an often overlooked element of policy development that has far-reaching implications. To produce effective policy, the security manager must be situationally aware and recognize those events that should trigger policy action.

ORGANIZATIONAL ROLE

Organizations come in all shapes, sizes, and missions. Organizations have been studied by many academics and there have been many theories that emanate from these studies. What remains common among all of these theories is the recognition of some common traits in all organizations. These common threads are:

- The presence of people
- The grouping of people together to accomplish a common mission
- The coordination of the people to accomplish the mission
- The combining and leveraging of individual strengths to overcome individual limitations
- The establishment of a leadership structure that generates decision making
- The presence of rules and policies

A critical thread in all of these is the necessity and role of people and the impact of leadership and policy. It is incumbent on leaders to move the organization (and its people) forward in an environment of threats and opportunities. An essential part of movement is sensing of the surroundings. Blind movement of any kind is not just less than optimal but downright dangerous. Leading an organization forward is no different.

ORGANIZATIONAL SENSING

It has been said Learn from the mistakes of others, you cannot live long enough to make them all yourself. I find this statement particularly on point for those who are running organizations. In the contemporary world, trial and error is not a viable business model. If as a leader you do not learn from the mistakes of those around you, particularly those in your industry, you and your organization will not be around long. The purpose of this chapter is to explore the concept of proactive policy making, which is to say, paying attention to your environment and adapting to it via policy changes and effective development of directives. This construct is called *sensing*.

We define sensing as an organization's ability to fathom its complex relationship with the outside world. The sensing process consists of three distinct stages: noticing, interpreting, and acting (Daft & Weick, 1984; Kiesler & Sproull, 1982). We examine the process at the lowest unit of an organization – the person.

Noticing

Noticing involves the act of recognizing some stimuli. This stimuli triggers an assessment to determine if it can be categorized and connected to some previous experience. If the stimuli can be understood on the basis of prior experience and is not presented in a novel way, the process ends. There is no need to move to the next stage of sensemaking. This level will indicate the necessity for action or inaction. In the case of a security officer, the detection of smoke from an area that contains machines that generate smoke would generate no action. Yet the stimuli of smoke in an area that does not normally have machines that cause the condition would trigger movement to the next phase of sensemaking, which is *interpretation*.

Interpretation

Interpretation is the process in which the receiver of the stimuli begins to analyze the potential causes of the stimulus. The interpretation is internal and relies on how the cues are identified in a meaningful form. The meaningful form can be identification of the stimulus as threat or nonthreat. This is like putting a puzzle together. How does the person put the stimuli in a frame of reference? In the case of the security officer and smoke, the frame of reference is the location of the smoke. The new location presents the smoke as a problem. This then leads to the final phase of sensemaking, which is *acting*.

Acting

Acting is the final step in this process. It is the purposeful behavior geared to addressing the stimuli as it has been interpreted. The action then affects the stimuli and starts the cycle all over again as new stimuli are produced. In the case of our security officer, the action could be calling the fire department, using a fire extinguisher, or evacuating the building.

As you can see, each phase of this process is highly dependent on the accuracy of the others. In the context of the security officer, the noticing skills can be sharpened through good training, capable supervision, and experience. The interpretation can be guided through effective policy that reduces the options for framing things. For example, the indoctrination of the security officer is to report everything observed. The final element is action. This is also effectively influenced through training and policy, for example, a rule that a security officer must contact a security supervisor anytime smoke is detected. Given that organizations are made up of people, sensemaking can be extrapolated to the organization.

Organizational sensing for our purposes is the act of using every tool at our disposal to detect and analyze streams of information that may be useful in establishing the current environment relative to our organization. Much in the same way we use our body's senses to determine the state of our surroundings, to dictate actions, an organization must use every sensing organ at its disposal. It is critical that all members of the organization be involved in sensemaking activities and that this occur at the internal and external level. It is critical that the organizational leadership are not the only ones to understand what is going on. The effective communication of policy and directives and timely training and effective follow-up by supervisors are essential.

In large organizations, formal structures engage in information gathering and reporting. The purpose of sensing is to produce intelligence, which is information that is substantial enough to act on. In the government, it is known as *actionable information*. In terms of policy development and directives a very basic form of this type of information gathering is used. The intent is not to gain intelligence on other companies or to gain a competitive edge but to gain an understanding of the environment so as to adapt and adjust policy. This type of sensing borrows from the intelligence cycle found in government intelligence organizations. The first element of sensing is to establish what information the organization requires. For the leader responsible for development of policy and drafting of directives, the information required is about industry best practices, industry crisis, and industry innovations.

The second element is collection of information. The collection of information can come from many sources and having different sources is desirable. These sources are discussed in detail in following sections, but the best source is usually from your peers in the industry, so efforts should be made to cultivate relationships.

The third element is called processing and exploitation, which is another way of saying sorting out what is useful and discarding what is not, then acting on the information. While all of this seems to be a very unwieldy process, the average organizational leader should be able to distill it down to a streamlined process – the simplest being paying attention to the information streams and zeroing in on what affects your organization.

SENSING RESOURCES

As a leader of a smaller sized organization, there are many ways to engage in sensing of this type. The following will detail a number of sensing tools and resources.

Industry Groups

In just about every industry, there are any number of interest groups that exist to advance the objectives of the industry. As a marginal example, there are many such groups that advocate for the sex industry despite its mostly illegal status. The group SWOP-USA, Sex Workers Outreach Project, is one such organization. Its website provides access to resources, area chapters, legislative updates, and membership (see http://www.swopusa.org/). Others groups are the Desiree Alliance and Sex Workers Without Borders.

For security professionals, there are numerous organizations, the foremost being ASIS International (formerly known as the American Society for Industrial Security), which has a robust website, as well as many programs and networks dedicated to the advancement of professional security. In addition to ASIS, the International Security Industry Organization (ISIO) is an excellent resource to monitor emerging trends and case studies in security. The number of organizations is staggering and a good leader can find his or her industry-specific organizations with minimal effort.

Human Resources Groups

The mission of human resources is intertwined in just about every aspect of every organization. Human resource issues are ubiquitous because there is a human factor in every organization. Human resource groups can be an excellent source of intelligence and can allow you to expand your sensing capabilities. For example, the Society for Human Resource Management is a highly developed organization that offers a wide range of resources, including a section focused solely on safety and security.

Anti-Industry Groups

Much in the same way industry groups advocate for the advancement of their own interests, you may be able to find groups dedicated to advancing goals that are not in your organization's interests. These groups can be an invaluable sensing tool as they will often expose weaknesses in an organization's operations and can foreshadow or even disclose tactics or strategies to be used against your industry or organization.

Public Relations Groups

The business of public relations is steeped in the concept of staying ahead of bad news. By monitoring these groups, you can get insight on emerging trends that can cause damage to your organization's image or reputation. In addition to this, you can find examples of problems and issues that other organizations are dealing with. Because public relations cuts across industries, these groups and their resources offer a good bird's-eye view of trends and challenges.

News Searches

Search engines can be set up to forward you alerts when certain key words are contained in news reports. Services such as Yahoo offer free news alert functions that allow you to select key words, sources such as the Web or newsfeeds, and how often the alerts are generated. Google also offers a similar function but has the added feature of limiting the region of the alerts.

News Providers

Much like Internet news alert functions on search engines, there are several news outlets that offer the news alert function. These include the *New York Times*, Fox News, CNN, and many others.

Social Media

No discussion about rapid sharing of information would be complete without mentioning social media. A great source of information is Twitter, which is a free application that allows you to follow people and organizations. While most people use it for socializing and entertainment, just about every organization has a Twitter presence. These organizations often provide real-time information of unfolding events. This can be a valuable tool for organizational sensing.

Research Sites

In addition to interest groups and news aggregators, a good leader should have the ability to perform sound research. This research can come from various sources, but it is important to assure that the information gathered is sound and reliable. The normal manner for ensuring this is to use the appropriate sources. Wikipedia is *not* a reliable source. As a starting point, I recommend using the Google Scholar search through the Google search engine. This will provide peer-reviewed information and can point you in the right direction for further research. In addition to Google Scholar, which is free, there are several fee-based resources that are also reliable. Westlaw and Lexis-Nexis both offer high-quality research platforms and are well worth the investment, especially if you have identified an emerging trend or threat to your organization. Aside from these paid sites, you can use the FindLaw site for regulatory and legal issues. For general information, the site RefSeek provides access to both sites and documents. The Digital Media Law Project Legal Threats database is a goldmine for keeping abreast of the legal threat environment.

Meta Searches

A meta search engine is an application that searches many databases and provides a single results list. This resource is good when researching from scratch without knowing anything about the subject. Consider it the largest part of a funnel. Some of the applications available are Dogpile, MetaCrawler, and Vivisimo.

Organizational sensing is more than just paying attention to external threats and emerging trends. It is just as important to pay attention to what is going on inside your organization. One of the most critical internal sensing tools is the scrutiny of internal reporting. Of these, scrutiny of accident and incident reports will provide actionable data that is relevant to policy development and directive drafting. Organizationally speaking, every report should be analyzed for trends. This analysis can serve as a risk management driver and is a regular feature in large organizations and smaller, yet sophisticated, ones. If your organization is large enough and has several layers of supervision, then this kind of analysis should be pushed down to the lowest supervisory level. In every accident or incident report, there should be an area that requires the supervisor to determine if the incident was caused by failure to follow directives, lack of training, or policy failure. Keep in mind that this determination is just a triggering event for follow-up by higher level supervisors. An important caveat is that the wording on documents should be toward remedying the situation. Therefore the initial supervisor would report that discipline, training, or policy issues should be changed to avoid further incidents. Some people reading this might be fearful of documenting perceived failures because it might be used against the organization in later court proceedings. This might be the case, yet doing so is a critical tool for the defense of the organization. By not addressing failures, the lack of oversight can be portrayed as negligence, and there would be little documentation to suggest otherwise. By going through the process of analyzing cause, the organization is actually showing that it is taking reasonable steps to supervise. Thus the act of documenting failures is actually a defensive action despite the counterintuitive nature of doing so. But more importantly, steps taken to remedy a condition claimed in a lawsuit may not be introduced into evidence. The rules are written so as to encourage the mitigation of dangerous conditions. If it were any other way, defendants would be reluctant to fix hazardous conditions after incidents because it would be an admission of guilt. Either way, not addressing negative events is tantamount to endorsing them. If you do not have a multilayered organization it will be up to you to assess accidents and incidents to determine if there was a failure in discipline, policy, or training.

As you can see, there is a need for formality in a successful directive system. There really is no way around it, investment in policy formality is a front-loaded one. In many organizations, failure to have an accurate situational awareness can lead to epic failures and in some cases, even more long-lasting consequences.

TRIGGERING EVENTS

A triggering event is an event that affects an organization and requires attention. This attention begins with analysis followed by action. For our purposes, the action triggered will focus on policy making or one of the supporting elements of training, supervision, or communication.

INTERNAL TRIGGERS

An internal trigger is any event or series of events that provide evidence that a policy change is needed. These can be workplace accidents, internal lawsuits, drops in productivity, or any other adverse incident. An internal trigger can also be recognition of sloppy or inefficient processes. An example of this is management by crisis; in a security agency, this is typically manifested in scheduling problems.

MANAGEMENT BY CRISIS

Management by crisis has no formal definition but it is a very real thing that affects organizations and people alike. It has been defined as "a reactive method of administration whereby strategies are formulated as events occur; basically shortsighted policy often leading to organizational confusion (Allbusiness.com, 2015). This phenomenon is one of the most common triggering events for policy change. It is typically self-inflicted and comes about because of internal causes. To be clear, this concept is not the same as crisis management. Crisis management is the method in which an organization deals with a major incident that has the potential to result in great harm. The issue we are examining here is less overtly dramatic and much more indirect in its harm to an organization. Management by crisis is a breakdown in the ordered process of labor in an organization. It may not be a stretch to say that many who read this book have lived management by crisis at least to some extent. This management style is typically not formally chosen, but it can become an informal practice nonetheless. As a commanding officer in the police department, I would often joke that I was so busy I now had the freedom to pick which deadlines I would not meet. This situation tends to occur when many action items are declared as urgent. These urgencies occur for many reasons, such as overpromising work, neglect of deadlines and political priority. This is short-term management and results in incremental tactical actions instead of actions that carry out the strategic goals. In other words, the organization moves from a collective of employees working together in a coordinated way to achieve the strategic policy, to an uncoordinated group that has redirected the efforts to satisfy short-term goals at the cost of supporting tasks. Management by crisis can compromise the ability of a leader to be proactive and can drastically affect organizational sensing. How can you be alert for problems when your time is completely devoted to dealing with crisis? The best way to identify if you are in a management by crisis situation is to recognize if you are dealing with urgencies routinely. If you are, then you are managing by crisis. As an attorney, this is a common occurrence, if for no other reason than clients wait until the last minute to see a lawyer about a case – sometimes the day before the court date and every now and then after it has passed. These events tend to shift the law office resources for planned events and can create inefficiencies or result in lawyers taking work home. But this is an example of outside influences affecting operations.

There are techniques that can be applied to dealing with the problem of management by crisis. For example, part of the job of a leader is to plan ahead. Planning ahead will allow for the determination of organizational priorities in chronological order. When you are tasked with something that is urgent, perform a triage and see if the task really requires immediate attention. This triage can be helped by determining what the cause of the urgency is. If it is the result of uncontrollable and unforeseeable factors, then it is indeed urgent. If the work is being deemed urgent because of neglect of deadlines or because of political factors, then it must be weighed against the importance of scheduled tasks and organizational priorities. From a policy perspective, management by crisis indicates a significant operational policy failure. The organizational processes have evolved outside of an orderly policy system and have become individual incident driven. As a leader with a responsibility for policy development, it is a warning that individual incidents are driving the organization through the co-opting of employees' time and attention. The operational policy must be examined to determine where the failure is occurring.

This type of management can be common in organizations that do not have a formal policy system. Without a formal set of operational policy directives, it is up to each individual to interpret how to conduct business. For a business that has a formal policy system, chronic management by crisis is an indication of the abandonment of formal directive for informal practices. For strategic and operational policy makers, management by crisis is a call to action. There has been a failure in either the policy structure or the supporting elements: The policy is flawed or there is a lack of supervision, training, communication, or discipline.

Internal triggers tend to be most common and are simply a part of the evolving nature of a policy system. Internal triggers can normally be addressed quickly and usually cost effectively. It is essential to identify if it is a policy failure or a failure of a supporting element. When responding to an internal trigger, the analysis must include looking at strategic policy, operational policy, training, supervision, and communication. Operational policy-making changes often occur when a member of the organization makes a mistake. It has often been joked that new directives that arise out of a workplace botch-up should be named after the offending party. While this is humorous, it does highlight a vulnerability in what I call remedial policy making. If an employee action creates a need to change or implement a new policy or adjust an existing one, is it really the employee's fault? I would argue that if a policy has to be changed, there was likely an operational policy failure. If there was a directive on point and should have provided direction, then the culprit was either training or supervision. In my experience, there is always at least one directive in place because someone made a mistake. The point is that a trigger may also implicate a training or supervision issue and not necessarily a policy failure. Simply adding another directive to the mix will not remedy the issue.

Regardless of the type of trigger, it is critical that it be analyzed and acted on. The analytic tools will be discussed in Chapter 6 and include scanning; strengths, weaknesses, opportunities, and threats (SWOT) analysis; and other tools to forecast outcomes and consequences. Actions resulting from sensemaking must take into account the actual best interests of the organization. We will examine a failure to address an internal trigger in the best interests of the organization in the Penn State football case study in Chapter 7.

EXTERNAL TRIGGERS

More often than not, the trigger for a policy change is external. External triggers can be new laws or regulations or influence from external stakeholders, such as customers or interest groups. They can also come in the form of external lawsuits or changes in the marketplace. These triggers can also be events that occur that change the entire environment. For example, when digital cameras first became affordable, the Eastman Kodak Company clearly sensed that an external trigger had occurred and made a policy decision to stay the course and remain focused on traditional photography. We all know that this was a critical error for Kodak.

External triggers can also be events or changes that occur to other organizations. It is very important that external sensing and sensemaking be a routine part of any organization. For example in 2010, the security firm G4S unveiled its tiered security officer system. This was a subtle game changer as it established classes within the same product. It branded officer qualifications as a marketing strategy and worked to bifurcate the markets. An alert security company executive would recognize this as both a threat and an opportunity. More recently the move by the Federal Aviation Administration to relax the rules for commercial use of unmanned aircraft systems (UAS) is a game changer. The use of UAS has obvious security applications and the company that can effectively exploit this opportunity can profit handsomely.

CASE STUDY: NETFLIX AND BANK OF AMERICA

In terms of external sensemaking, the business environment is ever-changing and organizations must adapt. The company Netflix revolutionized the video rental market through a company policy that did away with late fees. It effectively stole market share from brick-and-mortar rental stores. This allowed the company a meteoric rise and a huge stock price of $299 per share. But in 2011, the company adopted a policy of raising fees for customers and making additional structural changes. This change in policy was approved by its founder and leader Reed Hastings. This change was triggered by a desire to move the company forward. The result, however, was members leaving in droves, dropping stock prices to $53. The Netflix misstep was thoroughly covered by the media, and is a good example of an external trigger.

Losing a significant portion of your customer base definitely is an external trigger. A security leader who is paying attention could take some lessons from this with very little additional research. The first lesson is that the company got away from one of its core strengths, which in this case, was low cost. This was an example of faulty sensemaking regarding their place in the market. Netflix completely misread the situation. The second lesson is that even the leader of an organization can fail to anticipate unintended consequences. Most of you reading this book are not running mega corporations, yet the lessons of Netflix are applicable to whatever organization you are running. This is a story about a sensing failure and an external trigger. As an effective policy manager, this incident should prompt a few questions. For example, have we put into place any policy decisions or directives that are alienating our internal (employees) or external customers? Are any of our directives contrary to our core mission? Do those on the inside and outside understand what the organization is doing? Netflix, while clearly facilitating sensemaking internally in communicating the change, failed to have a clear situational awareness of the external client and the core mission of the organization.

On the flip side, an example of strong organizational sensing is the attempt by Bank of America to add a fee of $5 per month for customers to use their ATM cards. This was made in response to changes in the regulation of credit cards that put limits on credit card profits. Banks have become dependent on service fees with up to 40% of all profits coming from this source. When Bank of America instituted the $5 fee, their customers revolted and left the bank in droves, causing it to reverse its policy and rescind the fee. Other banks were paying attention and very quickly backed away from any ideas of charging a similar fee despite the huge financial incentive to do so. This is a good example of organizations recognizing external triggering events through sensing activities and responding with policy that serves the best interest of the organization.

While the effects of policy generally fall on the organization, sensemaking is a human endeavor and is value driven. Aside from the human factor, organizational structure can play a part. In a large diverse organization, internal structures can develop, which impede sensing and sensemaking. One of these structures is known as a *silo*. Silo theory suggests that in an organization subunits and subgroups can insulate themselves in a silo, similar to the structure found on a farm. A silo puts up boundaries where communication and perception can be limited. A critical step in countering silos and other sensing problems is to involve others who are not directly connected to the costs or benefits of an action arising out of sensemaking. In police agencies, evidence vaults are inspected by members who are not connected at all to the function. Fresh eyes and a lack of vestment in the outcome can be critical. Flawed sensemaking can occur especially when the policy maker is too narrowly focused. This can influence insiders to take actions that practically any outsider might consider foolish.

CASE STUDY: TOYOTA ACCELERATION CONTROVERSY

For many years, Toyota has been a popular auto brand that had the reputation for safety and value in the United States auto market. The company was able to surpass General Motors as the largest automaker by sound business practices and ethics. The company ethos was always safety first, quality second, and volume third. This process served the company well for many years and Toyota sold many cars because of their reputation for safety and value. This changed in 2006 when reports began to surface about unexpected and unintended acceleration. The problem may have been caused by a policy change in 2000 as part of an efficiency move by the company. The plan, Construction of Cost Competitiveness for the 21st Century, was intended to slash production costs through cost saving on car parts. The overall strategy was to cut costs by 30%, saving the company $10 billion by 2005, allowing Toyota to maintain its position as Japan's number one car maker. The plan came about after the merger of Chrysler and Daimler automakers, creating an organization that could gain a competitive edge against Toyota through economies of scale.

The policy change was heralded as a great success and was boasted about by the company president in 2005. In 2006, the unintended acceleration issue surfaced and resulted in massive recalls, lawsuits, and congressional hearings. Former employees and safety advocates allege that at the heart of the problem was the company policy of saving money at all costs. The "Construction of Cost Competitiveness" plan created engineering issues emanating from the need to stay within strict manufacturing constraints limiting parts. The quality of parts were reported to have been affected by demands to continually make them lighter and cheaper. The lean management process seems to have been taken to the limit. The initial reports of unintended acceleration were denied by company officials and blamed on driver error and then on faulty floor mats. What is clear is that an external trigger was occurring in the form of customer complaints about the apparent defect. Toyota noticed the stimulus of consumer complaints and made the interpretation that it was not an electrical or parts issue. They acted on this by insisting that it was not a parts issue and adamantly refused to take responsibility. But what was driving this outcome?

The trigger was clear; there were a significant number of reports that Toyota cars would simply accelerate without warning. The key to this initial response by Toyota was their interpretation. Did they make an honest assessment of the facts? There was certainly compelling reason not to take responsibility; the "Construction of Cost Competitiveness" plan was the cornerstone of the company's amazing cost savings and efficiency. Could the company now admit that perhaps the savings were all at the cost of safety and quality? It seems that anyone in their position might not want to admit that to themselves, let alone shareholders. Thus the initial interpretation may have been clouded by compelling reasons not to consider that the parts were to blame. Simply put, the leaders at Toyota failed to recognize the magnitude of the impending crisis and as a result, did not engage in an effective action resulting in an incremental response. Toyota had been recalling Lexus car mats in Europe and other nations since 2000 and had selectively been recalling car mats in other models before 2007.

In October 2009, the first universal response by Toyota was a floor mat recall, affecting 4.26 million vehicles. But the occurrences of unintended acceleration continued to worsen, with deaths being associated with Toyota vehicles. This led to a government investigation that revealed that Toyota vehicles had experienced a significant surge in unintended acceleration incidents as reported by the auto insurance industry and that the company had not been fully cooperative in granting access to vehicle black boxes to investigators. The ongoing problem that persisted in a new model year presented another triggering event and the company again responded in January of 2010 by blaming the issue on a mechanical issue, sticky brake pedals, but steadfastly refused to admit it was an electronic parts issue. This resulted in a second recall for brakes, yet the company instituted software upgrades on certain vehicles to address occasions where accelerator and brake pedals were depressed simultaneously giving braking priority. The upgrades were only effective in dealer-fixed vehicles when owners took action. This second opportunity to effectively interpret the situation was again missed.

In February 2010, the House of Representatives, Subcommittee on Oversight and Investigations, Committee on Energy and Commerce held a hearing on the unintended acceleration and heard testimony by company officials and victims of the apparent defect. The hearing showed that Toyota was dragging its feet in dealing with the issue. This was a third triggering event that was repeating the same stimulus, which was the unintended acceleration. At this point, the media was becoming involved and it was reported that between 2009 and 2011, 89 deaths, starting in 2003 and ending in 2010, could be attributed to certain Toyotas. In April 2010, Toyota was fined $16.4 million by the National Traffic Safety Board, the largest fine statutorily possible, for failing to react to the defect in a timely manner. Toyota suffered loss of prestige and sales and government prosecutions. In 2014, Toyota reached a settlement with the U.S. Justice Department, agreeing to pay a $1.2 billion fine, admitting that it misled American consumers by making deceptive statements about the safety problems regarding unintended acceleration. Also coming out in the investigation of Toyota was the presence of silos within the company. The silos were both geographic and cultural. Toyota is a Japanese company with 20 plus manufacturing plants in the United States. The geographic differences created a structural communication problem and contributed to the lack of effective interpretation of the triggering events from the acceleration incidents. In addition, there was a cultural silo created by the Japanese aversion to shame and the highly rigid corporate structure that inhibited communication between various levels of management.

The leaders at Toyota clearly employed organizational sensing as evidenced by the early recall of vehicles in Europe and other areas. The problem was known and the sensemaking process engaged. The information was simple: Certain Toyota vehicles were accelerating unintentionally. The interpretation of the data was faulty because of any number of reasons but certainly affected by the need to protect the reputation of the organization and its president with respect to the impressive gains made by the "Construction of Cost Competitiveness" plan. The prospect of having to admit the plan was a failure is cited as distorting the structure of the interpretation. The triggering events continued and yet the framing of the interpretation remained the same. The end result was damage to the organization in reputation and in profits. The company failed to consider that its two core assets were the reputation for safety and value. While the need to save face was an important consideration, the protection of the core company attributes was even more important. The most significant lesson here is that if the problem continues to be a triggering event, then it probably was not give a proper, honest analysis.

■ SUMMARY

Organizations must be moved forward by organizational leaders. To effectively move forward, there must be situational awareness. This awareness is accomplished through sensing and sensemaking. Sensing is the process of being alert for stimulus that is related to the well-being of the person or organization. Sensing is a multidisciplinary process that involves ongoing scanning and analysis. Sensemaking is the process that occurs when stimulus is recognized and leads to actions. The sensemaking process consists of three distinct stages: noticing, interpreting, and acting. Noticing is the detection of stimulus; interpreting is categorizing the stimulus; and acting is the action taken to deal with the stimulus. In organizational sensemaking, stimulus is identified as a triggering event. A triggering event is an event that affects an organization and requires attention. This attention begins with analysis followed by action. In some cases the action can be recognition and acceptance without mitigation or deed. Triggers can be internal or external. Internal triggers are typically those that occur within the organization and impact organizational stakeholders. One of the most common internal triggers is management by crisis. External triggers are those that come from outside the organization and can have both internal and external impacts to the organization. External triggers can also be incidents that occur to other organizations that highlight a vulnerability or opportunity.

PRACTICE POINTERS

- A security manager is always on the alert for internal and external triggering events.
- A basic way to engage in sensing is to subscribe and monitor industry and trade journals, as well as industry-specific court decisions.
- Once a triggering event is recognized, a thoughtful analysis must be undertaken and the cause identified as either a policy failure or a failure in supporting elements.
- A triggering event may not always be caused by a policy failure. The culprit may be training, communication, or supervision. Act accordingly.
- An effective way to deal with sensing vulnerabilities is to employ nonvested outsiders to provide a critical analysis of the situation.
- Ensure that any policy decision is based on what is in the interest of the organization and not other stakeholders.

Chapter Recap

- Organizations must be moved forward by organizational leaders. To effectively move forward, there must be situational awareness.
- Sensing is a critical part of organizational health and is the process of searching for triggering events.
- A triggering event is an event that affects an organization and requires attention. This attention begins with analysis followed by action.
- Triggering events can be internal or external.
- A triggering event can also be recognition of an inefficient organizational process, such as management by crisis.

BIBLIOGRAPHY

Bensinger, K., & Vartabedian, R. (2010, October 30). *Toyota faces new claims.* Chicago Tribune.

Boom, G. M., & Sha, B.-L. (2013). *Cutlip and Center's effective public relations* (11th ed.). Saddle Brook, NJ: Pearson.

Casstevens, S. R. (2012). Notable speech. *Be a lion. FBI Law Enforcement Bulletin, 81*(3), 10–12.

Dickson, D. M. (2010, February 10). *Toyota's bumpy ride began with race for growth.* McClatchy – Tribune Business News.

Dougherty, D. S., & Smythe, M. J. (2004). Sensemaking, organizational culture, and sexual harassment. *Journal of Applied Communication Research.*

Finch, J. (2009). Toyota sudden acceleration: A case study of the national highway traffic safety administration-recalls for change. *Loyola Consumer Law Review, 22,* 472.

G4s to feature its tiered officer program at ASIS. (2010, October 8). Retrieved from: <http://www.securityinfowatch.com/press_release/10486688/g4s-to-feature-its-tiered-officer-program-at-asis>.

Heller, V. L., & Darling, J. R. (2011). Toyota in crisis: Denial and mismanagement. *Journal of Business Strategy, 32*(5), 4–13.

Hewertson, R. (2013). 5 tips for breaking your habit of managing by crisis. *The Business Journals* Retrieved from: <http://www.bizjournals.com/bizjournals/feature/small-business/break-habit-of-managing-by-crisis.html?page=all>.

Ho, D. (2011, October 26). *Netflix – a classic MBA case study.* Retrieved from: <http://www.benzinga.com/news/earnings/11/10/2015570/netflix-a-classic-mba-case-study>.

Houck, D. W. (2012, August). Remembering the Paternos. *Cultural Studies – Critical Methodologies, 12*(4), 377–380. [first published May 14, 2012].

Jeong, H., Jeong, H. -S., & Brower, R. S. (2008). *Administration & society: Extending the present understanding of organizational sensemaking.* Thousand Oaks, CA: Sage.

Kappelman, L. A., McKeeman, R., & Zhang, L. (2006). Early warning signs of it project failure: The dominant dozen. *Information Systems Management, 23*(4), 31–36.

Kirchhoff, S. M., Peterman, D. R., & Library of Congress. (2010). *Unintended acceleration in passenger vehicles.* Washington, DC: Congressional Research Service.

Klayman, B., & Sullivan, C. (2012). Toyota poised to move past legal troubles; announces $1.1B settlement over acceleration issue. *Property & Casualty, 360.*

Lintilhac, L. (2014). *Management by crisis*: Land trust conservation engagement and methods in Vermont (Doctoral dissertation). Retrieved from ProQuest. (Order No. 1569881).

Management by crisis. (2015, January 3). *Dictionary of Business Terms.* Retrieved from: <http://www.allbusiness.com/barrons_dictionary/dictionary-management-by-crisis-4954912-1.html>.

McCrank, J. (2010, March 17). Toyota tardiness under fire; carmaker rapped for silence on safety problem. *The Province.*

Miel, R. (2011). Study cites mechanical issues for Toyota acceleration problem. *Plastics News, 22*(46), 5.

Oakley, C. A., Pesta, G. B., Ciftci, S., & Blomberg, T. G. (2013). A model and test of policymaking as process. *Journal of Politics and Law, 6*(4), 1–13.

Ohnsman, A., Green, J., & Inoue, K. (2010, March 11). The humbling of Toyota. *Bloomberg News*. Retrieved from: <http://www.bloomberg.com/bw/magazine/content/10_12/b4171032583967.htm>.

President of Toyota apologizes. (2010, June 25). Newsday, p. A.46. Retrieved from: <http://www.newsday.com/classifieds/cars/toyota-president-apologizes-for-safety-woes-1.1743786>.

Richardson, C. (2011, September 16). Netflix (NFLX) stock nosedives 19 percent after company ticks off customers. *Christian Science Monitor*.

Shepardson, D. (2010, May 21). Toyota's priorities come under fire. *Detroit News*.

Statt, D. A. (2014). *Routledge dictionary of business management*. London: Routledge.

Stensaker, I., Stensaker, I., Falkenberg, J., & Gronhaug, K. (2008, February 8). Implementation activities and organizational sensemaking. *The Journal of Applied Behavioral Science*.

Sysko, J., & Shinde, J. S. (2015). Crisis management at Toyota. *Advances in Management*, *8*(2), 16–21.

Toyota. (2005). 2005 annual report of Toyota Motor Corporation. Retrieved from: <http://www.toyota-global.com/investors/ir_library/annual/pdf/2005/pdf/ar05_e.pdf>.

U.S. House of Representatives, Subcommittee on Oversight and Investigations, Committee on Energy and Commerce. (2010). *Transcript of hearing on response by Toyota and NHTS*. Retrieved from: <http://democrats.energycommerce.house.gov/Press_111/20100223/Transcript.OI.02232010.pdf>.

Weick, K. E. (1988). Enacted sensemaking in crisis situations. *Journal of Management Studies*, *25*(4), 305–317.

Westhoff, M. (2011). Report: 7 insurers sue Toyota, cite acceleration issues. SNL *Insurance Weekly Life & Health Edition*.

Chapter **5**

Organizational Settings

An organization, although often viewed as a "thing," is actually mostly made up of people. Humans are very complicated, and to describe all of the potential aspects and effects people have on organizations is well outside the scope of this book. The important point to understand is that people significantly affect any organizational setting. Security-related policy almost always has a distinct human element, whether it is trying to influence human behavior or protecting the humans themselves. Human nature will also affect how security professionals do their job and presents a policy landscape that is ever evolving. Security policy must be adaptable to continuing change driven by human behavior. In addressing organizational settings relative to policy making, there are a few basic features that will be discussed. These features are office politics, the expectancy theory, the human factor, complacency, and organizational pecking orders. Each of these addresses how human interaction can have an effect on the development and implementation of policy.

OFFICE POLITICS

President Franklin D. Roosevelt allegedly commented on the benefits of competition: Competition has been shown to be useful up to a certain point and no further, but cooperation, which is the thing we must strive for today, begins where competition leaves off. Every organization faces competition; in fact, every organism on earth engages in competition in one form or another. There is a pronounced difference between healthy competition and unhealthy competition. The former encourages everyone to strive to be better. The latter is like a cancer that reduces the situation to a winner-take-all proposition, which effectively describes competition in the business world and is simply a feature in our capitalist system. And while the latter is understandable externally between organizations, it is toxic when it takes root internally in an organization. Unhealthy competition creates rivalries and breeds bad blood. Internal competition affects every facet of an organization and can be particularly pronounced when it comes to policy formulation and directive drafting. Policy making is often a collaborative process that relies on cooperation and not competition. Because unhealthy competition creates rivals, it also creates a situation where policy decisions can be influenced simply because of rivalries. For example, the security department may need a particular policy change that might be stymied by the human resources department because the heads of both consider themselves rivals. This can happen at any level in the organization and in the security department itself. As a leader who is responsible for policy, it is critical to understand the role internal competition and company politics play in this process. The phenomenon of office politics has been studied thoroughly and there are several factors that identify the presence of internal political action in your organization (Goltz, 2003). These identifiers are:

- The activities are not a core part of the employee's job function.
- The activities are not sanctioned by the organization.
- The activities are self-serving.
- The true motivations for the actions are concealed.
- The actions are at the expense of other employees or the organization.
- Political behaviors tend to occur in competitive environments with unclear rules about how resources and outcomes are allocated (Kacmar & Baron, 1999).

The last element speaks clearly to the role that an effective policy system plays on mitigating office politics. That said, as long as the financial reward, status, and advancement factors exist in an organization, there will be competition and attempts to gain a competitive edge. For our purposes, we only need look at the effect of politics on the formation and drafting of directives.

Every time a new directive is put in place or an existing one is changed, there will be winners and losers. Those who feel that their needs have not been met or, in the least, considered will be at risk of being alienated. These kinds of hurt feelings can wreak havoc in an organization and if left unchecked, can spread like cancer. Employing effective diplomacy during policy making is an essential skill that must be employed with protagonists and antagonists alike. An indispensable part of dealing with this is to understand and manage the expectations of those involved. Although we would like to dismiss office politics as simply people being childish or unprofessional, this phenomenon is linked to real science (Lawler & Suttle, 1973).

EXPECTANCY THEORY

In my experience, there is a psychological theory at the foundation of office politics. The principle involved in creating the environment in these situations is the expectancy theory. In short, this theory says that people are motivated by outcomes that they expect. In other words, if people do the job well, they feel they deserve a reward. For example, a security officer may feel that if he or she works longer hours, steps up and fills open shifts and is more productive, then he or she should get the next promotion. The security officer's actions are based on expectations of what will occur by engaging in this type of behavior. If the security officer does not get the promotion, then he or she is likely to be less productive and less engaged. On the flip side, those employees who have their expectations met tend to perform better and are more engaged in the workplace. This theory is well established in cognitive psychology and no doubt many of us have seen just this type of scenario play out in our own organizations. If results occur that are unexpected, the employee will seek a different avenue to achieve expectations and office politics is one of them.

As organizational leaders, how do we manage expectations? Expectations can be managed if everyone has the same understanding of how outcomes are achieved in the organization. This is where a strong directive system has a positive impact. Take our hardworking security officer for example. In the absence of a directive on how promotions are made, practically any expectation can be formulated. While it is reasonable to expect that high productivity and performing extra duties on behalf of an organization merits reward, a promotion may not be one of them. A directive that sets out the exact criteria for promotion will help employees manage the expectations regarding them. Perhaps the open-ended idea of having people expect good things from providing the organization high productivity and going the extra mile can be considered a benefit for the organization. In some cases it may be, but it also puts staff on the slippery slope of unguided competition. The use of competition in an organization is most effective when there are rules and boundaries involved. There is a reason why sports are highly regulated. Can you imagine professional football or mixed martial arts if access to the billions of dollars were not regulated? The end result would be chaos that normally comes from endeavors where anything goes. This is not to say that considering productivity and going above and beyond cannot be criteria for a promotion, but these criteria must be clearly spelled out.

Aside from promotions, there are other ways to meet employee's expectations for going above and beyond. In most security companies, there are programs to reward just that kind of behavior (Levine, 2014). Employee recognition programs are prevalent and can foster the desire to be productive and excel. The key is to ensure that the qualifications and operational performance requirements are spelled out clearly and are available to all members of the organization.

THE HUMAN FACTOR

Although psychological theory seems technical, it has real-world implications. The issue of employee expectancy has been investigated, at least in one study, to determine the effect on the function of security checks. Although the study was inconclusive, it was directed at security checks as a collateral function for police officers during unassigned time. The study indicated that core functions with defined parameters, such as verified security checks, have shown the impact of expectancy (Johnson, 2009). The act of providing security checks is a core function in any security regimen and is a foundational element to an effective security posture. It is also a function that is almost entirely dependent on people and vulnerable to realities of the human factor. A human factor is one that affects human performance and includes physical, cognitive, psychological, and social elements. Human factors can affect organizations through human error, poor performance, inefficiency, and human satisfaction. For example, a security-relevant human factor could be the reliance on a traditionally lower paid employee to exercise a high state of diligence and alert during a routine task. Many security professionals have started their careers performing this most basic security function. I suspect many reading this book have done so. It is an act that becomes so routine that complacency can sink in very rapidly. It is a task so ubiquitous that these tours are often just assumed to happen. That assumption is correct and there are undoubtedly security patrol tours going on right now. Herein lies the danger – the acceptance that simply mandating a task and the rote performance of the task equals getting the job done. Humans are not drones, and from a policy perspective, we have to ensure that the most basic and routine tasks are the best regulated and supported. I have witnessed this phenomenon personally in my security career.

While working as an account manager for the now defunct California Plant Protection, I was performing a security follow-up of an officer on a security tour. This particular tour was an exterior motor patrol and had multiple security tour verification system locations. The motor officer had to document the inspection with a clock and key system. As part of the follow-up, I waited at the most remote site on the property and remained for the tour stop to occur. After 90 minutes, the officer did not stop at the location, and I went to find out what the issue was. I located him, parked in the executive garage, asleep. When I confronted him, I noted that he had all of the tour keys in the vehicle with him. He had brought tools in from home and removed the keys on his first tour and replaced them on his last tour of the night. His justification was that he was forced to work midnights and should have been assigned day shift because of seniority.

The typical follow-up for tours was to verify that the records from the security tour verification system showed key strikes. The assumption was made that the routine of making tours was being followed, and because it always happened before, it would always happen. The likely time span of this security breach was approximately seven weeks, the time that elapsed from his failed shift bid. The factors in the organizational setting involved both human and functional factors. The human factor was the implication of the expectancy theory, job satisfaction, and supervisory complacency. The functional factor was that there was only one vehicle assigned to the security department, making inspections by line supervisors on remote key sites inconvenient. These, of course, resulted in a change in operational policy to include random daily checks of key sites by supervisors and additional training on the dangers of complacency and the importance of documented patrol tours. Sometimes the problems of organizational setting are not focused on the security personnel. Sometimes it is the perception of the members of the organization regarding their status.

ORGANIZATIONAL PECKING ORDERS

An organizational pecking order is nothing more than an informal and often unauthorized rank structure. The ranks come with perceived privileges and can either be fully unsanctioned or unsanctioned but tacitly permitted. As a security policy maker, it is essential to recognize the existence and extent of the pecking order and if it is completely unsanctioned or tacitly permitted. If tacitly permitted, this factor must be considered in any policy-making decision. Failure to recognize it can lead to complications and potentially, to security breaches.

Once when I was a security manager in a very large pharmaceutical company in the northeast United States, part of my responsibility was to manage a uniformed security force. The site was a modern and prestigious corporate office and housed many of the best and the brightest of the company. There was clearly a pecking order, and it went something like this: In the top tier were the executives of the company and their staff members. These persons had the best offices and the best amenities. Just under them were the company scientists and researchers, who were housed in the research areas and also had great amenities. Next came the administrative staff of the company and then the support staff employed by the company, who were typically union personnel. All in all, the top tier members were *actual* company employees.

The second tier consisted of the *experts*, who were the consultants or part-time staff, hired directly by the company. These second tier members, while not permanent members of the organization, still had a direct tie to the company and had perks, such as priority parking and access to the company store.

In the third tier were the contractors, who were the people who performed the actual day-to-day tasks that were essential to the operation of the company. The third tier members included the food service staff, janitorial staff, and of course, security staff. The third tier members did not have access to any of the company benefits, yet in the case of the security personnel and the cleaners, they had unrestricted access.

The higher the tier, the higher the perceived status in the company, and along with that came the sense of entitlement. This manifested itself in situations, more often than we would like to believe, particularly when it came to security operations. This sense of entitlement and unofficial political power had an inverse impact as well. The members of security were seen as drones and often not acknowledged. This had an effect on the self-perception of the security staff. As a young manager, I was not as in tune to this situation as I should have been and accepted it as just part of the job. After all, servicing the client is exactly what contractors do and client satisfaction is no minor thing. This all amounted to a very complex environment to perform some very basic security tasks. The security policies were carved in stone, but the application was subject to all kinds of exceptions. One such policy was that *any* company property leaving the property had to be accompanied by a special pass signed by the employee's supervisor and countersigned by a security manager. These forms were to be filled out in advance of the move of property. As you can imagine, the lower the position on the informal pecking order, the more stringent the enforcement was. Things did get very tricky when members of the research or executive clans were involved. Security officers were rebuked by the higher tier employees and oftentimes, the situation was worked out to the benefit of the employee against the letter of the rule. This type of situation was repeated in any number of situations, and I am sure they were not limited to my organization. This gray area left a significant effect on my security staff. They knew there was a set of formal directives that were supposed to be followed by everyone, but they also knew there was an unspoken pecking order for enforcement. This situation created performance issues in ways that I did not expect.

Aside from a security presence, part of the job entailed regular security tours at the site. These tours were directed tours that followed specific routes and were timed and tracked using a logging station at distinct locations along the tour route. One night while I was working, I went to observe one of my officers on a tour. On this particular tour, there was a timed gap between keys that lasted six minutes. A carefully undertaken patrol would take approximately that much time to complete. I came upon my officer sitting in a break area reading a magazine. When I asked him why he was not patrolling, he advised me that he still had four minutes before he had to hit the next key and it would only take him a minute to get there. I was obviously upset and I interrogated him on what he thought the purpose of the tour was. To my surprise, he understood that he was supposed to be performing a deliberate and careful patrol. Exasperated, I asked why he was not doing his duty. He asked, "What difference does it make?" Then he went on to explain that the company did not really want security, only the appearance of it, or why else would they have rules that did not apply to everyone? He also went on to say that security people mostly got into trouble when trying to enforce the rules, particularly when it was against the wrong tier of people. This left me speechless. It was a watershed moment in my life in the protective services. It underscored the effect the organizational setting has on the end results. It also started me along my lifelong pursuit of finding a way to make policy and fact reconcile.

From an analytical view, this is a case of a policy with good intent – control of company property leaving the company grounds – morphing into an undermining unintended consequence. The three-step premise of the property pass policy is simple and universally acceptable:

1. Implement a policy that calls for the safeguarding of company property. This is a staple of any for-profit enterprise – the more resources that you can retain the less you have to replace. This leaves the cost of replacement free to be used for profit taking or reinvestment that can generate more profit. This is a construct that is universally accepted by all members of the organization as each member has a vested interest (their job) in the health of the company.
2. Promulgate directives to support the policy. In this case, a directive that any company-owned property leaving the site must have authorization and must be accompanied by proof of authorization. Again there is nothing outrageous about this kind of rule. Everyone can likely agree that they should not be able to take something that does not belong to them without permission. Please note that this is not an absolute restriction against removing property, but a mechanism to accommodate people who may need to do so in the furtherance of their jobs.
3. Create a system to ensure compliance with the directive and in this case, the use of a countersigned form and checking with security. This is a process that requires some effort but cannot be portrayed as burdensome. Part of the system includes the enforcement of the rule.

This is where the organizational environment begins to be affected. Security officers are tasked with preventing loss and challenging people on the site who may be breaking the rules. When a security officer observes an employee leaving with company property, he or she is obliged to inquire about the authorization, no matter what tier the officer is a member of.

This premise worked up until the end of step three. When the policy decision was made and the directive designed, the impact of the corporate caste system was not factored into the outcome.

The end result of this operational policy was failure and what is worse, it ended up undermining security in other ways. What was the problem? Most of the essential elements of the way-means-ends formula were present. The failure occurred in the *means* fork of the formula. The missing component of the means was the political will component. While mutually agreeable constructs were included, the more difficult to identify and apply political factor was not addressed. Most policies and, later, supporting directives are constructed without an effective assessment of the organizational politics. Including culture and politics is uncomfortable in just about any situation and is often avoided at all costs in formal organizations. So how can policy makers and directive writers address the cultural and/or political factors? Sadly, I do not have a simple answer. Organizational politics and culture are fact specific and constantly evolving. There is no one-size-fits-all solution. The ability to recognize the mere existence of these policy landmines, however, does go a long way to mitigating the effects of this problem. In my scenario, the recognition of the unofficial caste system might have allowed for another component to be added to the rule. For example, why not include executive staff and research staff as exempt from the rule? After all, if the organization sees fit to exempt key staff from the rule, they are well within their rights to do so. This is nothing more than a formal recognition that rank comes with privilege. In effect, the risk of loss is being assumed by the company, based on the level of trust placed in this rank of employee. Of course politics being what they are, you must be prepared to justify where the cutoff in the exemption begins and ends. In addition, the exemption must be communicated to everyone, so there is no question as to the propriety of the directive. But this may not be acceptable and the leaders of the organization may not want to admit that a caste system exists. As part of the policy formulation process, it is not your job to tell the final decision makers what they feel. It is a losing battle even if you were tasked to do so. It is your job to educate and let the policy maker decide. In a case like that, you may have to simply accept that there will be unintended consequences and work to identify them. We will discuss this in greater detail in Chapter 8.

In the present case, with the benefit of hindsight, we know that the unintended consequence is that the security staff felt that the rules were for show. In this case, training may have been the proper response. You will need to provide training that is realistic, which acknowledges that there will be cases where security rules will have to yield to other concerns, and focus on officer professionalism. This training can go a long way to mitigating the unintended consequences. You can also adopt protocols that support the intent of the rule while not actually enforcing it. For example, a protocol can be put into place that calls for any security officer who is faced with an employee who has property and no pass is allowed to proceed after authorization by the security shift commander and a notation of the employee's identity and a description of the property entered onto the daily log. This protocol effectively meets the policy, just not the way the directive dictates. This type of action should be communicated to the security staff as a win-win and should be recognized as the team meeting its duty even when faced with difficulties.

COMPLACENCY

Complacency is defined by Merriam-Webster's online dictionary as "(1) self-satisfaction, especially when accompanied by unawareness of actual dangers or deficiencies; (2) an instance of usually unaware or uninformed self-satisfaction" (Webster, 2015). When it comes to organizational settings, people can become familiar and comfortable. This is not necessarily a negative state in the workplace and is acceptable to varying degrees, depending on the line of work or profession. For security professionals, the tolerance for complacency is very low. The nature of professional security require vigilance and the projection of a state of readiness. Vigilance is the practice of being alert and watchful, especially to avoid danger. This is the core of a security professional's obligation to those under protection. The danger of complacency comes from a number of different sources. The most basic is getting too comfortable for the surroundings, which leads to taking things for granted. This is known as *habituation*, which is when habit takes over for focused attention, in other words, working on autopilot. This occurs in many circumstances where it might be an asset. For example, a sanitation worker might no longer notice the rancid smell of garbage through the process of habituation. It is not an asset in the security profession. As we have examined in this chapter, complacency can come from acceptance of and satisfaction with the subordinate role of the security officer in a pecking order. The acquiescence that certain people are exempt from security policy is a form of complacency and creates a significant vulnerability for everyone. Complacency can also be as a result of the resignation of a security officer: The officer gives up because of an expectancy issue. In this case the complacency is not only on the part of the individual officer but on the organizational leadership.

Because of the effects of the technology in use today, complacency has an added dimension. Studies have shown that reliance on technology sometimes trumps decision making with disastrous effects as demonstrated in the following case study.

CASE STUDY: THE *ROYAL MAJESTY*

On June 10, 1995, the Panamanian passenger ship *Royal Majesty* grounded on Rose and Crown Shoal about 10 miles east of Nantucket Island, Massachusetts, and about 17 miles from where the watch officers thought the vessel was. The vessel, with 1509 persons on board, was on route from St. George's, Bermuda, to Boston, Massachusetts. In effect, the accident occurred because the GPS came unplugged and no one paid enough attention to realize the error. There were no deaths or injuries as a result of this accident. Damage to the vessel and lost revenue, however, were estimated at about $7 million (NTSB, 1997). Although no one was killed or injured, this event stands as an abject tale on the effect of technology on complacency. The *Royal Majesty* incident underscores the effect automation has on human work and safety processes. Automation changes the task it was meant to support; through complacency, it creates new error pathways, shifts consequences of error further into the future, and delays opportunities for error detection and recovery. Research shows that humans are poor monitors of automated systems and that they tend to rely on warning systems and not manual checks. To make matters worse, once systems are perceived as trustworthy by operators, they are deemed reliable (Lützhöft & Dekker, 2002).

In the *Royal Majesty* grounding, the National Transportation Safety Board investigation revealed the following facts:

- The highly experienced crew all failed to detect that the GPS had become unplugged.
- Because of it being unplugged, the GPS reset to a "dead reckoning mode."
- This mode had the ship 15 miles off course.
- Because of reliance on this technology, the officers on watch were lax and failed to spot buoys that could have warned them.
- To compound the situation, someone had silenced the depth alarm, which gives alarm when a ship goes below 10 feet of depth.
- The company had a policy that required a six-person watch, two officers and four crew members.

- The company required 30-minute-minimum course and position verifications.
- Just before the grounding, a fishing vessel radioed *Majesty* about its peril. The investigation was inconclusive as to whether the channel was monitored as required.
- The ship was on autopilot, using the GPS as its location data source.
- The ship's watches missed the incorrect course for 34 hours with three different watches.
- Had any of the officers on watch checked the Loran-C radar for course verification, the error would have been discovered.
- Watch officers relied on the GPS alarm indicator to determine if there were any problems with course.
- In this case, overreliance on technology removed the crew from active control of the vessel.

In terms of organizational setting, the environment on the ship contributed to the accident. There was a level of complacency that allowed the crew to rely on technology despite clear indications of error. Defined policies were in place and ignored, which shows a failure in supervision and a failure of the policy maker to take into account technology and complacency. The human factor and organizational rank were also unaccounted for in company policy, as in this case, ship's officers were delinquent in the execution of their duties.

Ship's officers are given a high level of trust and authority by their rank, and the crew are trained to defer to those of rank, similar to any military organization. There were many events in the causation chain that led to the accident, but there is a lesson to be learned for dealing with complacency.

The remedy for complacency is a thorough and well-thought-out policy system with sound strategic policy, carried out by effective operational policy. Both of these need to be supported by uncompromising training, supervision, communication, and discipline. In other words, correct behaviors must not only be set, they must be constantly reinforced and supervision verified. As policy makers, the issue of complacency must always be a consideration and counteractions factored into policy.

The issues of expectancy, the human factor, pecking orders, and complacency are all part of the organizational setting. The situation is circular in that humans are part of the organization and are there to advance organizational goals. Humans also, however, create the setting within the organization and, absent a strong direction through policy, there will be an uncontrolled effect on the quality of human performance and, by extension, organizational performance.

PRACTICE POINTERS

- A security manager must understand how the organizational setting can affect policy making and the accomplishment of organizational goals. Policy is not created in a vacuum and the internal organizational environment must be accounted for.
- Office politics are inevitable because of workplace competition. Security policy makers must recognize the presence of office politics and work to mitigate existing rivals and avoid creating new ones.
- Managing employee expectations through clearly defined policy will mitigate this issue.
- Complacency is inevitable and must be relentlessly addressed through policy and policy support elements, such as training and supervision.
- Complacency is particularly problematic in supervisors and requires diligence and honest self-assessment as an ongoing process.
- Do not permit unauthorized rank structures to affect the delivery of security services. Insist that everyone be treated equally.

Chapter Recap

- Organizations are made up of people and are subject to issues of human nature.
- Competition is a natural state between humans, but it must be healthy because unhealthy competition breeds rivalries and office politics. This can negatively impact policy making.
- People who perform for organizations expect to be rewarded. When the reality does not match the expectation, problems can occur. These issues can be dealt with through effective policy making, policy support, and reward systems.
- The human factor is present in all organizations and includes physical, cognitive, psychological, and social elements. These must be managed through policy.
- Organizational pecking orders are often unauthorized, although sometimes tier structures are tolerated. Policy must be constructed to mitigate this; otherwise, security policy will be undermined.
- All humans are vulnerable to complacency, which can only be solved through the proper application and reinforcement of effective policy.

BIBLIOGRAPHY

Ajzen, I., & Fishbein, M. (2005). The influence of attitudes on behavior. In D. Albarracín, B. T. Johnson, & M. P. Zanna (Eds.), *The handbook of attitudes* (pp. 173–221). Mahwah, NJ: Erlbaum.

Bailey, N. R. (2004). *The effects of operator trust, complacency potential, and task complexity on monitoring a highly reliable automated system* (Doctoral dissertation). ProQuest. (Order No. 3160637).

Berry, J. M., & Maisel, L. S. (2010). *The Oxford handbook of American political parties and interest groups.* Oxford: Oxford University Press.

Browning, L. D. (1977). Diagnosing teams in organizational settings. *Group & Organization Studies (Pre-1986), 2*(2), 187.

Burstein, P., & Linton, A. (2002). The impact of political parties, interest groups, and social movement organizations on public policy: Some recent evidence and theoretical concerns. *Social Forces, 81*(2), 380–408.

Competition, (2004). In J. M. Burns, G. J. Sorenson & G. R. Goethals (Eds.), *Encyclopedia of Leadership (pp. i).* Thousand Oaks, CA: Sage.

Complacency. (2015, April 11). *Merriam-Webster's online dictionary.* Retrieved from: <http://www.merriam-webster.com/dictionary/complacency>.

Goltz, S. M. (2003). Considering political behavior in organizations. *Behavior Analyst Today, 4*(3), 78–87.

Johnson, R. R. (2009). Using expectancy theory to explain officer security check activity. *International Journal of Police Science & Management, 11*(3), 274–284.

Kacmar, K. M., & Baron, R. A. (1999). Organizational politics: The state of the field, links to related processes, and an agenda for future research. *Research in Personnel and Human Resources Management, 17,* 1–39.

Kearney, P. (2010). *Security: The human factor.* Ely: IT Governance Pub.

Lawler, E. E., III, & Suttle, J. (1973). Expectancy theory and job behavior. *Organizational Behavior and Human Performance, 9*(3), 482–503.

Levine, D. (2014, April 1). G4s all stars. *G4S News,* Retrieved from: <http://www.g4s.us/~/media/Files/USA/G4S-News/G4S News Spring 2014 web.ashx>.

Liden, R. C., & Mitchell, T. R. (1988). Ingratiatory behaviors in organizational settings. *Academy of Management Review, 13*(4), 572.

Ludiwg, T. (2015). When complacency creeps in. *Industrial Safety & Hygiene News, 49*(2), 58.

Lützhöft, M. H., & Dekker, S. W. A. (2002). On your watch: Automation on the bridge. *Journal of Navigation, 55*(1), 83–96.

Matejka, K., & Murphy, A. (2005). *Making change happen on time, on target, on budget.* Mountain View, CA: Davies-Black.

National Transportation Safety Board (NTSB). (1997). *Grounding of the Panamanian passenger ship Royal Majesty on Rose and Crown Shoal near Nantucket, Massachusetts, June 10, 1995* (Marine Accident Report PB97-916401). Washington, DC: NTSB.

Overreliance on automation led to cruise ship grounding. (1999). *Mobility Forum, 8*(3), 26–27.

Roosevelt, F. D. (n.d.). *Competition and cooperation (quote).* Retrieved from: BrainyMedia.com, <http://www.brainyquote.com/quotes/quotes/f/franklind404172.html>.

Smith, M. J. (1990). Pluralism, reformed pluralism and neopluralism: The role of pressure groups in policy-making. *Political Studies*, *38*(2), 302–322.

Sullivan, L. E. (2009). *The Sage glossary of the social and behavioral sciences*. London: Sage.

Vickers, R. (2009). Training in human factor skills: lessons from aviation. *Clinical Risk*, *15*(1), 8–10.

The Analytical Process for Policy Makers

According to the *Encyclopedia of Governance,*

Policy analysis is primarily concerned with the consideration of a number of different policy alternatives that are expected to produce different policy consequences or outputs, varying the quality or quantity of policy output for a given amount of resources to be used. Policy analysis requires careful systematic and empirical study. Policy analysis focuses on all aspects of the policy process, from the early stages of policy adoption and formulation to the implementation and evaluation of public policies.

(Bevir, 2007)

It has been my experience that when people hear the word *analysis*, they tend to feel a bit uncomfortable or even intimidated. An analysis is nothing more than an investigation and should be treated as such. In dealing with the policy-making process, efforts should be made to treat it as a natural process, starting with an ongoing curiosity about what is happening. Pay attention to what is happening and when something is noticed, investigate. This describes the sensing and sensemaking process. The analytic processes described are basic tools to ensure that your investigation is as thorough as it is practical. The intent is to explore all aspects of a policy change. For our purposes, a policy change is a new strategic or operational policy or a substantive change to an existing one that occurs as a result of a triggering event or routine updates.

RISK ANALYSIS

Often policy changes and the adoption of news ones come because of the identification of a risk. This is a normal result of organizational sensing and sensemaking as discussed in Chapter 4. One of the tools employed in organizational sensing is the risk analysis. There are many ways to diagnose risk and there are many different tools that can be employed. For simplicity sake, I have employed the strengths, weaknesses, opportunities, and threats

(SWOT) analysis. A SWOT analysis is an established strategic planning tool. A SWOT analysis provides situational awareness for an organization at a specific point in time, normally a current or future. The elements of a SWOT analysis can be internal or external. The analysis is a detailed examination of each of the elements as they apply to the strategic policy (goals) of the organization. From the SWOT analysis, the policy maker can detect emerging problems or add a better understanding of an existing problem.

Strengths (Internal)

In performing a SWOT analysis, the first step is to look to the strengths of the organization. Strengths are the internal attributes or resources that can be leveraged to accomplish organizational goals. The list can be broad, and all relevant attributes and resources should be considered. An example might be that a burglar alarm company currently has the most effective alarm system on the market. The strengths of this could be both technological superiority and/or reputational good will.

Weaknesses (Internal)

Weaknesses are attributes or resource issues that undermine the ability of an organization to accomplish strategic policy. The weakness assessment is the most difficult to fully explore, as members of an organization may be reluctant to discuss or address shortcomings. An example of a weakness might be that a contract security service may have too many sites and have exceeded their capacity to recruit and staff the accounts. The weakness in this case is structural and would definitely be a critical part of the decision to take on additional accounts.

Opportunities (External)

An opportunity is a set of conditions that are present that give rise to an environment that presents a chance to accomplish something. The key to assessing opportunities is that they must be realistic and achievable. Opportunity assessment is not a science and caution must be taken to make grounded decisions using as many facts as possible. An example would be a proprietary security force transitioning to a fully contract force. The obvious opportunity would be a cost savings but in making a policy change of this magnitude, there are many other factors to consider.

Threats (External)

Threats are any impending or potential hazards to the health of the organization. Threats should be assessed broadly and should include even minor threats. A threat in the security policy context can be to physical security or it might be financial. Threats come in all shapes and sizes and require proactive approaches to uncover. An example of a threat could be a rising crime in the geographic area of the organization or a subunit of the organization. It could also be a mandatory $15-an-hour minimum wage if you are a security officer contractor. This element of the analysis is critical and is intended to identify all potential threats or problems. This will provide practically all of the problem streams for the multiple streams theory and drives virtually all of the following inquiries.

The SWOT analysis works well for policy making because it offers a sensible method for identifying factors that impact risk in both a positive or negative manner. When considering a policy change, the first step is to get a sense of the current environment. This is accomplished through the SWOT analysis and provides a situational awareness and framework for the next step, the *Seven Question Inquiry*. In addition, it compels an examination of not only external factors but internal as well. It also permits a rudimentary process for exposing the potential relationship between variables, leading to a more thorough assessment of both intended and unintended outcomes.

The SWOT analysis works well when broken down into a graphic. There are any number of examples available and most can be used without modification. I have provided a sample graphic that can be used in a policy-making analysis (Figure 6.1). The intent is to provide context for the

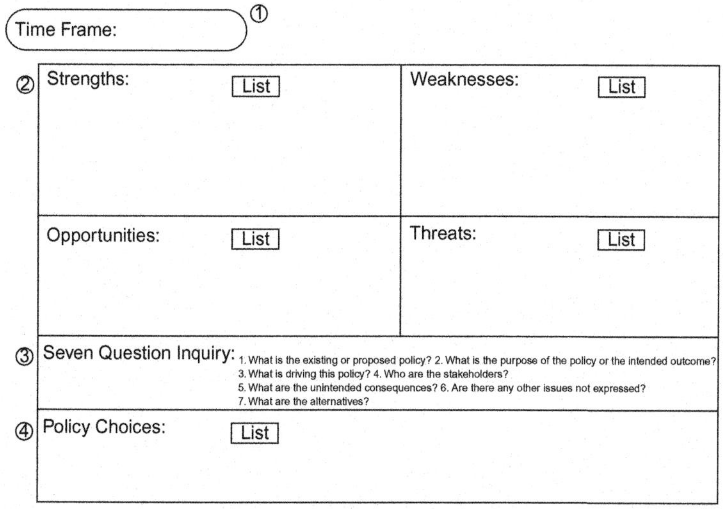

Time Frame: ①

② Strengths: List   Weaknesses: List

Opportunities: List   Threats: List

③ Seven Question Inquiry: 1. What is the existing or proposed policy? 2. What is the purpose of the policy or the intended outcome? 3. What is driving this policy? 4. Who are the stakeholders? 5. What are the unintended consequences? 6. Are there any other issues not expressed? 7. What are the alternatives?

④ Policy Choices: List

■ **FIGURE 6.1** Graphic by Matthew Bremer.

analysis and use as a tool to aid in the investigation of the listed elements. The first step is to record the time frame of the analysis, the second step is to list all strengths, weaknesses, opportunities, and threats. This step helps identify the current reality facing the organization and is also instructive on framing the political environment.

The most critical part of this step is to be extremely thorough in the threat element of the SWOT analysis. The identification of threats must be exclusive and will drive step three. Step three is the Seven Question Inquiry, in which the policy situation is further detailed and outcomes are considered. Step three will be completed for all of the potential policy options. Step four is to identify all of the viable potential policy choices.

The graphic depiction of the process is not intended to be linear, and information found in the Seven Question Inquiry can alter the SWOT analysis. The process is intended to be fluid and evolving. When completed, there will be a graphic depiction of all of the policy choices along with the outcomes of each based on a grounded situational awareness.

SEVEN QUESTION INQUIRY

The discussion of policy analysis normally involves public policy and implicates any number of theories and processes. The policy analysis for our purposes deals with organizational strategic and operational policy. It is not the usual policy analysis practiced by academia. The common discipline of policy analysis is often supported through significant statistical study. The tools discussed herein are more operational in nature, but they do contain elements from traditional policy analysis. Every effort has been made to simplify this process and make it as user friendly as possible. That said, these processes have their limitations and are designed to be shorthand techniques.

We discussed policy-making theories in Chapter 1, with multiple streams theory as the focus. The multiple streams theory identifies three separate and distinct streams: the problem stream, the policy or solutions stream, and the political stream. These streams are always engaged simultaneously. There may be times when there are multiple policy streams that are in play as a result of the problem stream. This is just like in real life when there may be competing solutions to a problem. The opportunity for the streams to converge occurs when the political stream supports the solution stream. In other words, there may be many solution streams but only one solution stream will achieve political support. When the three streams – problem, solution, and political – do actually converge, the situation is ripe for the emergence of a new policy. The problem stream is based on the belief or perceptions of those inside and outside the organization. The observations of both internal and external stakeholders can prompt a policy maker to address a particular problem. The driving force is the realization that a problem exists that requires a policy to address it. The solution stream, otherwise known as the policy stream, is engaged when all of the options are weighed and presented. This is the domain of the policy makers and before a decision is made, the options may be beta tested to gauge acceptance by the various stakeholders. Finally, the political stream is engaged when the policy makers of an organization begin to set an agenda. The agenda is effectively the list of problems that must be solved by the organization. The agenda is influenced by political factors, such as interest groups (internal and external), public and employee opinion, and the dynamics of the organization. If a consensus can be achieved, then the policy stream is viable. That is, if there is political will to deal with the problem, then a policy can emerge.

This analysis takes into account all three streams and is question based. By answering each of these questions, issues relating to problems, policy alternatives, and political realities should be uncovered. As with anything involving humans, this analysis is only as thorough as its application and there will always be an element of unpredictability. The utility of this analysis is that it is basic and can be used by novice and skilled security practitioners alike. The process is to answer the seven relevant questions as thoroughly as possible.

The Seven Question Inquiry, that is, the seven elements of the process, are:

1. What is the existing or proposed policy?
2. What is the purpose of the policy or the intended outcome?
3. What is driving this policy?
4. Who are the stakeholders?
5. What are the unintended consequences?
6. Are there any other issues not expressed?
7. What are the alternatives?

Problem Stream

In addressing the problem stream, several factors must be considered. First, what is the actual problem that needs to be addressed? A primary task in identifying a problem is to determine the cause of the problem. A cause is defined by *West's Encyclopedia of American Law* as "a separate antecedent of any event. An event or element that precedes and brings about an effect or a result. A reason for an action or condition. An agent that brings something about" (West's Am Law, 2005).

Once a cause is identified, the next step is to determine if the problem under consideration is the true cause or the proximate cause. *True cause* refers to the factor that if unchanged will prompt a reoccurrence of the problem. It has been called *root cause* or *underlying cause* and as these names suggest, it is not easy or obvious to detect. When policy making in response to a problem, the identification of the true cause will be essential for the success of the policy.

For our purposes, proximate cause is the event that appears to be the primary cause of damage. It is normally not the closest cause in time or space. It is the last event that occurred in the causal chain leading to the damage.

In simpler terms, think of the true cause as an infection with the proximate cause as the fever. Treating a fever may provide relief and can be a very necessary part of enacting a solution, but if the true cause of the fever, the infection, is not dealt with, there will be no solution. Determining true cause requires investigation. It can also be complicated because proximate causes are often the most obvious and the simple to fix. This can be problematic as fixing a proximate cause of a problem provides instant gratification. But the gratification is illusory; the true cause is still lurking and the problem will re-manifest with potentially more drastic consequences. Organizational problems work the same way. Take, for example, an excessively high turnover rate at a contract security site. The obviously concerned district manager reaches out to the account manager who advises that this is one of the lowest paying sites in the security company portfolio. This response seems reasonable and there is an obvious solution, which is to raise the pay to a comparable level with other job sites. This may be attractive to the district manager, as paying the cost of overtime is bad enough to justify a pay increase in return for a stable workforce. It makes sense, right? But what if there is something more? Changing the rate of pay at the site is a policy change and it is straightforward. But is the rate of pay the true cause? There are only two ways to find out, go forward with the policy change and hope things get better, or investigate more thoroughly. In this case, there may be other issues at play that may be the true cause. The working conditions at the site may be so bad that security officers do not want to work there, regardless of the pay rate. It may also be a leadership failure; the account manager may be a poor leader who alienates staff. These two causes are both more difficult to deal with than the pay issue. The solutions to these causes may be more complex and painful. The bad job site conditions are probably out of the control of the security contractor, and even if they were not, expending funds to deal with the conditions is not likely in the best interests of the security company.

The second cause presents a chance for a remedy, but it is also more complex. It involves retraining or even reassigning the account manager. It represents a loss in human capital and is much harder to do on a personal level. Many leaders have fallen prey to believing the problem targeted is the true cause when in fact, it is the proximate cause. The danger of focusing on a proximate cause is that the root of the problem still exists. In diagnosing proximate or true cause, analysis elements include questions 3 and 4: What is driving this policy – is it internal pressure, external, regulatory? And who are the stakeholders and what are their motives?

Policy Stream

The policy stream is the mechanism for identifying and assessing competing solutions to the problem. These solutions can be existing or new, but they all have the same opportunity to be the final policy. Much like identifying the true cause in the problem stream, the organization has to pick the solution that has the greatest potential for solving the problem. The analysis of the solution stream incorporates questions 2 through 7.

2. What is the purpose of the policy or the intended outcome?
3. What is driving this policy?
4. Who are the stakeholders?
5. What are the unintended consequences?
6. Are there any other issues not expressed?
7. What are the alternatives?

In vetting potential solutions, understanding the end result is critical. This involves a direct query of the chief executive of the organization to ensure that the proffered solutions are in line with the stated goals of the organization. When the goals are unclear, the choice of solution may undermine the organization. In this case, having a clear and formal strategic policy is essential. As part of this analysis when there is no formal organizational goal, it is an opportunity to enact one.

The second part of this analysis deals with understanding the purpose of the new solution. Does it actually remedy the problem? A policy (solution) may be offered that only partially deals with the problem. This is a reality of life and may very well be the best option, but when analyzing this and other elements of the process, be cautious of something called *satisficing*.

Satisficing refers to the act of picking the first solution that meets the requirements at hand. It is picking a workable solution but not the optimal solution. I am sure that we have all heard the phrase "that's good enough"; the technical term for this is satisficing. From a policy perspective, satisficing should be avoided if practical. As we have mentioned, leaving out a formal directive or a communication of how things should be done is tantamount to giving unfettered discretion and results in patterns and practices that can be used as evidence of negligence in a lawsuit or regulatory investigation. There may be circumstances where satisficing is appropriate; these are usually situations where a decision is critically needed and there is no time to go through a long analytical process. Satisficing equals an acceptable minimal level of direction.

The caveat here is that when time becomes available, there must be a more thorough analysis and policy adjustment if necessary. One key concern with routine satisficing is that it may encourage performance satisficing. That is, you may be encouraging your staff to just do the minimal acceptable work.

Political Stream

The political stream is the investigation of the relevant political environment. Whether we like it or not, politics play a part in every organization, regardless of type. The politics can be internal politics such as office politics or even partisan political beliefs. They can also be external, originating from elected politicians or established interest groups. The influence exerted could be public or private and the communication of influence can be positive or negative. In any event, policy must have political support to come to fruition.

It is important to recognize what policy choices may or may not be viable because of the political factor. The analysis of the political stream implicates responses to questions 2 through 4 of the seven question analysis.

2. What is the purpose of the policy or the intended outcome?
3. What is driving this policy?
4. Who are the stakeholders?

The political stream is really all about who wields influence on the policy maker. This influence can be persuasive or coercive. In a persuasive situation, the policy maker may make the decision out of deference or attachment to a group or individual. The decision maker may be persuaded through personal gain or notoriety. In a coercive situation, the decision maker may be compelled to make a decision out of fear of negative repercussion, personally or against the organization. The goal in identifying the influencers is to give the decision maker defenses and options to mitigate these influences.

In some situations, the policy decision maker may be the subject of multiple political influences and there may be several competing policy windows coinciding with competing interests. In this case, as in all cases, the best interests of the organizations must be the primary concern.

What is the Existing or Proposed Policy?

Identifying the existing or proposed policy option is an examination of the policy or solution stream dictated in the multiple streams theory. In some cases, there will be existing policy, either formal or informal; in other cases, the policy option will be totally new; and in other situations, an entirely new policy approach will be an option replacing the existing policy.

In most situations, there will be an existing policy and the accompanying directives or there will be an unofficial policy and a generally accepted method of accomplishing a task. Identifying the existing policy only requires finding the formal written document. There can be two types of written policy that affect this investigation. First is the strategic policy, for example, the policy set by the chief executive that lays out the goals of the organization. Second is the operational policy, also known as the directives, which tell members of the organization how things are to be done. In a well-developed policy system, there should be both strategic and operational policy. If there is no operational policy, but there is strategic policy, then the goals of the organization are available for analysis. If there is no written strategic or operational policy, then an examination of existing informal policy must be undertaken. The unofficial policy, which is known as a *pattern* or *practice*, is a little more abstract. Identifying and quantifying these practices takes a little detective work and you might be tempted to accept that nothing exists. Keep looking as there will be clues.

When searching for clues of informal policy, look to see if staff members are taking repetitive common actions in the furtherance of the organization's mission, then you are witnessing a practice. A simple test to determine if there is a practice is to question staff members about why they are doing something the way they are doing it. More often than not, you may find a response such as, "We have always done it that way" or "They said that's how it is to be done." It is also possible that employees may simply be performing tasks on the basis of behavior modeling. That is, watching how others are doing a task and emulating those actions. A pattern or practice can be dangerous to an organization for several reasons. The most significant is that it is undirected and unsupervised activity. Failing to supervise can lead to legal liability and unpredictable actions and outcomes. In addition, this type of action can result in staff members that determine the outcomes from the bottom up and not the top down. In the worst case, it can allow staff to engage in any manner of misconduct, which could lead to not only lost productivity and lack of efficiency, but harm. Thus it is highly important to identify the current policy or practice.

If this is a situation that involves a new policy instead of altering an existing policy, the goal will be to detail the elements of the new policy as specifically as possible. A situation involving new policy solutions typically has multiple, sometimes contradictory, options. Each policy option must be detailed. Once identified, the next step is to analyze the policy or practice to determine if the existing process should be incorporated into the new policy. It should be noted that the input from the operational level should be considered as the staff may be performing tasks in the most effective manner through trial and error.

What is the Purpose of the Policy or the Intended Outcome?

When examining the purpose of a policy, the question to answer is "Why?" Why is this policy appropriate? Is the predicted outcome in line with the strategic policy of the organization? In answering these questions, the investigation should be broad and inclusive. The strategic policy should not be a starting point, but the questions should be answered and then tested against the strategic policy. In some cases, the investigation may reveal a need to change the strategic policy. For example, prior to the tragic shooting at Columbine High School, the strategic policy for active shooters was to contain the scene and intervene when sufficient resources were ready. In response to the incident, the investigation into a new operational policy uncovered a need to change the strategic policy. Today, active shooter events are countered by rapid intervention tactics, and waiting for a full force response is unthinkable.

What is Driving This Policy?

When investigating a policy change or new policy, the driving forces must be considered. If the driving forces behind the change are not considered, the political stream may not be available and the change will not occur. Thus understanding what is motivating the change will allow the policy maker to have sufficient information to advocate for or against the change. The driving forces can be internal or external. They can be for good faith reasons or for reasons of self-interest. Understanding motivations will permit a more accurate interpretation of how the change will affect the strategic policy and can assist in clarifying the role and political power wielded by stakeholders. In some cases, tragedies have prompted individuals and interest groups to advocate for changes in laws – changes that are well meaning, personal, but may not be in the best interests of the organization or the public. Changes driven by emotion tend to be narrow and make an analysis of unintended consequences difficult.

Who are the Stakeholders?

Identifying the people and groups who have a stake in the policy change is critical. The investigation of stakeholders should be undertaken with a broad approach. Stakeholders are defined as any individual or group who is impacted or can be impacted by organizational objectives. Stakeholders can be internal or external. They can be overt or covert and can work inside the system or seek change outside the system. Understanding who the stakeholders are will give context to the true purpose of a policy change and will help uncover changes that are advanced through pretext. Stakeholders can include interest groups (internal and external), public and employee opinion, and the dynamics of the organization. One often overlooked stakeholder in the investigation is yourself. A thorough investigation will include the recognition of the investigator's bias, which should be accounted for in the process.

What are the Unintended Consequences?

In virtually every policy-making process, the outcomes are specified and fully intended. A common issue plaguing policy making is the occurrence of unintended consequences. This question is an attempt to identify consequences that may occur aside from those that are intended. This examination requires some discipline and creativity to detect and identify an event that only has the potential for occurring. Identifying true causes is an investment for the organization, as unintended consequences can be extreme. It is often the case that when a highly adverse negative consequence occurs, someone needs to be held accountable. It does not matter that the outcome was unintended, failure to predict and mitigate these outcomes is the only effective means to protect yourself and the organization. And legally, if the harm was at all foreseeable, liability will attach. One of the most obvious examples of unintended consequences is the impact of the passage of the Eighteenth Amendment to the Constitution. This amendment ushered in the Volstead Act, also known as the National Prohibition Act. The amendment was driven by interest groups with political power and the good intention of doing away with the adverse effects of alcoholic beverages. In the end, the unintended consequences were the rise of organized crime and a public health issue brought on by drinking adulterated black market alcohol. The amendment was repealed and organized crime became entrenched in the United States. At its most basic, the unintended consequences inquiry is nothing more than playing "What if?" The what-if game is an exercise in playing out all of the potential outcomes of a given situation. Used by public safety professionals prior to engaging in an action, one team member asks, "If we do this…" and the other team members respond with as many "this will happen" responses until there are none left.

Are there Any Other Issues Not Expressed?

This is the catch-all question of the investigation. It is the place to raise any other issues regardless of how unlikely or unreasonable. This is the due diligence prong of the inquiry and looks to issues that may or may not affect policy but may have other types of impact. The rationale is that in examining these areas, situational awareness is expanded, and it may lead to the discovery of additional relevant policy-related information.

What are the Alternatives?

This analysis examines whether there are any ways to accomplish dealing with a problem without a change in strategic or operational policy. Not every problem rises to the level of an organization-wide solution. This step in the investigation can often be performed earlier in the process if there is an indication that a policy change may not be in order.

CASE STUDY: FAST-FOOD BAN AND THE SEVEN QUESTION INQUIRY

In various locations in the United States, there have been proposed or enacted bans on fast food and the restaurants that sell them. The underlying theory is that obesity is a dangerous and compelling public health issue that is deserving of regulation. The problem stream in this scenario is increasing obesity; one of the solution streams is a ban on fast food. The political stream depends on the situational reality of the organization as known through a SWOT analysis. In the case of South Los Angeles, it was a politically viable option and did in fact occur in 2008. A sample Seven Question Inquiry follows:

1. What is the existing or proposed policy?
  - Tax or ban high-fat or high-calorie food to coerce people to make healthy eating choices
  - Better health through legislation

2. What is the purpose of the policy or the intended outcome?
   - Force people to make healthy choices by financial incentive or denial of opportunity, thereby making people healthier and lessening the impact on healthcare services
   - Save people from themselves
3. What is driving this policy?
   - Worldwide obesity epidemic; India, China, and Africa also affected
   - Social engineering – healthcare costs borne by society, so society can regulate
   - Emotion – sick overweight children; people dying of heart attacks
   - Interest groups – World Health Organization (WHO), National Institutes of Health (NIH), Center for Science in the Public Interest ($17 million annual budget)
   - Good intentions – get people healthy
4. Who are the stakeholders?
   - The public (fewer overweight people)
   - Parents (no overweight children)
   - Society (less funds spent on healthcare)
   - Lawmakers (political points?)
   - Interest groups (WHO, NIH)
   - Insurance companies
   - Healthcare companies
   - Diet and exercise industry
5. What are the unintended consequences?
   - Loss of freedom of choice
   - Defiance – people refuse to comply; black market develops
   - Statutory neglect – regulators will not enforce
   - Feel-good law only – will not actually reduce obesity (several studies show that exercise has more significant impact)
   - Impact on poor – good food costs more
   - Economic losses – more people out of work
6. Are there any other issues not expressed?
   - Floodgates – open the door to regulate other types of high-risk health behavior
   - Require daily exercise at work and school
   - Restrictions on other types of food
   - Backlash against the obese
   - Constitutional issues
7. What are the alternatives? What could have been done instead?
   - Public awareness campaign
   - Bring back physical education in schools
   - Offer health insurance breaks for healthy weight as mandated by regulation
   - Community programs, buying cooperatives for poor to get healthy food

At the end of the day, the answers to the questions in this inquiry will be fact specific and depend on the current situation facing your organization. The purpose of the SWOT analysis and the Seven Question Inquiry is to make policy decisions with as much information as possible. If you can identify issues in advance, then steps can be taken to manage them. There are many different policy-making analytics available; my intention is to provide a practical approach that can be implemented by most anyone. The drawback is that the process is not scientific and simply employing an educated deduction. In cases where the ability to employ scientific analysis is available and practical, it should be used.

PRACTICE POINTERS

- Every situation where a policy change is suggested should trigger an analysis to determine if and how the change should be made.
- A SWOT analysis should be a routine practice for security management and policy professionals.
- A policy change has many moving parts and many people or individuals that can influence the final policy; identification of these elements can ensure that the policy change is in the best interests of the organization.
- Undertaking a policy analysis may seem daunting and complicated: It is not; the focus should be on determining what the current situation is and how changes will play out.
- Play the what-if game when assessing outcomes of an action.
- Employ a regular process when policy making, as it will give the decision maker the best chance at getting full information and preventing unforeseen adverse impacts.

Chapter Recap

- Policy making must be guided by sound information. This information is obtained through a process of analysis.
- A basic analysis tool is a SWOT analysis, which gives a snapshot of the current environment facing the organization.
- Once situational awareness is obtained through the SWOT analysis, any policy change should be analyzed through the Seven Question Inquiry.
- The Seven Question Inquiry is a basic tool to establish the motives behind a policy option, the players and influencers involved, the potential unintended consequences, and alternatives to a policy change and related issues.
- When engaging in an inquiry, determining the true cause of a problem is critical; be cautious of proximate causes driving policy change.

BIBLIOGRAPHY

Bevir, M. (2007). *Encyclopedia of governance*. Thousand Oaks, CA: Sage.

Broder, J. F., & Tucker, E. (2006). Risk analysis methodologies. *Security, 43*(9), 92–93.

Cadle, J., Paul, D., & Turner, P. (2010). *Business analysis techniques: 72 essential tools for success*. Swindon: British Computer Society.

Causation, (2005). In M. C. (2005). Horowitz (Ed.) *New dictionary of the history of ideas* (Vol. 1, pp. 280–289). Detroit: Scribner.

Cause, (2005). (2nd ed.). In S. Phelps & J. Lehman (Eds.), *West's encyclopedia of American Law* (Vol. 8, pp. 161). Detroit, MI: Gale.

Coman, A., & Ronen, B. (2009). Focused SWOT: Diagnosing critical strengths and weaknesses. *International Journal of Production Research, 47*(20), 5677–5689.

Escobar, O. (2013). Commentary: Public engagers and the political craft of participatory policy making. *Public Administration Review, 73*(1), 36–37. http://dx.doi.org/10.1111/puar.12008.

Friedman, A. L., & Miles, S. (2006). *Stakeholders: Theory and practice*. Oxford: Oxford University Press.

Gale encyclopedia of American law. (2011). Farmington Hills, MI: Gale/Cengage Learning.

Hagen, R., Statler, M., & Penuel, K. B. (2013). *Encyclopedia of crisis management*. Los Angeles, CA: Sage.

Hindle, T. (2008). *Guide to management ideas and gurus*. London: Profile.

Krishnamoorthy, J. S., Hart, C., & Jelalian, E. (2006). The epidemic of childhood obesity: Review of research and implications for public policy. *Social Policy Report, 20*(2).

Kuchler, F., Golan, E., Variyam, J. N., & Crutchfield, S. R. (2005). Obesity policy and the law of unintended consequences. *Amber Waves, 3*(3), 26–33.

Lavrakas, P. J. (2008). *Encyclopedia of survey research methods*. Thousand Oaks, CA: Sage.

Lessiter, M. J. (1998). Give your business a SWOT. *Modern Casting, 88*(1), 9.

Lissner, K. X. (2001). Leadership and unintended consequences. *Marine Corps Gazette, 85*(1), 41–42.

Maruca, R. F. (2008). *The way we work: An encyclopedia of business culture*. Westport, CT: Greenwood.

Mawson, T. (2003). Risk: Evaluation and control. *Security, 40*(7), 45.

Mesenbrink, J. (2002). Ten steps to reducing your security risk. *Security, 39*(9), 11–12.

Nixon, W. B. (2009). Assessing workplace violence risk to the business. *Security, 46*(5), 28–32.

Proximate Cause, (2005). (2nd ed.). In S. Phelps & J. Lehman (Eds.), *West's encyclopedia of American Law* (Vol. 8, pp. 161). Detroit, MI: Gale.

Rendeiro, J. (2013). Threat analysis and ratings for the security manager: The broad view. *Security, 50*(1), 22–26.

Scartascini, C., & Tommasi, M. (2012). The making of policy: Institutionalized or not? *American Journal of Political Science, 56*(4), 787–801.

Sharkansky, I. (1992). What a political scientist can tell a policymaker about the likelihood of success or failure. *Policy Studies Review, 11*(3/4), 406–422.

Sturm, R., & Cohen, D. A. (2009). Zoning for health? The year-old ban on new fast-food restaurants in South LA. *Health Affairs, 28*(6), w1088–w1097.

Sulitzeanu-Kenan, R., & Halperin, E. (2013). Making a difference: Political efficacy and policy preference construction. *British Journal of Political Science, 43*(2), 295–322.

Total risk management and ROI: It's priceless. 2010. *Security, 47*(11), 67–77.

Vile, J. R. (1996). *Encyclopedia of constitutional amendments, proposed amendments, and amending issues, 1789–1995*. Santa Barbara, CA: ABC-CLIO.

Policy Influences

"You didn't build that…"

Life is not lived in a vacuum; just about every aspect of our existence is affected by any number of variables. The policy world is no different. Organizations are interconnected more than ever. It has been said we act locally, but we must think globally. This is indeed true in the policy construct. There are interactions with outside organizations, both public and private, with internal groups whether unions or other departments, interactions with clients, and even interactions with the general public that have no substantial contacts with the organization. Yet when policy is being developed, each of these relationships must be considered. Essential to the discussion of these influencers are the group known as *stakeholders*. Stakeholders are those persons or groups that have an interest in the operation of your organization, that is, they can either benefit or suffer from a policy decision. Stakeholders can wield influence on your organization in many expected and unexpected ways. Stakeholders can also be part of multiple stakeholder categories and may shift between others. Policy making plays a foundational role in attaining organizational goals. It is a process that can be influenced at many different levels and is driven by stakeholders. In every policy decision, there stands to be winners and losers, and oftentimes the nature and depth of the gain or loss can determine the standing of the stakeholder.

Aside from the role stakeholders play in policy formation, they can also play a part in the mitigation of unintended consequences. Having identified and won, stakeholders will help mitigate damage to the organization from policy-related black swan events or poor policy outcomes. The indispensable fact is that an organization exists within a broader system, and every member of that system can have a stake. This is often a fact that is taken for granted.

During the 2012 presidential election, President Barack Obama was credited with saying that no person created a business by him- or herself;

everything we do in our society is supported by public funding (C-Span, 2012). He suggested that in order to have a business, we all rely on services, such as roads, and that employees are educated in public schools and businesses are protected by taxpayer-funded police and fire departments. Of course his opponents latched onto the statement and some media organizations were able to create a controversy by focusing the message on the idea that the President was advancing the ideals of socialism and inferring that individual enterprise was not the American way. It literally took on a life of its own and was a very effective campaign attack for Republican presidential contender Mitt Romney (Smerconish, 2012). This is a good example of how stakeholders can be taken for granted, as the President was alluding to, and how other stakeholders, such as the media (opportunistic stakeholders), can affect an organization, which in this case was President Obama's campaign organization.

IDENTIFYING STAKEHOLDERS

The most obvious stakeholders are those who directly benefit from the policy action contemplated. In the academic sense, a stakeholder is defined as "any group or individual who can affect or is affected by the achievement of the organization objectives" (Freeman, 1984). Stakeholder identification is not a science and is subject to interpretation; the process of identifying stakeholders should be inclusive and broad. The categories of stakeholders are subject to interpretation and may change because of the facts of the situation. The categories included represent the most common from my experience and there are some basic traits for each. The most basic qualities of stakeholders represent the interest of the stakeholder and the relationship to the organization. They can be internal or external stakeholders.

Equity Stakeholders

First and foremost are the equity owners of the organization. In the private sector, this means either the proprietary owners or the shareholders. These individuals derive profit from the operation of the organization and as such, their interests are highly intertwined with the policy decision and their outcomes.

Financial Motive Stakeholders

The second group of stakeholders are those who make their living from the organization or can benefit financially some other way. Although similar to equity stakeholders, these individuals are the executives, employees, subcontractors, or anyone who draws a paycheck from the organization. In these cases, policy shifts can result in loss of relevance to the organization and potentially threaten job security. Policy shifts can also result in loss of staffing and resources, which can impact the necessity for supervisory positions and thus impact upward job mobility. Policy changes can also directly impact those outsiders who support the organization. For example, a company may decide that it wants to exercise greater control over its security staff and thus move to a fully proprietary staffed unit. If there is an existing contractor providing service, then that company and its employees are very much stakeholders in the policy decision. In addition to internal stakeholders, there are also external financial motive stakeholders that would benefit from adverse effects on the organization. Typically, these are business competitors who would benefit by taking market share or minimizing competition.

Commerce Stakeholders

In some cases individuals or groups may have ties to the organization as consumers of the organization's goods or services. The relationship between the organization and this stakeholder group cannot be overstated. Both private and public organizations have clients, and these represent a class of external stakeholders that can often have significant interests in policy decisions as there may be a reliance on the good or service. In addition, a policy decision that could produce an adverse effect on an end user must be scrutinized against the interests of this group. As with all other stakeholders, individuals and groups may be included in multiple stakeholder categories or may shift between them. Oftentimes policy decisions may be driven by perceptions of client needs or desires. It is critical that any policy change being driven by this kind of perception be scrutinized. The failure to take into account the category and bias of stakeholders, particularly commerce stakeholders, can lead to adverse impacts as the Coca-Cola Company found out in 1984 with its rollout of New Coke.

Ego-Vested Stakeholders

The third group of stakeholders are the ego-vested stakeholders. These are people with an identity with the organization. For example, there are some people who are not just simply football fans. There are people who are so hugely ego invested that they will act to influence a team policy decision. In 1995, the Los Angeles Rams football team of the National Football League made the policy decision to depart California and move the team to St. Louis, Missouri. In formulating that decision, the owner of the team (a St. Louis native) undoubtedly weighed the benefits and consequences of making the move. No doubt, the team owner expected to be demonized in California but applauded in Missouri, which she was. It is likely that she did not expect a fan to sue her over the move. The fan, Larry Charpentier actually filed suit in federal court under the title, Save the Rams. Mr. Charpentier, a season ticket holder for many years, followed the team from Los Angeles to Anaheim and was extremely disturbed by the move out of state. In his suit, he argued that he was subjected to ongoing losing seasons by the Rams yet continued to support the team through annual season ticket renewals. His argument included the proposition that even in the event of a move, he should be eligible for season tickets. Despite suffering no actual monetary loss as he did not have a multiyear prepaid season ticket contract, he was prevented from buying future tickets. The suit was based on the legal arguments of contract breach, intentional misrepresentation, concealment, and breach of the implied covenant of good faith and fair dealing. As part of his suit, Mr. Charpentier sought an injunction, presumably (although legally ineffective) to keep the team in southern California. Despite the obviously futile nature of his suit, the lesson here is that a person with no financial motivations can be just as much of a stakeholder as a person who is fully financially vested.

Interest Group Stakeholders

Because we do not exist in a vacuum, there may be groups who are acutely interested in a policy change or adoption in your organization. These groups can be affiliated collective groups that have ties to the organization. They are not always obvious and even if they are, their impacts may not be obvious. I recall a story about a company that I knew that had a small but high-end art gallery on their site, and there was a group within the company that supported the various exhibits. The group was diverse and had members across the membership of the company, as many people enjoy art. Because of the cross section of members from senior executive to service personnel and members of the community at large, this group exercised a very subtle yet powerful informal political power. During the year, a major construction project was undertaken in which it was necessary to shut down the museum for a week. The plans were approved, the work started, and the closing of the gallery began. The group was well known and it was abundantly clear that they would not like closing the gallery. Within two hours, the construction was stopped and the plans reworked to ensure that the gallery remained open. The expense to accommodate this was significant and included staff hours for planning and hiring of additional security personnel to ensure safe traffic into and out of the gallery. The analysis was good in identifying the group as a stakeholder in the project but the analysis was incomplete because it failed to recognize the informal political power of the group.

There are other interest groups that have clear formal political power and are clearly stakeholders. Labor unions are a good example of this type of group. But it is not limited to the internal labor groups; in fact, your organization may not even have organized labor, which does not mean they should not be considered stakeholders.

Proximity Stakeholders

There may be stakeholders involved in your organization simply by nature of proximity to your operations. These local stakeholders are usually easily identified simply by assessing who is near your operations. The key to this assessment is to take a global approach to the idea of proximity. It is not just the people next door. This class of people can also include those in the area of your transportation corridors, or even in the areas where your suppliers are operating. In addition, the simple fact that local stakeholders may receive a benefit from your activities does not necessarily make them an advocate. For example, in my home state of New Jersey, space is at a premium. It is the most densely populated state in the union and is also highly industrialized. The state has faced a staggering economic downturn and is wracked with exceptionally high property taxes. The most common fix to the property tax issue is the luring of a new tax ratable to the town. This can lower property taxes for residents and also has an added benefit of bringing in new jobs. It only stands to reason that members of the community are clearly stakeholders – lower property taxes are a benefit to anyone and new jobs are positive. Yet the norm for New Jersey is for local residents to fight against new businesses. Typically the fight centers on quality-of-life issues and pits neighbor against neighbor. Sometimes these stakeholders even resort to taking the town and businesses to court to stop the move. If your organization had plans to expand to a new location, this is an issue that you would need to address in your analysis.

Opportunistic Stakeholders

Opportunistic stakeholders are those who have no specific ties or interests related to the organization. A good example of this are local, state, or national politicians. Opportunistic stakeholders impact organizations through publicity and legislative action. This group of stakeholders are typically involved through other stakeholders, such as interest groups. Although usually involved to garner political support, these stakeholders are not always driven by self-interest. Legislators come from all walks of life and can naturally be members of any of the other stakeholder groups. A politician with a personal stake in your organizational policy can be a tremendous asset or threat. In assessing policy influences, it is critical that politicians with an interest or tie to the geographic location be considered. It is good practice to reach out to the politicians and create a relationship, particularly with local politicians and state politicians in relevant districts.

There are other opportunistic stakeholders who must be considered; of particular importance are the media. Virtually every community is served by various news organizations. It is important that a good working relationship be established with at least the local members. News professionals and amateurs are not looking out for your organization's interests, no matter the relationship. They have a job to do and will not hesitate to do it. From a policy perspective, the effect on the news cycle should be considered and the clarity of policies should be scrutinized. A vague policy leaves room for the media and lawyers to make inferences. In the case of politicians and the news media, it is essential to have a media crisis plan and to have at least one person who has rudimentary public relations skills or a plan to rapidly contract for a public relations consultant if needed.

There are any number of opportunistic stakeholders that can and should be involved in a policy analysis. Determining who might be a player is fact specific, and the key to investigating potential parties is to look at what opportunities are presented to unidentified stakeholders. Any person or organization that stands to lose or gain from a policy decision should be identified and assessed.

STAKEHOLDER BIAS

In policy making, security professionals will often find themselves faced with passive or active resistance when attempting to implement policy that is in the best interest of the organization. Once stakeholders are identified, they should be classified by their level of support for the contemplated policy change.

Positive Bias

Some stakeholders are in a position to actively support the policy shift or development. These members are advocates for the proposed strategic or operational policy change. Examples are employees who support a policy change that will allow for four-day workweeks. They can also be external stakeholders who support a policy change, such as a change in product packaging for environmental concerns. Think of these people and groups as allies.

Negative Bias

Some stakeholders are in a position to resist your policy shift or implementation. These are the groups and people who stand to lose if the policy advances. This could be essential employees who would not benefit from a four-day workweek or middle managers who fear productivity could drop as a result of the shorter schedule. External stakeholders could have a negative bias against a packaging change as it could result in more expense or job loss for the companies that provide materials or service for the old packaging. Think of these people or groups as opponents.

Lukewarm Bias

Some stakeholders are in a position to be either lukewarm defenders or opponents. Like the undecided voter in national elections, this group can be critical in gaining support for a policy option or to otherwise gaining support for the organization. Influence on policy making can often be achieved by majority consensus. Often there will be multiple opinions and competing policy options. To advance the most effective policy, the security professional has to be able to understand the significance of stakeholder bias and take steps to move the lukewarm stakeholders into the appropriate side. Think of these people or groups as potential allies or opponents.

Unidentified Bias

These are stakeholders who have escaped the analysis. This is the most dangerous type of stakeholder bias as it represents a failure in the organizational sensemaking. This category exists because groups and individuals often keep their opinions or positions purposely vague or unknown. Investigating stakeholders with this bias must be done with great care, as repetitive inquiry may be seen as harassment. In my experience I designated this type of bias as a negative bias. It was a cautious approach, but it gave a clear understanding of the worst-case situation and allowed me to respond accordingly. Oftentimes I would simply ask these groups or people what they wanted; surprisingly they told me, and I was able to accommodate their desire and get them to change bias. Being this direct may not be appropriate in all cases, but I have had success simply asking.

The identification of stakeholders can be as sophisticated or expedient as desired or practical. The bottom line is to understand who the players are and how they can impact the policy-making process and the organization. This process is not a science and for the purposes of this book, the information is intended to be applied as basically as possible. The goal is to provide the policy maker with the best possible understanding of potential influencers. Employing a basic assessment of stakeholders does not mean that it will be less effective than an assessment that a huge corporation, such as Coca-Cola might engage in; even the sophisticated attempts can be ineffective as described in the following case study.

CASE STUDY: NEW COKE

The Coca-Cola Company is among the largest of corporations and throughout their history, has had a strong grasp on who their stakeholders were and what their biases were. Even in organizations with sound strategic policy and well-defined operational policy, errors are made. In this case, the error was a change to a foundational process that the company was built on, which was the flagship beverage recipe. The change was a result of internal and external policy influences. Externally the company believed they were losing ground in the cola wars, and internally key executives felt pressured to make a change. Coca-Cola undertook a radical change in their leading product in 1984. This was a result of the mistaken belief that the critical stakeholder in the equation – the public – favored the sweeter taste of their main rival, Pepsi. Coke had lost some market share, and the internal equity stakeholders – the company executives – felt compelled to act. The driving force behind this belief was the marketing strategy of Pepsi in the blind taste tests of the Pepsi challenge. The Coca-Cola executives made an assumption that their loss of market share coupled with the slight rise in Pepsi's market share equated to the need to make the change. It is unknown if a strengths, weaknesses, opportunities, and threats (SWOT) analysis was performed, but if it was, it was inaccurate. The equity stakeholders failed to understand the complex nature of ego-vested stakeholder loyalty and brand identification. They did not identify real public opinion and accepted perceived public opinion. Coca-Cola is perhaps the most successful brand in world history – in 2011 being recognized as such. Most major organizations strive to have a branding even remotely as successful as Coke. The good memories and association with the Coke brand was extremely high. Whereas the company executives (equity stakeholders) reacted to the threat of the Pepsi challenge, the customers (ego-vested stakeholders) had different ideas. The Coca-Cola Company engaged in what can only be described as corporate tunnel vision. They confused test subjects' opinions that were narrowly tailored to a specific instance, the test, with their attitude about Coke. The journey from one of the most recognized brands in the world to one of the most significant public relations blunders exhibits evidence of failed recognition of stakeholders and outcome analysis. This breakdown of communication led to a crisis in the company when they introduced their answer to Pepsi – New Coke. This undoubtedly had elements of failed analysis of stakeholders, including the public, employees, stockholders, the media, and perhaps worst of all, between the executive policy decision makers.

The Coca-Cola Company failed recognize the true bias of customers, who were their ego-vested stakeholders. They bought into the marketing strategy of Pepsi's taste test campaign and viewed the loss of market share (Coke had loss of market share and Pepsi picked up a small amount) as tantamount to the public actually choosing the sweeter taste of Pepsi over that of Coke. Coca-Cola also failed to recognize the intense bias of their customers. The company viewed the intensity of the preference communicated in the Pepsi taste test campaign as being the actual feelings about the product Coke and not the product of a situational environment. They gave too much credence to Pepsi (as a financial stakeholder) and its consumer testing. Coca-Cola fixated on a single element of stakeholder bias – taste – which was proven to be shortsighted.

In terms of influence of stakeholders, the Coca-Cola Company clearly misunderstood the depth and longevity of the feelings their public had for the Coca-Cola brand. It did not seem to contemplate the issue of brand loyalty. Over the years Coke has been the beneficiary of very successful marketing strategies, making the brand and its logo an ingrained part of the public's life. If there was ever a case for ego investment in a product, Coke had to be it. In effect, the company allowed themselves to believe that more than a century's worth of building trust and product identity could be eradicated with a half a decade of Pepsi marketing.

The focus by Coca-Cola on a stakeholder (Pepsi) they could not control drove this radical policy change. The emotional investment of the public to more than 50 years of advertising should have been evident to everyone. Instead, the executives at Coke were stunned by the negative public response. This indicates a faulty analysis of consequences and unintended consequences. Perhaps the impact of tunnel vison affected the assessment of potential outcomes. The rollout of New Coke was not done with an accompanying public relations program, in fact it was a two-year process that was undertaken with extreme secrecy. This lack of understanding and communication with its customer base (ego-based stakeholders) resulted in outright hostility. The only thing people like less than change is radical unexpected change that is sprung on them without warning. This lack of informational support led to a vacuum of information that allowed aggrieved members of the public to portray the action as a surrender to Pepsi. Even worse, it was portrayed as a callous attempt by the Coca-Cola Company to steal or, at the very least, diminish stakeholders' cherished memories. Coke was aware of its customers as stakeholders but apparently did not understand the category or bias and did nothing to try and determine them.

The Coca-Cola Company clearly underestimated the effect that this change would have on its ego-vested stakeholders. The change itself was news and opened the door for opportunistic stakeholders to become involved. The formula change stopped being news and the negativity of the public response, in turn, became news driven by the media who now had a tangible stake in exposing their blunder. The news of the negative response merely fed more people to respond with hostility, and this hostility became a movement. Coke, because it failed to recognize the media as stakeholders, quite frankly, had no advocates to respond effectively. The story of New Coke had a good ending with Coca-Cola recovering, but the whole mess underscores how complex the stakeholder organization relationship can be. The obvious lesson in this story is that if the change is radical and foundational, then the analysis should be extensive.

It is not just mega corporations that have missteps because of external information and external stakeholders' actions, organizations can also be misled by internal stakeholders. Sometimes the damage from failing to understand the influence of internal stakeholders can be unimaginable. Not all stakeholders are created equally and some stakeholders, although small in size, can exert extreme levels of influence. In cases such as this, policy makers must have the ethical courage to not only identify these circumstances but to act in the best interests of the organization. A good friend of mine, and a mentor, Dr. Michael Krantz, has always reminded me to do what is right rather than the "right thing," as demonstrated in the following case study. This includes identifying stakeholders and understanding what they have to win or lose in any policy decision.

CASE STUDY: PENN STATE FOOTBALL

The Penn State University mission statement reads in part: "Penn State is a multi-campus public research university that educates students from Pennsylvania, the nation, and the world, and improves the well-being and health of individuals and communities through integrated programs of teaching, research, and service" (Penn State University, 2006). A highly reputable university well known for its football team, the school was rocked by a scandal in 2010 when it came to light that well-known former player and defensive coach Jerry Sandusky had used a nonprofit organization, The Second Mile, which Sandusky founded, for pedophilic purposes – to prey on young boys.

The grand jury testimony was particularly damning, showing that Sandusky had victimized at least 25 boys during his tenure at Penn State. The media coverage of this event, called the worst scandal in collegiate sports history, included testimony by a graduate assistant, Mike McQueary, who was a witness to an assault on school grounds. McQueary testified that in 2001, he observed Sandusky sodomizing a nine-year-old boy in the showers at the Lasch Football Building. McQueary then reported the incident to Joe Paterno, Penn State legend and football coach. Paterno then notified Athletic Director Tim Curley who met with university Vice President of Finance and Business Gary Schultz. Schultz and Curley met with university President Graham Spanier to discuss the incident. They determined to meet with Sandusky and confront him. It was decided that if Sandusky did not come clean and admit he had a problem, then the investigation would be turned over to public safety.

Prior to the meeting, Curley contacted Spanier and Shultz and advised them that after consulting with Paterno, it was determined that Sandusky would be offered help and dealt with internally. This measure determined by the athletic director was simply accepted by both the vice president and the president of the university.

Later in 2001, Sandusky was prohibited from bringing Second Mile children on campus, a measure largely known to be unenforceable. During this time, Sandusky continued to assault young boys, using his ties to Penn State football to exploit victims, including bringing them to football games. In 2008, after one of his victims entered freshman year at high school, the victim's mother became aware of the assaults and reported them to local school authorities and an investigation finally began.

When the investigation by school officials lagged, the mother reported the assaults to the Pennsylvania attorney general's office and a law enforcement investigation commenced in 2009. Their investigation revealed that Penn State University executives were aware of Sandusky's attacks since 1998. Evidence included a handwritten note by Schultz regarding the 1998 incident that read, "Behavior—at best inappropriate @ worst sexual improprieties." Also, "ay min—Poor Judgment""Is this opening of Pandora's box? Other children?" (Freeh, Sporkin, & Sullivan, 2012). The evidence indicated that warning flags about Sandusky were know at the highest decision-making levels in the university since 1998.

On November 4, 2011, the story hit the media. Sandusky was arrested the next day and charged with 40 criminal counts. On November 7, the Pennsylvania attorney general reported that Paterno was not a target of the investigation but other members of the school administration were. Both Curley and Schultz were charged and stepped down from their positions. Media coverage turned into a frenzy as the lurid accounts of the scandal come to light.

On November 7, when it was reported that Paterno did nothing to stop Sandusky, outcry from outside of Penn State University grew, demanding the firing of Paterno and President Spanier. On November 9, both Paterno and Spanier were fired. This led to many media stories that painted the Penn State football culture as a cult.

Although the university is in actuality an open system, a taxpayer-funded school with ties to communities, alumni, and so forth, in this case, it acted as if it were a closed system. The football program was a silo located within the perceived closed system. A communications silo is exactly like a grain silo found on a Midwestern farm. It is completely isolated. On a farm, the grain would be isolated; in an organization, a function or department is isolated. In the case of Penn State, it is clear that not only was the football program a silo, but it was a silo with practically unlimited clout with school officials.

The incident report, the Freeh Report, cited both cultural and policy failures on the part of the university. The impact of stakeholders was clearly present in the findings of the investigation, and this sad case serves as an abject lesson. The football program and Coach Paterno, although a small segment of the many stakeholders involved, became the focus of policy decisions to the exclusion of the other stakeholders. The underrepresented stakeholders – the victims, students, and people of Pennsylvania – were not effectively recognized as critical, or worse, they were recognized and ignored.

When you find yourself in a position to do this kind of analysis, remember to do what is right.

PRACTICE POINTERS

- Before engaging in policy making, a security leader must know who the potential players will be and what their intentions are. A stakeholder analysis can be instrumental in providing these answers.
- Stakeholders can take many forms, and identifying them can take creativity. Be inclusive and do not neglect any potential stakeholders regardless of perceived insignificance.
- Stakeholders can sometimes purposely conceal their bias or be noncommittal in order to maximize their own interests. Do not be afraid to ask these stakeholders what they want; it can be very effective in identifying intentions and winning supporters.
- Do not forget about opportunistic stakeholders, such as the media; if they can profit from an adverse outcome they will.
- Regardless of the influence and power of stakeholders, never do anything that will be unethical or create damage to the innocent. Remember the story of Penn State.
- Do what is right not just the "right thing."

Chapter Recap

- Policy is primarily influenced by stakeholders. A stakeholder is a person or group that can impact or be impacted by organizational policy.
- Stakeholders can be internal or external.
- There is no universally accepted formula for identifying stakeholders; the process should be inclusive and broad.
- Stakeholders can be categorized by the relationship they have to the organization or the policy.
- Failure to identify stakeholders can lead to flawed policy-making decisions. This can also include failing to identify the influence of specific stakeholders.

- Stakeholders will have varying biases toward policy options and this bias should be identified as accurately as possible.
- Stakeholder power and influence may be significantly disproportionate to size or relationship. Caution should be exercised if excessive influence is identified in any particular stakeholder, as it could lead to policy decisions that are against the interests of the organization.
- As an organizational leader, you have an obligation to yourself and the company to ensure that policy decisions are ethical regardless of the influence of stakeholders.

BIBLIOGRAPHY

Abramovitch S. (2011). South Park finishes season 15 with a bunch of Penn State jokes. Retrieved from: <http://www.tv.com/news/south-park-finishes-season-15-with-a-bunch-of-penn-state-jokes-27192/>.

Bailey, J. R., & Clegg, S. (2007). *International encyclopedia of organization studies.* London: Sage.

Bérubé M. (2011, November 17). At Penn State, a bitter reckoning. *The New York Times.* Retrieved from: <http://www.nytimes.com/2011/11/18/opinion/at-penn-state-a-bitter-reckoning.html>.

Boom, G. M., & Sha, B. -L. (Eds.), (2013). *Cutlip and Center's effective public relations.* Saddle Brook, NJ: Pearson.

Brady S. (2011, December 8). Penn State of shock: Jerry Sandusky arrest drags brand through mud (again). *Brandchannel.* Retrieved from: <http://www.brandchannel.com/home/post/2011/12/08/Penn-State-Sandusky-Arrest-120811.aspx>.

Buchholz, R. A., & Rosenthal, S. B. (2004). Stakeholder theory and public policy: How governments matter. *Journal of Business Ethics, 51*(2), 143–153.

By, G.C. (1995, April 11). Ten years later, Coca-Cola laughs at 'new coke.' *The New York Times.*

Cooky, C. (2012, May 17). Success without honor: Cultures of silence and the Penn State scandal. *Cultural Studies - Critical Methodologies, 12*, 326–329.

C-Span. (2012, July 13). *President Obama campaign rally in Roanoke (Television broadcast).* Washington, DC: National Cable Satellite Corporation. Available from: <http://www.c-span.org/video/?307056-2/president-obama-campaign-rally-roanoke>.

Houck, D. W. (2012, August). Remembering the Paternos. *Cultural Studies - Critical Methodologies, 12*(4), 377–380. (first published May 14, 2012).

Emerson, W. M., Alves, H., & Raposo, M. (2011). Stakeholder theory: Issues to resolve. *Management Decision, 49*(2), 226–252.

Fitzpatrick F. (2011). Paterno's Greek tragedy plays out. Retrieved from: <http://articles.philly.com/2011-11-30/sports/30459132_1_joe-paterno-jerry-sandusky-virgil>.

Freeman, R. E. (1984). *Strategic management: A stakeholder approach.* Boston, MA: Pitman.

Freeman, R. E., Wicks, A. C., & Parmar, B. (2004). Stakeholder theory and 'the corporate objective revisited.' *Organization Science*, *15*(3), 364–369.

Freeh, L. J., Freeh Sporkin & Sullivan, LLP., & Pennsylvania State University. (2012). Report of the Special Investigative Counsel regarding the actions of The Pennsylvania State University related to the child sexual abuse committed by Gerald A. Sandusky. S.L.: Freeh Sporkin & Sullivan LLP. Retrieved from: <http://health-equity.pitt.edu/3956/1/REPORT_FINAL_071212.pdf>.

Friedman, A. L., & Miles, S. (2006). *Stakeholders: Theory and practice*. Oxford: Oxford University Press.

Graves, P. (2010). *Consumerology: The market research myth, the truth about consumers and the psychology of shopping*. Boston, MA: Nicholas Brealey.

Gelb, B. D., & Gelb, G. M. (1986). SMR forum: New coke's fizzle lessons for the rest of us. *Sloan Management Review*, *28*(1), 71.

Giroux H.A., & Giroux, S.S. (2012). Universities gone wild: Big money, big sports, and scandalous abuse at Penn State. Retrieved from: <http://www.truth-out.org/universities-gone-wild/1325615231>.

Hamilton M. (2011, November 8). Is Penn State the Catholic Church? *The Huffington Post*. Retrieved from <http://www.huffingtonpost.com/marci-hamilton/is-penn-state-the-catholi_b_1082595.html>.

Hruby P. (2011, November 16). What the Catholic Church can teach us about the Penn State scandal. *The Atlantic*. Retrieved from: <http://www.theatlantic.com/entertainment/print/2011/11/what-the-catholic-church-can-teach-us-about-the-penn-state-scandal/248588/>.

Jerry Sandusky grand jury testimony. (2011, November 4). Retrieved from: <http://www.freep.com/assets/freep/pdf/C4181508116.PDF>.

Lueck, D. (2000). Unintended consequences. *Forum for Applied Research and Public Policy*, *15*(3), 16–22.

Keevil, A.A.C. (2014). *Behavioral stakeholder theory* (Doctoral dissertation). ProQuest. *(Order No. 3584640)*.

Neville, B. A., & Menguc, B. (2006). Stakeholder multiplicity: Toward an understanding of the interactions between stakeholders. *Journal of Business Ethics*, *66*(4), 377–391.

Pollitt K. (2011, November 16). Penn State's patriarchal pastimes. *The Nation*. Retrieved from: <http://draweb.njcu.edu:2390/article/164655/penn-states-patriarchal-pastimes>.

Processing the new coke fiasco. (1993). *Science*, *261*(5126), 1271.

Reimer S. (2011, November 8). Penn State has lost the high ground: School's squeaky clean image has been tarnished by charges cover up and molestation. *The Baltimore Sun*. Retrieved from: <http://articles.baltimoresun.com/2011-11-08/features/bs-gl-reimer-penn-state-20111108_1_joe-paterno-penn-state-joepa>.

Rossi, R. (2012). The representation of a scandal: A case study of the Jerry Sandusky sex abuse scandal (Doctoral dissertation, Gonzaga University). ProQuest. (Order No. 1514333).

Schindler, R. M. (1992). The real lesson of new coke: The value of focus groups for predicting the effects of social influence. *Marketing Research*, *4*(4), 22.

Schweber N. (2011, November 10). Penn State students clash with police in unrest after announcement. *The New York Times*. Retrieved from: <http://www.nytimes.com/2011/11/11/sports/ncaafootball/penn-state-students-in-clashes-after-joe-paterno-is-ousted.html>.

Sileo L. (2012, January 26). Penn State students: We're being punished. HLNtv. Retrieved from: <http://www.hlntv.com/video/2011/11/16/penn-state-student-panel-punished-sandusky>.

Smerconish, M. (2012, July 30). The context behind Obama's 'you didn't build that.' Philly.com. <http://articles.philly.com/2012-07-30/news/32924415_1_elizabeth-warren-american-crossroads-president-obama>.

Thomaselli R. (2011, November 11). Penn State sponsors start to flee in wake of sex abuse scandal. *Advertising Age*. Retrieved from: <http://adage.com/article/news/penn-state-sponsors-back-wake-scandal/230967/>.

Thompson C. (2011, November 20). Penn State trustees say Jerry Sandusky scandal caught them by surprise. PennLive.com. Retrieved from: <http://blog.pennlive.com/midstate_impact/print.html?entry=/2011/11/penn>.

Chapter 8

Surprise?

UNINTENDED CONSEQUENCES

A policy by its nature is intended to have consequences. These consequences might be better identified as *outcomes*. These outcomes can be either positive or negative and there are times when they can be unintended. The process of identifying outcomes can be found in military doctrine prior to World War II. The concept of identifying *branches and sequels* is the study of potential outcomes for each action in a campaign. This type of outcome analysis survives today and is particularly well executed in elite military units such as the U.S. Navy's Sea, Air, Land teams (Navy SEALs). The extensive what-if analysis is performed to prepare for any eventuality in the field. An unintended consequences analysis is essentially the same thing. The goal is to first determine all of the probable outcomes and when completed with that analysis, move onto the possible outcomes. In some cases, it may be worthwhile to even consider the impossible outcomes, particularly if the stakes to the organization are high. Once these outcomes are identified, they can be managed or mitigated.

The negative impacts in the civil world may not be as dramatic as for the Navy SEALs, but unintended consequences occur every day and are part of every policy decision. For example, a company could enact a policy that prohibits smoking with the intention that the consequences or outcomes would be that employees would refrain from lighting up at work. Notwithstanding the outcomes the policy was intended to create, there will certainly be consequences that are unintended. These unintended consequences result from several factors with the most significant being the human factor. Our nonsmoking policy experience has shown us that humans will find a way to engage in smoking one way or another. This means that the behavior the policy was intended to stop will simply be driven underground. Because smoking is a habit, people will find a way to do it. This recently occurred on a Canadian flight from Canada to the Caribbean when three members of a family took a smoke break in the airplane's lavatory, causing a confrontation with the flight crew, ultimately forcing the plane to land in Bermuda because the cigarette butts could not be located. On landing, everyone was removed from the plane while the family was arrested. The following year a Southwest Airline flight from Florida had to make an emergency landing in Baltimore, Maryland, when a passenger set off a smoke alarm in the lavatory using an electronic cigarette. Human nature will always be a strong factor in the outcomes of a policy.

When we consider the personal stake in the safe operation of an aircraft in flight, it might be expected that everyone would not only understand the policy of not smoking on board but also gladly comply. But when it comes to policy, good will and common sense should not be a factor in expecting compliance. People routinely subvert the common good and personal responsibility from the equation and will act out of purely selfish motivation. So if you want to stop employees smoking on your work site, how effective will the formation of a policy be? The answer is that it will only be as strong as the supporting directives and the will to enforce them. The unintended consequences of a nonsmoking policy might be underground smoking in that employees sneak to hidden places to indulge in a smoke break, which is a blatant disregard of the directives. The lack of nicotine might also result in a loss of worker productivity or even the loss of employees.

In the university where I teach, a full-campus no-smoking policy was put into effect. There was a huge advertising campaign and new signage everywhere. The net result was a group of smokers at just about every doorway. The unintended consequence was that every person attending the school now gets a large dose of second-hand smoke coming and going to class.

I am sure you have witnessed the same phenomenon in your own travels. The end result of attempting to make the area healthier through removal of harmful second-hand smoke is the almost uniform dosing of just about everyone. In the world of unintended consequences, this is the worst – the anti-goal, if you will.

So what are the options in dealing with this huge unintended consequence? The obvious is simply zero tolerance enforcement of the policy. But as we have already discussed, when implementing a policy and directives, both have to pass the reality test. That is, is this element, which is zero tolerance for smoking, realistic? On a large college campus where the violation is practically ubiquitous, I would assess that it is not a realistic expectation. To enforce the no-smoking directive would require additional security personnel and would monopolize resources. It also may not be politically appealing; one thing college campuses are not meant to be are police states. This type of aggressive enforcement might cause all kinds of political issues, although not because of smokers' rights but because of the heightened security posture.

Enforcement of zero tolerance is probably not a viable response. The policy could be amended back to the original one where certain areas were designated as smoking zones. This was not perfect, but there were certainly fewer people lighting up in the entry points. This is realistic as it was already in place and did deliver some of the intended results that the no smoking on campus policy was looking to achieve. However, to do this, someone will lose face.

Usually policy makers are not open to decisions that make them lose face. Politically this would likely fail, not because of its effect on the masses but because of the impact at the top. Other options might include the employment of technology, such as cameras at entry points or enhanced education programs about the dangers of smoking in places that force others to be exposed to second-hand smoke. The technology solution is likely unrealistic in the same way most technology-based solutions are – cost. It would be cost prohibitive to install that many cameras and just as expensive because more people would have to be hired to monitor them. Politically it would probably be fine, as technology is usually politically friendly and allows for nice photo opportunities.

The educational solution has merit, yet given that smoking is a habit and it is not uncommon for some smokers to ignore everything but their needs to indulge, the return on investment may be limited. The education program is also fairly politically inert. But again, the cost factor must be considered and the investment of training instructors and producing materials can be quite significant. There does not seem to be an easy and reasonable response to this unintended consequence.

I posed this question to one of my policy classes and sought a solution. After much debate, the students came up with a modified zero tolerance policy. The enforcement would come from the end users of the college. Students would be encouraged to take cell photos of smokers at the doorways and forward them to campus security for investigation and enforcement. The enforcement actions would be limited to those people smoking in locations that are entry or exit points. The person reporting the violator would get free tuition to a class the following semester and the violator would be fined two-thirds of the cost of a course. The school would pay the remaining one-third.

This certainly would encourage people to enforce the no-smoking rule. It would also be a very strong inducement for smokers to avoid the behavior. Of course, during our discussions, I did bring up the reality test. It was my feeling that this type of bounty hunter behavior could create all kinds of unintended consequences. Yet the students themselves were convinced that the mere publication of the program would go a very long way to curtailing the behavior. They strongly believed that once the first person had to pay the fine, the effect on everyone else would be dramatic. I still have reservations about this solution, but it was a lesson to me about thinking outside the box in trying to come up with policy answers. Is having a bounty system any worse than having a no-smoking rule that is so broadly violated that it makes a mockery of the school administration?

UNINTENDED CONSEQUENCES OF OTHERS' ACTIONS

During one of my many training sessions as a police commander, I was fortunate enough to attend a seminar by well-known risk expert Gordon Graham. Mr. Graham has devoted a significant part of his professional life to preventing adverse consequences in the public safety field. He is an exceptional speaker and his company is a leader in the risk management world. If you get the chance to see or host one of his courses, I highly recommend you take advantage of the opportunity.

Part of his presentation highlights the adventures of the first person to fly across the United States and how the decisions of the pilot and crew provided a lesson to the aviation industry. The concept is that predictable events are preventable, which is a cornerstone of risk management but clearly has applications in management of outcomes. This represents an often unrealized opportunity to benefit from unintended consequences of decisions made by others. This is a dimension of unintended consequences that can be an advantage to the alert policy maker as discussed in the following case study.

CASE STUDY: VIN FIZ FLYER

The challenge was made part as a publicity stunt and part as a way to advance aviation by William Randolph Hearst, a well-known publisher of the day. In 1911, Hearst offered $50,000, an exceptionally large sum in those days, for anyone who could fly ocean to ocean in 30 days or less. Knowing how far modern aviation has advanced, this does not seem to be particularly daunting in our modern world. But back in those days, people had yet to take mechanical flight in any form other than rudimentary flights. The man who accepted the challenge was Calbraith Perry Rodgers. To engage in the contest, Cal Rodgers purchased the first aircraft offered to a private party from the Wright brothers. The aircraft was a Wright Model B and even being generous, it was a very basic airframe. The plane had a wingspan of 32 feet, 21 feet in length, and moved using two pusher propellers driven by bicycle chains. It weighed 903 pounds, including Rodgers. The craft was powered by a 35-horsepower Wright four-cylinder engine. The aircraft only had enough fuel for a little more than three hours of sustained flight. Its maximum sustained flight speed was 55 miles per hour, provided there were no headwinds. The craft's cruising altitude was approximately 1500 feet. This was literally the first private plane and was wholly unregulated. The sum of Cal's pilot training consisted of approximately an hour and a half instruction from the Wright brothers. To facilitate the mission, Rodgers was able to get a sponsor, a grape soda company under the product name Vin Fiz. The sponsor provided a second Model B and a train to follow Rodgers' flight across the country. The flight started on September 17, 1911, with takeoff occurring at 4:30 from Sheepshead Bay, New York. The first leg of the flight was uneventful, despite bets to the contrary, and Cal logged approximately 100 miles that day, landing in Middletown, New York's Dolson Avenue Pleasure Grounds. This was no small event, with a majority of the town turning out for the landing, adding up to approximately 10,000 people. This was the first time they had actually seen a real airplane.

The next day the Vin Fiz Flyer took off in the presence of a large crowd and promptly crashed into a chicken coop near Fulton Street. Luckily Rodgers only nursed a scalp wound. It seemed that the first lesson was learning the minimum distance of runway needed to effect a safe takeoff. The plane was fixed with the help of spectators and took off from a different location with a longer runway. He landed next in Hancock, New York, because of engine problems and poor wind conditions. The second lesson was that the aircraft will often dictate the landing point, not necessarily the flight plan or the pilot. Rodgers next landed in Binghamton, New York, after a collision with some crows, highlighting the dangers of bird strikes on aircraft.

This situation bears similarities to a policy situation, particularly a policy shift into an area where the organization does not have past experience. Much like the inexperienced Cal Rodgers, a policy maker or directive drafter may not have any practical experience in the new policy area. And like Cal, the policy maker may simply have to engage in a process of trial and error. It is not farfetched to see how this type of situation can occur particularly in areas of new or rapidly expanding technology. When social media began to take off several years ago, there were no textbooks that policy makers could look to frame directives or policies. The process was trial and error. Yet like the Vin Fiz Flyer, there are probably people who have been pioneers and have made the common mistakes. As an organizational leader, it is up to you to look to these mistakes in an effort to anticipate the outcomes of policy actions.

The Vin Fiz Flyer is a great example of the value of exploiting organizational sensing to predict pitfalls that may apply to your policy change. Those pilots who flew after the Vin Fiz Flyer had a listing of practically all of the hazards that could impact a flight. They would only need to examine the news of the flight and its many crashes to import significant institutional knowledge. Sadly, even today, aircraft still fall victim to the causes of some of the crashes experienced by Cal Rodgers.

TUNNEL VISION AND UNINTENDED CONSEQUENCES

The process of policy making is normally driven by a triggering event, and because the process is problem-driven, analytical focus can be compromised. This can be even more applicable in the field of professional security. Even in less-intensive environments, the pressure to find a solution to a problem in a timely fashion is common. Circumstances such as a compressed time frame, internal or external pressure to act, and even an existing safety threat can narrow the focus of policy makers. This type of pressure can result in a very narrow outlook on dealing with the problem. Even highly skilled professionals, such as lawyers whose job it is to analyze decisions and potential outcomes, can be misled. In 1956, actor William Holden was negotiating his contract with Columbia Pictures and the clause of profit sharing was negotiated into the contract. He successfully negotiated a 10% share of the film's gross earnings. The average gross for films in 1956 was approximately $4 million. Out of a concern for tax consequences, Holden negotiated a clause to only receive up to $50,000 in any one year and that payouts would be disbursed over the course of years. The film grossed between $20 and $30 million, giving Holden a share of $2 to $3 million. Because of the clause, the studio simply banked the cash and paid Holden out of the interest from the money over 40 years. This effectively meant that he did not participate in any real profit sharing (Segall, 2002). The clause was clearly intended to mitigate the impact of taxes and was successful, but the unintended consequences were rather extreme. By using a simple what-if analysis, it would have likely revealed the potential adverse outcomes like this one, especially because every year there were movies that were statistical outliers that grossed at least $20 million. So the possibility of a major hit was very realistic.

We all love a story where a lawyer messes up, but there is a bit more value to this story than simply getting a modicum of happiness at the expense of celebrities and attorneys. The issue in this case was that neither the lawyers drafting the contract nor the star gave enough attention to the possibility that the contract could actually be against his interest. Their focus was clearly solely on tax consequences, which are a legitimate concern. It is unclear if the contract was drafted by a tax lawyer or one who had expertise in contracts. At the end of the day, the scope of the analysis was too narrow. It is human nature to focus narrowly on perceived threats and to act accordingly; it is part of our genetic makeup and allowed our ancestors to survive. Although this worked well for prehistoric people, it does not always help in our contemporary civilized world. As a policy maker, the recognition of threats and effectively responding is just part of the job, but to avoid tunnel vision, a process should be employed. Using a defined process can help break policy-making tunnel vison and mitigate unintended consequences. The policy analysis process was covered in detail in Chapter 6. It involves performing a strengths, weaknesses, opportunities, and threats (SWOT) analysis followed by the Seven Question Inquiry. The SWOT analysis requires a detailed listing of all of the actual or potential factors that can impact strategic policy (goals). The listing of these elements should continue until there is nothing left to list. This exhaustive listing is especially true for the threats element. Employing this process hopefully can provide structure in identifying and assessing policy options and their outcomes. The process relies on a broad approach to analyzing the circumstances, and engaging in tunnel vision can significantly limit the effectiveness.

Sometimes policy decisions are made that do not contemplate the adverse impacts of a new technology. This can be a result of policy makers performing an analysis without fully grasping the nuances of the new technology. In contemporary society, the evolution of technology is sometimes hard to comprehend itself. In cases of new technology, it is important to have subject matter experts weigh in on the policy options. If an expert is not available, then it can be fruitful to do some basic research to find out if there is a contemporary Vin Fiz Flyer. Search for another person or organization that has gone before and made mistakes. Given the invasive nature of news media, both amateur and professional, a thorough search should uncover examples to learn from.

EMERGING TECHNOLOGY AND UNINTENDED CONSEQUENCES

The assessment of unintended consequences can be complicated by new technology. By its nature, new and disruptive technology creates situations where policy struggles to catch up to the practical reality. We can see that in contemporary society, technology evolves rapidly, and the benefits of use sometimes create situations where adverse impacts of the use cannot be forecast. In cases of emerging or rapidly evolving technology, it is important to assess these opportunities through a SWOT analysis against the backdrop of the organizational strengths and weaknesses and the relation to the technology. When a policy option includes a technology that the policy maker is not fully knowledgeable about, a subject matter expert should be employed to assist in the policy-making process. In the event that a subject matter expert is not available or appropriate, then the policy maker should look to the experience of others. A search of the Internet for a contemporary Vin Fiz Flyer can reveal potential adverse impacts and can be instructional in operational policy. Give the extensive amateur and professional news offerings, the likelihood of information on early adopters of technology should be available. There is also a danger of hubris in that the policy maker or stakeholders may feel that they have an expertise in the subject. This is a red flag and if the new technology seems simple and common, you need to seek assistance. A subject matter expert should be considered – one that has formal training and credentials or years of proven experience and results. Misguided appreciation for the complexity of new technology is common and can impact even the most sophisticated of organizations.

CASE STUDY: THE NEW YORK POLICE DEPARTMENT AND SOCIAL MEDIA

The New York City Police Department (NYPD) is arguably the best in the world. It is massive and has the ability to drawn on a diverse set of skill sets brought to the agency by its members. Presumably this would include Internet technology professionals. In April 2014, the NYPD began a new policy of public engagement through social media. This engagement of the public was meant to show interactions with the police and the public that were positive. Like most policy shifts, it was undoubtedly conceived with good intentions and expectations of success. The outcome was anything but positive, with tweets showing police using force, sleeping on duty, and all manner of unflattering and inflammatory photos. The question in this case is whether the potential for this kind of response was considered. The negative portrayal of the police was certainly foreseeable, as it is the nature of Twitter to have spontaneous and uncontrolled content and responses. Yet a more significant consideration for the assessment of unintended consequences in the use of this social media platform is the human factor. In the policy process, it seems surprising that this kind of response would not be expected and thus planned for. Another factor that might have been considered in this situation is the level of inexperience in the use of a technology like Twitter. It did not end there. Aside from the Twitter picture fiasco, police officers were very clumsy in using Twitter, sometimes posting sarcastic comments on official tweets or in response to them. This is clearly not the image that the police department or any organization for that matter wants to send. As a result, officers were disciplined, and large-scale follow-on policy changes were made to remedy the situation, including sending cops to school to learn about how to properly use social media. The lesson here is that had a thorough analysis been undertaken, all of this could have been prevented. Despite the relative newness of Twitter to the NYPD, it was not a new phenomenon in the private sector. There were plenty of examples similar to the Vin Fiz Flyer, which could have been found using the most basic of policy-sensing tools – the Google search. It looks like it was the Vin Fiz Flyer all over again. The NYPD made just about every mistake that could be made in their foray into the Twitter-verse.

While unfortunate for New York's finest, it represents a learning opportunity for other police agencies. It was highly publicized and provided an abject lesson in how things can go bad when making this kind of change. Despite policy changes and hard lessons in unintended consequences learned from their past Twitter issues, the NYPD continued to show a lack of grasp of the social media impacts. Another misstep occurred when the department tweeted after the controversial Eric Garner grand jury decision, setting off a firestorm of negative responses to the ill-timed tweet. Clearly the idea of avoiding a social networking medium with which the organization had limited success and an apparent lack of skill was not contemplated. The lesson in the latest Twitter fail might be that the unintended consequences have not all been factored and limiting use is a viable policy. From the outside, the NYPD looked to be in over their heads and they failed to recognize that the public at large is much more skilled at the use of social media than the department. A SWOT analysis with an honest assessment of the environment may have prevented these missteps.

STRUCTURALLY DRIVEN UNINTENDED CONSEQUENCES

In some cases unintended consequences can arise from more basic origins and not external factors. One of the most difficult sources of unintended consequences is the organization itself. Sometimes it is a matter of strategic policy that drives the organization into situations that breed unintended consequences. Other times it can be the disproportionate influence of a stakeholder who is driving policy for self-enrichment. Self-serving stakeholders will not concern themselves with the adverse impacts of a policy decision as the effect will be on the organization and not them. In either case, a meaningful and honest SWOT assessment can detect structural issues that can lead to unintended consequences. Attention should be paid to the strengths and weaknesses section of the analysis, which should be instructional as to whether the organization is involved in actions that are outside its abilities or scope. Although unintended consequences often occur because of a failure in outcome analysis, structurally driven outcomes can happen to even the most professional organizations.

CASE STUDY: SECRET SERVICE

Protecting the president of the United States is surely a task that requires laser focus and clarity of purpose. In recent years, the focus and clarity of purpose of the United States Secret Service (USSS) has increasingly been called into question. There have been many instances of penetrations of the security system provided by the USSS, but the nature of security is not a zero-sum game and requires an exacting process and vigilance. The USSS has taken a beating in the press for many lapses that have made the organization appear careless. This is not exactly a desirable attribute for a group entrusted with the safety of the president and our monetary system. Typically in failures at the operational level, there are the usual suspects: failure to supervise, failure to train, and organizational culture.

In 2014, the head of the USSS was fired after a man was able to get inside the White House after jumping the fence. We might make the assumption that there was a failure to supervise, based on the dismissal of the head of the USSS. In other cases, revelations about calling off countersniper teams as the White House was under fire and allowing an armed security contractor near the president in an elevator created outrage on Capitol Hill. But the issue may be more fundamental than supervision or simple carelessness. These are proximate causes to be sure, but the true cause may be that these incidents were just unintended consequences of much more fundamental and structural issues.

The mission of the USSS is not just to protect national leaders: "The mission of the United States Secret Service (USSS) is to safeguard the nation's financial infrastructure and payment systems to preserve the integrity of the economy, and to protect national leaders, visiting heads of state and government, designated sites and National Special Security Events" (Reese, 2014). The USSS has two vital missions and thus must make value judgments as to how to employ limited resources to fulfill the mission. The expectation of the USSS preventing every attack is unreasonable. Part of risk management requires that there be an assumption of some risk. In this case, it is the balance between maximum accessibility of the president and the White House and protection. In fact, historically there have been criticisms that the USSS is too heavy handed. In a 1992, a little over a year after a sitting president was shot, an article by George Will condemned the service as too officious and creating great inconvenience to the public (Will, 1992). Thus the USSS must constantly balance openness with security, which are two contradictory missions at best.

The incidents at the White House are nothing new and there will be more. It is a fixed target with a highly observable routine. Outside of measures that will limit access, the security at the White House will be reactive. The USSS cannot screen everyone who is outside the perimeter. The incidents that have led to the controversy surrounding the USSS can be linked to failures in parts of the system, and not necessarily the entire system. The fence jumper was able to penetrate several layers of security, but elements of the system worked. The jumper was delayed by the fence and was almost immediately detected. The failure appears to be that the exterior door accessed was not locked. We have no evidence that the jumper was under countersniper surveillance and that there was a calculated decision to allow for the subject to be dealt with by other assets.

The incident where an armed contractor got near the president also represents a failure in part of the system – the advance work. Yet the man was challenged by USSS agents and neutralized in the elevator. The shots fired at the White House present a failure in decision making and lack of technology. The search by the countersniper teams was called off because a commanding officer believed erroneous information. Also, there appeared to be a lack of gunfire spotting technology that would have been able to quickly identify the threat. Yet, in this case, the physical security of the building protected the occupants.

The USSS is an agency that faces multiple unrelated missions. The protection of the nation's currency and financial crime investigation are massive undertakings in their own right. The skill set and resources required to effectively deal with this mission alone are daunting. The USSS is an organization with two radically different mandates, which presents an almost schizophrenic organization. What is clear is that the threat profiles of both missions are growing. The pressure on the protection side can be illustrated by the $53 million increase requested for 2015. To add to the dilution of the protective missions, Congress continues to add mandates. The USSS is also responsible for security at events designated as "nationally important" and have also been tasked with providing support for missing and exploited children (Powers, Authorities, and Duties of the United States Secret Service, 2015).

While it may more comforting to look to proximate causes of incidents, such as complacency (unlocked doors, poor advance screening) or human error (leadership failures), looking at the mission is more likely to fix the problem. Having the USSS divest itself from the economic investigations mission will clearly be politically unpopular and may even result in loss of prestige. Yet, from a policy perspective, the mission of protecting our currency and investigating financial crime might be better served as a function of the Treasury Department. In the alternative, a new organization could be created in the Department of Homeland Security.

In the end, having the lead agency responsible for protecting the president trying to perform two completely unrelated missions is not optimal and leads to unintended consequences. Contemporary reporting shows the lapses in protecting the president are arguably the unintended consequences of the USSS being overtasked. Additionally, the balance between trying to maintain accessibility and protection at the same time will always be a fertile ground for incidents to occur. Given that the occurrence, unintended consequences are virtually assured in trying to reconcile two competing missions, which makes the operational policy-making process even more critical.

The necessity to identify and mitigate unintended consequences is not simply being a matter of being a good corporate citizen or doing the right thing; there can be consequences as well. It can also present a legal threat to an organization that fails to perform a reasonable inquiry of potential adverse outcomes. When a person or organization undertakes an action, in our case a policy, the person or organization is legally responsible for all of the outcomes. The highest degree of responsibility is attached to those outcomes that were foreseeable. In assessing foreseeability, the inquiry focuses on the impacts and those who are affected and from an action that can be reasonably predicted. Any person or organization that has a relationship with the actor is considered foreseeably involved. This means that any person or group who could potentially be a stakeholder is owed a duty to be protected from hazards or at a minimum notify them of the threat. An organization that does not thoroughly assess all of the potential outcomes will not be able to claim lack of knowledge as a defense. If anything, this admission will indicate negligence. As we discussed in Chapter 2, the impact of a lawsuit on an organization can be significant, and this alone should drive meaningful outcome analysis.

PRACTICE POINTERS

- The prediction of unintended consequences is difficult but necessary. It is a formal process of identifying the potential outcomes of any given decision.
- As an organizational leader, you are responsible for ensuring that a meaningful and honest assessment of the possible outcomes for each policy option is considered. The analysis will not just happen on its own.
- The essential part of an outcome analysis is to mitigate the unintended consequences. This can require being direct with stakeholders even if they do not wish to hear it.
- In analyzing policy options for unintended consequences, take advantage of the mistakes of other similarly situated organizations. It is an effective way to gain institutional knowledge and frame the search for outcomes. This is particularly true in cases of emerging technology.
- Structurally driven outcomes are very dangerous and will be a source of ongoing unintended consequences unless dealt with. Make sure that any policy choices are in the best interests of the organization and are actually attainable.
- Failing to perform an outcome analysis can result in legal liability to the organization. Protect yourself and the group by insisting on a meaningful assessment.

Chapter Recap

- The analysis of unintended consequences is really the recognition of all probable, possible, and even impossible outcomes of a given policy choice or option.
- The goal of an inquiry into unintended consequences is to mitigate them.
- Virtually any policy option will have unintended consequences.
- Unintended consequences can be predicted through lessons learned by the missteps of other people or organizations.
- When investigating unintended consequences, tunnel vison may be a problem, particularly if under pressure to act or if ongoing harm is occurring. Tunnel vison can be countered by methodically following an analytic process.
- New technology can present difficulties in predicting outcomes because policy normally lags behind emerging technology. This can be addressed by looking for the contemporary Vin Fiz Flyer examples of early adopters.
- One of the most difficult issues confronting the management of unintended consequences are structurally driven outcomes. These can be addressed through an honest and thorough SWOT analysis.
- Failure to identify and mitigate unintended consequences will result in legal liability if a harm to a person or organization results.

BIBLIOGRAPHY

Bevir, M. (2007). *Encyclopedia of governance*. Thousand Oaks, CA: Sage.

Blackstock, J. (2010). Vin Fiz Flyer landed in Pomona on its way into aviation history. Inland Valley Daily Bulletin (Ontario, CA). McClatchy-Tribune Information Services. Retrieved July 8, 2015 from HighBeam Research: <http://www.highbeam.com/doc/1P2-26108843.html>.

Cortell, A. P., Cortell, A. P., & Peterson, S. (2001). *Comparative political studies: Limiting the unintended consequences of institutional change*. Thousand Oaks, CA: Sage.

Daniel, K. J. (1988). Gasoline conservation versus pollution control unintended consequences, continued. *Journal of Policy Analysis and Management, 7*(4), 710.

Department of Homeland Security, United States Secret Service. (2014). U.S. secret service strategic plan (FY 2014–FY 2018). Retrieved from: <http://www.secretservice.gov/usss_strategic_plan_2014_2018.pdf>.

Fern, T. (2002). Up, up and away (sort of). *Boys' Life, 92,* 8.

Fisher, D. B. (2013). Law of unintended consequences. *Aircraft Maintenance Technology, 24* 30–30.

Gains, F. (2003). Executive agencies in government: The impact of bureaucratic networks on policy outcomes. *Journal of Public Policy, 23*, 55–79.

Goldsmith, A. J. (2010, September). Policing's new visibility. *The British Journal of Criminology, 50*(5), 914–934.

Greenberg, S. (2011, September 17). Middletown celebrates 100th anniversary of the Vin Fiz airplane's flight from New York to California. *Hudson Valley Magazine*, Retrieved from: <http://www.hvmag.com/Hudson-Valley-Magazine/September-2011/Middletown-Celebrates-100th-Anniversary-of-the-Vin-Fiz-Airplanes-Flight-from-New-York-to-California/>.

Hawken, A., Kulick, J., & Prieger, J.E. (2013). Unintended consequences of cigarette taxation and regulation. Retrieved from <http://papers.ssrn.com/sol3/papers.cfm?abstract_id=2354772>.

Ho, E. (2013, February 5). Family accused of smoking on plane forces emergency landing, gets arrested. *Time Magazine*. Retrieved from: <http://newsfeed.time.com/2013/02/05/family-accused-of-smoking-on-plane-forces-emergency-landing-gets-arrested/>.

Houle, B., & Siegel, M. (2009). Smoker-free workplace policies: Developing a model of public health consequences of workplace policies barring employment to smokers. *Tobacco Control, 18*(1), 64–69.

House, J. M. (1989). *Do doctrinal buzzwords obscure the meaning of operational art?* Fort Leavenworth, KS: US Army Command and General Staff College.

Lave, L. (1975, December). Coal or nuclear: The unintended consequences of electricity generation. American Economic Association Annual meeting, Dallas Texas. Retrieved from: <http://repository.cmu.edu/cgi/viewcontent.cgi?article=2135&context=tepper>.

Leonnig, C., & Nakamura, D. (2014, October 1). Julia Pierson resigns as Secret Service director after series of security lapses. *The Washington Post*. Retrieved from: <http://www.washingtonpost.com/politics/julia-pierson-resigns-as-secret-service-director/2014/10/01/ea39a396-499f-11e4-891d-713f052086a0_story.html>.

Levy, G. (2014). Julia Pierson resigns as head of Secret Service. *UPI Top News*, Retrieved from: <http://www.upi.com/Top_News/US/2014/10/01/Secret-Service-Director-Julia-Pierson-to-step-down/5351412191209/>.

Mackin, M. (2008, December 4). The Vin Fiz Flyer. *Pittsburgh Post - Gazette*, D5.

Negligence, (2005). (2nd ed.). In S. Phelps & J. Lehman (Eds.), *West's encyclopedia of American law* (Vol. 7, pp. 221–228). Detroit, MI: Gale.

Oh, I. (2014, April 23). This NYPD idea backfired horribly on twitter. *The Huffington Post*, Retrieved from: <http://www.huffingtonpost.com/2014/04/22/mynypd-nypd-twitter_n_5193523.html>.

Powers, authorities, and duties of the United States Secret Service 18 U.S.C. 3056(e)-(f). (2015).

Prieger, J. E., & Kulick, J. (2014). Unintended consequences of enforcement in illicit markets. *Economics Letters, 125*(2), 295–297.

Read, S. N., & Army Command And General Staff Coll Fort Leavenworth KS School Of Advanced Military Studies, (1990). *Planning for the unplannable: Branches, sequels and reserves*. Ft. Belvoir, VA: Defense Technical Information Center. Retrieved from: <http://cdm16040.contentdm.oclc.org/cdm/ref/collection/p4013coll3/id/1851>.

Reese, S. (2009). *U.S. Secret Service: An examination and analysis of its evolving missions*. Washington, DC: Congressional Research Service, Library of Congress.

Reese, S. (2014). *The U.S. secret service: History and missions.* Washington, DC: Congressional Research Service, Library of Congress.

Roots, R. I. (2004). When laws backfire: Unintended consequences of public policy. *The American Behavioral Scientist, 47*(11), 1376–1394.

Segall, H. A. (2002). Drafting: An essential skill. Fordham Urb. LJ, 30, 751.

Sherden, W. A. (2011). *Best laid plans : The tyranny of unintended consequences and how to avoid them.* Santa Barbara, CA: ABC-CLIO.

Sleeper, M., Cranshaw, J., Kelley, P. G., Ur, B., Acquisti, A., Cranor, L. F., et al. (2013, April). I read my Twitter the next morning and was astonished: A conversational perspective on Twitter regrets: *Proceedings of the SIGCHI conference on human factors in computing systems* (pp. 3277–3286). New York: ACM.

Sommer, A. A., Jr. (1997). Preempting unintended consequences. *Law and Contemporary Problems, 60,* 231.

Stittleburg, P. C. (2012). Law of unintended consequences. *Fire Chief, 56*(3), 20–23.

Valez, N., & Celona, L. (2014, September 2). NYPD sends top cops to twitter school. New York Post. Retrieved from: <http://nypost.com/2014/09/02/nypd-commanders-to-take-twitter-courses/>.

WBAL. (2014, December 11). Southwest: Passenger's e-cigarette use caused emergency landing (Television broadcast). Retrieved from <http://www.wbaltv.com/news/airline-pilot-declares-emergency-after-passenger-uses-ecigarette-in-bathroom/30170064>.

Will, G. (1992, February 24). Getting back to Truman's stroll. *Newsweek, 119,* 74. http://dx.doi.org/200602.

Williams, D. (2011, February). Charities hurt by law of unintended consequences. *Public Finance,* 8–9.

Policy Construction

When we speak of policy construction, what we are really talking about are the elements contained in the actual written product used to communicate strategic and operational policy. An essential facet of policy construction is the continuity of documents and document structure. That is, each policy document should be drafted with a common structure, which should be as intuitive as possible. The proper terminology to use in any policy document is the term *directive*. It should be used when describing, in general, the material end product of the formal policy-making process. When referring to a known directive, use the common name, numeric identifier, or the exact type of document. In my years as a law enforcement accreditation assessor and commissioner I have observed agencies operating with multiple types of policy documents that have little in common. This may be an effective way to draft and quickly disburse policy but in the long run, it is far from optimal. The manner in which the policy documents are constructed requires some forethought and a lot depends on the type of organization that is involved. Each of the elements covered in this chapter are essential to the drafting of coherent and defensible directives. The following sections describe the elements of a directive and hopefully can guide you on developing your own for your organization.

DIRECTIVE HEADER
Directive Type

Directive type indicates the category of directive being employed. The types of directives can be rules, orders, procedures, policy, or memorandum among others. The identity of each type of directive is tied to the level of discretion permitted, with the rule being the least and the policy being the most. The designation of directive also serves as a categorizing and cataloging tool for directives and allows for each type to be filed with their own categories.

Policy Identification System

The second element of this directive will be the manner in which directives will be identified. Directives have been known to be identified strictly by name, especially when contained as part of a policy manual. A common name identifier is appropriate for very small organizations that are structured as flat and with personnel directly supervised by the chief executive. A flat organization has minimal or no middle management and a skilled workforce. This is typical of start-ups and creativity-driven organizations. This identifier can also be appropriate for a solo practitioner. A common name identifier is workable as it is intuitive to generally reference. It has several drawbacks: It cannot be cited with precision and can be confusing. Eventually it will require additional effort in constructing future directives, as the title must be unique enough to allow for ready identification. It also has the drawback of limiting expansion. For example, there could be several directives that affect harassment. Although this type of identifier does exist, it is inappropriate for all but the smallest organizations.

Identifiers can also use numeric or alphanumeric identifier systems. A strictly numeric identifier is appropriate for most organizations, including those structured as flat or tall. A flat organization has minimal middle management and a skilled workforce. A strictly numeric identifier is workable, as it is intuitive to construct and offers a way to cite directives with specificity. The danger of this type of identifier is that it can become confusing unless it is organized in chunks. For example all directives that apply to the administration of the organization would have the primary identifier of "1." All directives that apply to manufacturing have a primary identifier of "2," and all directives that apply to sales would be "3." Thus, if looking for a directive that applies to sales you would seek out the category that starts with "3." It might look like this: 3.27. The addition of an alpha character provides even more flexibility. In my experience, the optimal system is to use an alphanumeric identifier system. The application of the alpha character would be in front of the numeral and would indicate what type of directive is involved.

As we have seen, there are different types of directives for different purposes. Generally, directives are organized along the lines of the amount of discretion allowed. This pyramid of directives starts with rules at the top and works its way down to the strategic policy with a rule being at the apex and the strategic policy at the base. An alphanumeric identifier allows for the designation of the type of directive that are applicable. For example, a rule that deals with company dress code, which is administrative in nature, might be cited as: R.1.33, where R = a rule, 1 = administrative directives, and 33 = dress code. So the format is a letter followed by a single number followed by the assigned directive number. The final numeric employed will be the heading identifier. This final numeric will be a number and will be limited to identifying the relevant heading in the body of directive document. For example, heading number "1" will always be the policy statement. Heading number "2" will always be the purpose statement. Heading number "3" varies depending on the requirement of a definitions heading. If the definitions heading is present then it will be numbered as "3" otherwise the procedure heading will be number "3" and number "4" if definitions are included. The heading designator is only used for citing specificity and will complement the identification of the subheadings. Thus if a sales manager wanted to cite an employee to the purpose statement in a training session or counseling for dress code rule infraction, it would be cited like this: R.1.33.2.

Date Issued

The date issued refers to the date the directive is actually published. Publishing a directive can only occur after the chief executive has approved the directive. Having a clearly defined date on directives is important to establish exactly when the policy change was adopted. This can be very important in future litigation and employee discipline.

Author's Identification Number

Each directive must have an author and for continuity and other reasons, the person must be identified. This will allow the chief executive to immediately know who drafted the document and who to contact if revisions are required. It also provides recognition for the author and demonstrates a level of subject matter expertise. It is recommended that the author's identity be exhibited through the use of an employee identification (ID) number. This is an important privacy element in cases of future litigation or public release of the directive. To have a healthy policy-making system, there should be many contributors to the drafting of directives and having only a few drafters can be problematic and result in tunnel vison. In cases of multiple authors, the ID numbers of each should be included. In addition, if an existing directive is updated, the original author's ID should still remain first with the contributing author as second.

Issuing Authority

The first element of this directive is to establish the single person who is the issuing authority. This is typically the chief executive of the organization. Having a single identified issuing authority is important because it allows the organization to ensure that the operational policy supports the strategic policy and that competing and contradictory policy is not issued.

Revision Date

The revision date fulfills the same purpose as the issue date and the date recorded should be the exact date the directive is published. As with the original effective date, a revision cannot be published until after the issuing authority has signed off on the directive and given permission to publish.

Sources

In many cases, policy changes will be required as a result of a new law or regulation. In these circumstances, the underlying law or regulation should be referenced. If the directive is technical in nature, the sources of the definitions or other important data should be cited. There is a limit and only cite information that will help readers get context in carrying out the directive. Sources should be cited very specifically to allow readers to find the source quickly and effectively.

Old Number

This section will only be used if there is an obsolete directive on the same topic and it has a different identifier, otherwise it should reflect "N/A," meaning not applicable.

Appendix

When drafting a directive, the use of an appendix should be limited to essential information that supports the directive. Additionally, if the directive contains information that is subject to routine changes, this information should be included as an appendix. For example, if the security department has to interact with an outside regulatory body and the points of contact frequently change, the contact list should be an appendix. It is my suggestion that the enabling directives for the policy system provide for an exception to the changing of an appendix. A change to the appendix should not be considered a revision to the directive and therefore can be changed without issuing authority approval.

Page Numbers

The number of pages in the directive should be recorded in the heading to include the appendix. This is often an area where mistakes are made and it is essential to ensure that the proper number of pages is reflected. It often creates problems when the document is in hard-copy form and readers are unsure if the document they possess is complete. Also, in the event of litigation, a properly paginated document can lead to questions about missing information.

BODY OF THE DIRECTIVE

Figure 9.1 is an example of a directive form. The following sections will examine the body of the directive in more detail.

ANYTOWN SECURITY DEPARTMENT

General Order (This indicates the type of directive)		**Response to Unmanned Aerial System Incidents** **G.1.4** (This is the title and the numerical designation)	
DATE(s)	**AUTHOR ID NO.**	**AUTHORITY**	
Effective: **03/18/20XX** (The date issued)	Computer # **34** (Identification number or the name of author)	**John Doe, CEO** (The issuing authority)	
Revised: **09/18/20XX** (Revision date if any)	Computer # **34/108**	**John Doe, CEO**	
Revised:	Computer #		
Revised:	Computer #		
Revised:	Computer #		
Source(s): **NJ Common Law, FAA Regulations**			
Old Number:**N/A** (Referral to any obsolete related directives)	Appendix: **None** (Listing of any appendix)		Pages: **5** (Number of pages)

■ **FIGURE 9.1** Example of a Directive Header.

Policy Statement

The policy statement is the first heading of the document and is related directly to the strategic policy of the organization. It is a restatement of what the organization hopes to achieve. The policy statement is also the failsafe in a directive in that if the employee cannot understand the procedure or instruction contained in the directive, the policy statement provides context. For example, in a security department directive on highway drug enforcement, the policy statement would likely speak about the agency's goal of stopping the flow of drugs *while* preserving and protecting all citizens' constitutional rights. A directive might be confusing in how to stop and search cars, but if the confused employee looks to the policy statement for reference, he or she will understand that whatever action is taken must comport with the Constitution.

Purpose Statement

The next element of a directive is the purpose statement. A purpose statement is included in a document to ensure that the employee understands the purpose of the directive. This narrows down the directive to be specific or in some cases can identify the directive to be read broadly. The purpose also provides context as to why the employee is performing the function a certain way. It also should be written to underscore the importance of the directive. This has always been an important part of the document as it explains the "why" and understanding the mission is an important part of employee buy-in and to the overall success of the task. This is even more significant now because of generational differences in the workforce. The baby boom generation may have accepted direction without question, but successive generations want more information.

Definitions

In situations where there is specific terminology used or there is a need to specifically define a word or a construct a definition, a heading would be appropriate. The general rule is that if anyone in the company could pick up the directive and know exactly what is being described, then a definitions section is not required. However, given that we have already identified at least three different parts of the organization – administration, manufacturing, and sales – it is likely that the job functions in the organization are sufficiently different and segregated such that a definitions section will be required. If the directive uses only terminology that has only one commonly accepted definition, then you may also be able to forego a definitions heading. The test is if two people can see the word and have different meanings for it, then it must be defined. Defining words is contingent on commonly accepted and formally published definitions. It is not appropriate to set your own definitions unless there are no formal sources to define the word. You can only set a definition on your own if you researched the word and could not find an appropriate definition. This is a very subjective area of the directive and caution should be used when straying from formal definitions.

Procedure

The procedure section is the area where the reader is told how things are expected to be done. A procedural section is part of all directives not just procedures. The procedure section should not be confused with the directive titled "procedure." Orders and other types of directives will also contain the procedure section. The difference is the level of discretion allowed in carrying out the process. The information presented in this area should be written as simply and plainly as possible. It should be broken down into its component parts and these main parts should serve as the headings using an uppercase letter to designate the heading. The information in this section should be focused on the specific processes required to complete the task and should detail each step that is required. The processes should be in chronological order as much as possible and they should be separated by employee function under a separate heading if applicable. For example, in the case of a theft report, the responding security officer will be required to take specific actions, but there might be actions required by the dispatcher. Thus for each function, officers and dispatchers will have their own section of guidance. An additional section will always be contained for the supervisory function. The supervisor should have the conditions of routine follow-up as well as any specific supervisory action detailed. In addition, if there is any time limitation for any actions, these should be detailed in the functional area required to complete them. If a task is assigned to any particular function or unit, it must clearly be stated. If there are any training requirements affiliated with the directive, they should be clearly and precisely spelled out under their own heading, and if time sensitive, the deadlines should be noted. The point of the procedure section of a directive is to explain the process in unambiguous steps and in a chronological order, specifying exactly who is responsible to do what and when. The stream of the procedural steps should be intuitive yet very thorough. The following case study is a sample process that we all should engage in every day.

CASE STUDY: BRUSHING TEETH

If you were providing the procedural section of a directive on brushing your teeth, it would look something like this:

A. Pre-brushing activities
   1. Enter the bathroom and select your toothbrush.
   2. Fill up cup with water.
   3. Rinse toothbrush with water for 10 seconds.
   4. Select toothpaste.
   5. Apply toothpaste to your toothbrush bristle section.
   6. Rinse out mouth with water from cup leaving half for later.
B. Brushing activities
   1. Bring toothbrush to the inside of mouth.
   2. Place bristles with attached toothpaste to front of teeth.
   3. Move toothbrush against teeth in an up and down motion.
   4. Continue this motion until all of the teeth are brushed.
   5. Brush for three full minutes.
C. Post-brushing activities
   1. Remove brush from mouth and rinse it in sink.
   2. Take cup and rinse mouth.
   3. Refill cup with mouthwash.
   4. Rinse mouth with mouthwash.
   5. Hold mouthwash in mouth and gargle.
   6. Spit mouthwash into sink.
   7. Rinse off toothbrush and put away.
   8. Rinse out cup and put away.
   9. Dry face off with towel.
   10. Leave bathroom.

If you are like me, this seems like an awful lot of writing to describe a very simple task. But is it really that simple? The key to drafting the procedural section of a directive is to draft it with sufficient information to allow someone who knows very little about the function to perform it in a manner that the organization has determined is the best way. There are people out there who do not brush their teeth in the most effective way, just as there are employees in the workplace who do not perform tasks in the most effective ways. By clearly stating the preferred steps of a process, the organization ensures that there is uniformity in performance and that when there are any questions, there is a detailed and specific reference. The toothbrushing example may feel a bit comical or oversimplified in that the design of the procedure section is broken down too basically. But I firmly believe that at least some people reading this book have never written a directive before, and as simple as this information seems, it is useful to some. This underscores the point I am trying to make: A procedure must be basic in order to work for every member of the organization.

CRISIS

There is another reason why the procedural section of a directive must be written to the lowest common denominator and that reason is crisis. Not every need to reference a procedure will be in calm circumstances with lots of available time. There will be times when personnel will need to reference a procedure under extreme stress in the midst of a crisis. This happens all the time, and there is nothing worse than needing an answer and having to interpret the document that is intended to tell you how to do something. Over the years, I have instructed thousands of security officers and many college students as well. I teach them the same thing when it comes to the most fundamental truth about a crisis; you do not get to pick the day. One never knows when an outcome during a crisis may depend on how clearly written a directive is.

CASE STUDY: OCEAN RANGER

Drilling for oil in the ocean is a risky endeavor and many things can go wrong. Seaborne oil rigs are marvels of engineering and it could be expected that they are highly regulated. Sadly, this is not always the case, and often organizations leave much to chance. The Ocean Ranger oil drilling vessel was at 16,500 tons making it the largest self-propelled, semi-submersible, offshore drilling unit in the world at the time. The Ocean Ranger met its end while in the North Atlantic 170 miles east of Newfoundland, Canada. In the early morning hours of February 15, 1982, it was sunk by a storm lashing it with 100 miles per hour winds. The ocean roiled with waves, hitting the top of the rig and flooding the upper decks. During the storm, the rig began to list and eventually capsized, killing 84 crew members.

The Ocean Ranger was constructed similar to an end table with four main supports and two large pontoon stabilizers. The stabilizers were hollow and contained ballast tanks, storage for fuel and water, and operating equipment for the rig, including control valves. The legs that supported the rig were also hollow and contained chain lockers and anchors. One of them contained the control room and was very close to the water. This room curiously also had a porthole. The balance and buoyancy of the rig was controlled by shifting ballast through the control room, contained in one of the two shorter middle legs on the starboard side. The room was staffed by a trained operator on duty at all times. The ballast control was a skill and it required training and knowledge to operate. This was demonstrated when a new captain took over the rig and while relieving the control room operator, almost capsized the vessel by activating an incorrect button because of his inexperience. The vessel was saved by the hasty return of the operator. To complicate matters, the electrical system that controlled the ballast was unreliable and a manual override system of brass actuator rods was installed to compensate. More ominously, there was a general lack of discipline and policy, the owners of the rig had failed to inspect it for some time, and there were many safety protocols not followed or implemented. Training was almost nonexistent and there were not enough lifeboats or survival suits for the crew.

The Ocean Ranger trained ballast operators mostly by on-the-job training. This training consisted of having crew members qualify for the ballast control job by spending several hours each day of their sparse free time hanging out in the control room, observing the ballast operator at work. Once the deck boss thought that the crew member was able to do the job, the crew member left his or her original assignment and started work in the control room. This was contrary to company policy that required employees to have 80 weeks of offshore training prior to their shipboard on-the-job training. The investigation revealed that the approach to control room training was based on the assumption that the ballast controls were failsafe. This is an odd assertion considering that a manual override system was in place to compensate for the inconsistent performance of the electric controls. Aside from a failure in policy, supervision, and training, complacency driven by overreliance on technology was involved. The control room did in fact have an operations manual that was complicated and provided guidance for operating the electronic controls and the use of formulas and calibrations. It was not routinely used and those undergoing on-the-job training were told to look it over. There were no written instructions in how to operate the brass manual control rods or specific testing.

On February 14, 1982, the storm struck the Ocean Ranger and a wave broke the control room porthole. No one had shut the steel porthole cover on the approaching storm. The crew did not know it yet, but the seawater rushing through the porthole had shorted out the ballast control panel, causing random opening and closing of the ballast tanks. Tragically, shutting down the electronic panel would have caused the tanks to close and may have stopped the listing. This left only the brass control rods to save their lives. A few hours later the Ocean Ranger began to list and the fight to save it began in the control room using the brass rods. These brass rods were found threaded into the controls by rescue divers after the disaster. Ultimately the actions of control room operators, failing to control the ballast tanks, contributed to the sinking of the Ocean Ranger. Given the lack of formal training and supervision, the control room operators were at a serious disadvantage that night. If there was ever a need for very clear and detailed procedures, the control room on the Ocean Ranger needed them.

This tragedy is a demonstration of how the lack of effective operational policy can be deadly, but it also shows that in any high-risk endeavor, there needs to be very detailed instruction and direction.

The procedure section of directives should be drafted very thoroughly so as to work in situations like the Ocean Ranger. If they will stand up to a crisis, they can work in all other situations.

DIRECTIVE FORMAT AND DISCIPLINE

The procedural section is written in an outline format and this is by design (see Appendix A). The idea is to break down the information into manageable chunks of data much like you would for class notes in college. In an organizational sense, there is an added benefit to this kind of informational structure, which is specificity in citing sections of the directive. For example, if a supervisor was getting reports that one of the workers was not effectively brushing his or her teeth and it needed investigation, the directive would clearly show what steps were required. In our fictional toothbrushing investigation, let us say the employee was not using mouthwash. The supervisor would be able to rapidly diagnose the missing step and the underlying cause of the deficiency. The situation could be remedied by directing the offending employee to section C(3) and C(4) of the directive. It leaves no question as to what the employee should have been doing, and it serves as notice to the employee on what must be done in the future. This type of structure also has the benefit of allowing for specific identification of the exact element of a directive violated if discipline is to be imposed. The more focused and clear the charge of the violation, the more likely the offender will relate the discipline to the offense. In the alternative, it requires the supervisor to charge exactly what the violation is and support that exact violation with evidence. It serves to take personal bias and perception out of the discipline process and allows for a more objective outcome. One key point here is that if the procedure section is contained in an order, then the discretion is significantly limited and the employee must provide justification for departing from the steps in the procedure. If however the procedural section is in a standard operating procedure, then the employee is entitled to depart from the process with a reason.

WRITING STYLE

When drafting a directive, it is important to write as plainly as possible and avoid jargon and overly technical words. The idea is to write to the lowest common denominator and without trying to be sarcastic. This means imagining the laziest and dumbest person in the organization when writing. Having reviewed thousands of strategic and operational policies, I can tell you that it looks like many drafters are paid by the word. Although I know this not to be the case, it is prevalent in most policies. I believe that people feel pressured to draft lengthy and wordy documents because they may feel that a short document indicates a lack of effort. This is definitely not the case in policy writing. I know this because it is something I struggle with when I write. Avoid adding content for padding purposes; short and to the point is the best work product when it comes to directives. When drafting directives, it is essential to base everything on facts because opinions in documents that people will be using to carry out a process can lead to all kinds of trouble. This is one reason why I advocate for the author to be identified in directives. It keeps the writer honest. Grammar and spelling count. I know this is not what anyone wants to hear, but take the time to have the work product proofread prior to sending it out for approval. Read it out loud to yourself and test the contents against the policy statement to be sure the procedures advance the strategic policy of the organization. These directives will undoubtedly be seen by outsiders at some point and are a reflection on you and the organization. Besides, if the chief executive signs off on a document that is full of errors, it will be you making him or her look bad, which is definitely not a great career move. A well-written directive will require several drafts and revisions, much like any other well-written document.

When writing a directive, authors will be tempted to find a similar existing document and take a shortcut of cutting and pasting into the directive. At best, this is shoddy workmanship, and at worse, it can get you sued for failing to perform due diligence. In addition, taking someone else's work without express permission is copyright infringement. I have heard the saying "no need to reinvent the wheel" hundreds if not thousands of times in my various capacities. In the world of policy making and directive drafting, you *really* do need to reinvent the wheel. Organizations are all unique and have their own identities and realities; simply taking someone else's directives will not work. Even if you did take someone else's work, you are legally obliged to fact-check every item in the procedure to ensure that it will not result in injury to someone inside or outside the organization. Passing off a directive as your own without this fact checking is negligence and it could lead to consequences. That said, looking at other similarly situated organizations' directives can be a starting point and can provide ideas but cutting and pasting someone else's work is not a good idea.

Writing a directive is a lasting and essential tool in the effectiveness of the organization. It allows the author to affect how the organization functions and should be treated with a level of respect that comes with a task of this importance. If you are responsible for creating directives and you have others drafting them, be sure to train them properly and hold them accountable. Writing directives is not a task enjoyed by many, and unless held to high standards, the submission will be deficient. Do not accept incomplete or minimalistic work products, you never know when the directive might be needed in a crisis.

PRACTICE POINTERS

- Remember that the intent of a written directive is to communicate the strategic or operational policy.
- When preparing to draft a directive, ensure that the intended actions are consistent with the strategic policy of the organization.
- Avoid simply cutting and pasting another organization's directive and taking it as your own. It may result in legal liability and can be a copyright violation.
- The bottom line when drafting a directive is to keep it as simple and straightforward as possible. Avoid the temptation to pad the directive.
- It is essential that the information contained in a directive be factually correct; avoid opinion and if necessary, collaborate with a subject matter expert.

Chapter Recap

- The term *directive* is the proper terminology to describe a strategic or operational policy committed to writing.
- It is important to have a set format for all directives. This will help with the continuity of communicating the organizational policy.
- The header of the directive contains information that identifies the directive and documents the approval process.
- The approving authority is usually the chief executive officer of the organization. It is essential that only one person be designated as the approving authority to avoid conflicting directives.
- The document identifier should be unique and should contain both a descriptive title and an alphanumeric designator.
- Every directive must contain a policy statement that provides notice of the strategic policy and can provide context to the procedure section of the directive.

- The directive should be formatted in the manner of an outline. This allows for specificity in citation of the parts of the procedure. Specificity in citation allows for precise understanding of content in training and disciplinary situations.
- The procedural section of a directive should be written to the lowest common denominator and should provide sufficient information to allow an uninitiated employee to understand the process steps and have a reasonable chance of carrying them out.
- Sadly, grammar and spelling count. The document is a representation of the author and the organization.

BIBLIOGRAPHY

Barnett, R. (2008). *Practical playscript: Writing procedure manuals that people can use.* Canberra: Robert Barnett.

Bhadwal, S., & Swanson, D. (2009). *Creating adaptive policies : A guide for policymaking in an uncertain world.* Los Angeles, CA: Sage Publications.

Chiles, J. R. (2002). *Inviting disaster: Lessons from the edge of technology: An inside look at catastrophes and why they happen.* New York: Harper Business.

Copeland, C. W., & Lee, P. (2010). *Federal rulemaking and regulations.* New York: Nova Science.

Cushway, B., & Hallsworth, I. (2012). *The employer's handbook 2012–13: An essential guide to employment law, personnel policies and procedures.* London: Kogan Page.

Davis, J. B. (2003, February). Sorting out Sarbanes-Oxley. *ABA Journal, 89,* 44–49.

Dodd, S. (2013, April). Remembering the ocean ranger disaster. *Our Times, 32,* 35–38.

Gunn, A. M. (2008). *Encyclopedia of disasters: Environmental catastrophes and human tragedies.* Westport, CT: Greenwood Press.

Hotta, T. A. (2013). Developing a policy manual. *Plastic Surgical Nursing, 33*(1), 36–37.

Means, R. (2014). Improving your policy manual. *Law and Order, 62*(6), 12–13.

National Transportation Board (NTSB). (1983). *Marine accident report: Capsizing and sinking of the U.S. mobile offshore drilling unit Ocean Ranger off the west coast of Canada, 166 nautical miles east of St. John's, Newfoundland, February 15, 1982.* Washington, DC: NTSB.

Nishman, R. F. (1991). Through the Portlights of the Ocean Ranger: Federalism, Energy, and the American Development of the Canadian Eastern Offshore, 1955–1985. Thèse (M.A.), Kingston, Queen's University.

Smith, C. B. (2006). *Extreme waves.* Washington, DC: Joseph Henry Press.

Smith, T. W. (1982). Developing a policy manual. *Personnel Journal, 61*(6), 446–449.

Ward, S. F. (2015). A crisis of consent. *ABA Journal, 101,* 15–17.

White, N. (2010). Make it a policy. *PT in Motion, 2*(9), 54–57.

APPENDIX A: RULEMAKING DIRECTIVE SAMPLE FORMAT

ANYTOWN SECURITY DEPARTMENT

General Order	Drafting Company Directives G.1.18

DATE(s)	AUTHOR ID NUMBER	AUTHORITY
Effective: **03/18/2015**	Computer # **34**	**Daniel V. Morghulis, CEO**
Revised: **09/18/2015**	Computer # **34/108**	**Daniel V. Morghulis, CEO**
Revised:	Computer #	
Revised:	Computer #	
Revised:	Computer #	

Source(s): **NJ Common Law**		
Old Number: **N/A**	Appendix: **None**	Pages: **4**

G.1.18.1 POLICY

It shall be the policy of the Anytown Security Department to conduct business and security operations in a fiscally, technically, and customer-friendly sound manner while complying with the Agency's core values (appendix A), mission statement (appendix B), and vision statement (appendix C). The chief executive officer has final authority to issue, modify, and approve all security department directives.

G.1.18.2 PURPOSE

The purpose of this directive is to implement the Anytown Security Department directive system and to explain its features, organization, and use. This system contains all directives in a codified form. All personnel are responsible for knowing and carrying out the provisions of all orders.

G.1.18.3 DEFINITIONS

Directive: An order or instruction, issued by a central authority for the purpose directing or guiding some organizational task or activity.

Divisional order: A directive issued at the company division level dealing with procedures and operations within the specific division, usually in the form of memorandum.

General order: Broadly based directive dealing with policy and procedures affecting one or more organizational divisions of the company. This directive has limited discretion.

Memorandum: Written information not warranting a formal order, used to direct any segment of company personnel in specific situations or to inform them of coming events.

Order: A written or oral directive issued by a superior officer to any subordinate or group of subordinates in the course of security duty and which is lawful in nature.

Personnel orders: A formal directive initiating and announcing a change in the assignment, rank, or status of personnel.

Rules and regulations: Formal and strict direction established and promulgated by the appropriate authority and instituted in detail by the chief executive officer. A rule or regulation leaves no room for employee discretion.

Special order: A directive dealing with a specific circumstance or event that is usually self-canceling.

Standard operating procedure: The official method of dealing with any given situation prescribed by the Security Chief's order or procedural guide. Standard operating procedures allow for discretion in those cases where it is reasonably necessary to accomplish the given task.

A. DIRECTIVE SYSTEM FORMAT

1. Directive type
2. Directive organizational category
   a. Administrative designated by the number "1"
   b. Manufacturing designated by the number "2"
   c. Sales designated by the number "3"
3. Directive number
   a. Directive numbers shall be as assigned and shall range from 1 to 999 and shall identify a particular directive.

B. HEADINGS

1. Headings shall include
   a. Alphabetical designator
   b. Numeric category designator

    c. Directive number

    d. Directive sections

2. Each directive section shall contain the following headings

    a. Policy

    b. Purpose

    c. Procedure

3. Directive may contain any other headings as necessary to intelligently display the information such as

    a. Definitions

    b. Any other pertinent information

C. DIRECTIVE SUBSECTION

1. The directive subsections shall be written in the following outline format

    a. The directive subsection shall be used to outline the directives distinct parts and shall be used in such a manner as to allow citation of applicable parts of the directive.

    b. The labeling of subsections shall start with the capital letters: (A).

    c. Subcategories of capital letters shall be labeled with numbers: (A)(1).

    d. Subcategories of numbers shall be labeled with lowercase letters: (A)(1)(a).

    e. Subcategories of lowercase letters shall be labeled with lower case Roman numerals. Uppercase Roman numerals shall not be used in departmental directives: (A)(1)(a)(i).

D. DIRECTIVE SUCCESSION

1. Upon effective date of a new directive, all old or previous editions of the directive shall be void and no longer in force.

2. Clearly erroneous portions of a new directive shall be immediately reported and the directive shall be interpreted to best meet the policy and purpose of the directive.

E. DISTRIBUTION

1. All employees are responsible for keeping abreast of all directives and revisions thereof.

2. All changes to the directives will be posted on the policy management system (PMS).

3. Directives will be stored on the PMS server and accessible 24 hours a day via the PMS portal.

4. All supervisors will be notified by electronic notification of any changes in the directives.
5. Employees shall check the PMS each workday.
6. Each unit supervisor or manager will ensure that employees under his or her authority are aware of any directives revisions and have completed and signed off on any documents within a reasonable time period. No member shall have unsigned documents in DMS for longer than 30 days unless they are on an excused absence.

F. AMENDMENTS

1. All suggested revisions of existing directives and proposals to add or delete directives must be submitted via the chain of command. These will be forwarded to the chief executive officer who will have the final approval on any revision of the current directives.

The chief executive officer may empower any employee of any company division, section, unit, or function to develop and propose directives. All members of the organization are encouraged to submit revisions or propose new sections for directives.

G. REVIEW AND REVISION

1. The company rules and regulations shall be reviewed at least once every three years from the most recent revision date.
2. If circumstances change or occurrences happen during the previous year, the issuing authority will review every associated written directive to determine if changes should be made.
3. The designated company manager in conjunction with human resources will conduct a yearly random review of department directives in order to detect and revise any obsolete directives.

Policy Implementation through Communication and Training

The goal of this chapter is to examine the functions that support the implementation of sound policy choices and outcomes. In this chapter we will study the impact of training and communication. Communication is the first of the three steps necessary for effective policy implementation. Supervision is the third step and it plays a part in both implementation and assessment and will be covered in Chapter 11.

The second step, training, includes indoctrination into the policy process and an understanding of how each policy affects the operation and the employee's role in the process. An effective security professional and leader should work tirelessly to create a culture of training in the organization. This can be accomplished by making training a priority through policy statements and actions. Every employee should be encouraged to request training unilaterally and then impart what they learn to others. By holding every member of the organization accountable to not only attend training but to lead training helps ensure that everyone has a stake.

As we discussed in Chapter 3, a policy system is a hierarchy with the top representing highly specific policy and the bottom being general. The policy system can be viewed as a pyramid, just like the kind that are found in Egypt. A pyramid has four triangular sides with the base of the structure being the widest and the top the apex. The pyramid represents how policy making is organized through the use of discretion in a policy system. The base of the pyramid represents the strategic policy of the organization. It is the goal or end result desired by the organization, and represents the general direction that the organization intends to pursue. It allows for the broadest amount of discretion. If you look closer, you will also recognize that the base is the critical first building block of the pyramid and in the construction of the structure, the starting point. Thus the strategic policy is the foundational building block of the policy system. As the pyramid moves up toward the apex, it begins to narrow. This is how a policy system works, the higher up the structure, the more narrow the focus of the directive and the less discretion allowed the employee. At the top of the pyramid is the rule. The rule is also the apex of operation policy and the directive that allows virtually no discretion. From apex to foundation, the order of directives is rule, order, special order, procedure, and strategic policy. In reality the pyramid is built upon something that is not actually part of the pyramid, the foundation, the earth. In the same way the ground supports a physical pyramid structure, the policy structure is also supported. The support in a policy system is provided by the functions of training, supervision, communication, and discipline. Quite simply, without the support of these functions, the policy system would inevitably fail regardless of how sound the policy-making process or compelling the goals. The elements of training and communication go hand in hand as do the elements of supervision and discipline.

COMMUNICATION

Communication is an essential supporting function of the policy system and is involved at every step of the process. Communication is not simply written or verbal. It has an action component as well. This action component has a lot to do with the manner the organizational executives and supervisors act when discussing or implementing policy.

When a supervisor has to communicate a newly implemented directive, the manner in which it is presented goes a long way to the weight assigned to the directive. There will always be two distinct levels of importance assigned to a policy. For our purposes I will designate these different importance echelons as *formally* important and *informally* important. A formally important policy is any policy that is formally approved and distributed. In effect, every formal policy is important. Some might assert that some polices are more important than others, but in reality, the only thing that differentiates a policy is the level of risk and the corresponding level of discretion in the policy. Although the discretion is different, every formal policy is important. The other side of the equation is the informal importance of the policy. This is the value assigned by the individual members of the organization and is a function of the human factor of organizations. There will only be two different variables in this equation: formally important/informally important and formally important/ informally unimportant. The optimal condition for a policy is formally important/informally important, which equates to understanding and buy-in of all members of the organization. The undesirable condition is formally important/informally unimportant, which indicates that there are persons or subgroups within the organization that do not accept the policy in question as valid. This situation can be isolated, sporadic, or systemic, meaning that it can be a matter of degrees. This is not a scientific measure, but anyone who has worked in the real world knows that some policies are ignored. This condition has several factors and the first one is how the individual directive is communicated through action. For example, if the organization adopts a policy of mandatory wearing of identification cards, the members of the organization will be watching to see if the chief executive wears his or hers at all times. If the chief executive conforms to the policy, it is likely that it will be considered informally important as well. In addition, if the line supervisors present the new directive in a positive light, citing safety concerns and using professional positive body language it will reinforce the informal importance.

I have seen this situation play out in real life. When I was a young police officer, the police chief issued a directive that restricted exiting from a particular driveway unless on official business. The denial of the use of this exit point required many employees to take a rather circuitous route to get home, adding an extra five minutes to the ride because of a traffic signal. As you might imagine, this was unpopular and some of the line supervisors presented the change professionally and some presented it by complaining about it. The very first day the restriction went into effect, I recall watching out the window with many other employees to see what the chief would do as he also had to take the now longer route. I have to admit it was a bit of a surprise when he did exactly that, even though he had a take-home police car and as the chief was always on official business. For the remainder of his tenure, the prohibition was not violated. The message was clear, aside from being formally important, it was also informally important and would be enforced. The simple fact that the leaders of the organization communicate the importance and, the intention to enforce, a directive will create the environment of formal and informal importance.

CASE STUDY: SEX IN THE CITY

This phenomenon plays out in actual statutory laws as well. There are no shortage of state laws that are still in effect but are absolutely not enforced. Take, for example, New York State where it is still very much against the law to engage in adultery. Under New York Penal Law, a person can be prosecuted for sleeping with a married person and the married person can be prosecuted as well (Adultery, N.Y. Pen. Law § 255.17). Even when being advised that it is against the law, most people do not actually believe that the law matters. But why? The law is still on the books and the state legislature has had decades to remove it, therefore it is still formally important. The reason most people do not believe it is because it has been communicated to the public that adultery will not be prosecuted and is no longer relevant. Rather than get into a long-winded discussion about social mores and prosecutorial neglect, I will sum up the issue a different way. Consider this, former New York Governor Eliot Spitzer, a successful prosecutor with a reputation as an incorruptible and a tireless reformer, was brought down by evidence that he frequented high-class prostitutes. He was not charged with the crime of adultery even though he was investigated for improper financial transactions related to his patronage of call girls and there was sufficient evidence to support the charge. A celebrated prosecutor known for aggressively pursuing criminals knowingly and willingly broke the adultery law. This was a clear signal to the public that although the law is formally important, it was certainly informally unimportant. To reinforce the unimportance of the law, Spitzer's successor, Governor David Paterson, was also caught up in an adultery scandal. When publicly addressing it, Paterson, a graduate of law school said he did not break the law by engaging in the affairs. Two chief executives of New York, were both educated in the law, admitted adulterous affairs, but received no prosecution. It seems clear that although it is illegal to commit adultery, the law is unimportant.

Policy communication is about channels, the content and the manner of the message. If both of these channels are done right, then the first major step in policy implementation is complete and the next step is training.

POLICY DISTRIBUTION SYSTEMS

An expertly applied policy-making process resulting in a well-drafted directive counts for nothing unless it can be effectively communicated to *all* members of the organization. An integral part of communicating policies both strategically and operationally is the manner in which they are distributed. Prior to the emergence of the computer, paper hard copies were the common tool in organizations for the distribution of policies. These physical copies were either handed out individually to organization members or were distributed through manuals. Typically, members were required to sign off on the new directive to indicate receipt and understanding. This was an inefficient way to distribute directives as it required many work hours to catalog and manually file the receipt forms. It also required extensive follow-up by supervisors to ensure that the hard copies were completely distributed and signed for by all employees. As computer networks became ubiquitous in the workplace, the medium for distribution was through email and the documents were held in an accessible folder or computer network drive. This was better than the hard copy system but still had filing and access limitations. It also required someone to keep track of activities in the folders and maintain a record of emails indicating distribution and sign offs. Today the gold standard for communicating policy is the policy management system, a specialty computer program that is designed for just this task. These specialty programs have addressed the shortfalls of previous methods and have ushered in a new level of policy communication. When exploring the potential benefits of a policy management system, there are certain functions that are particularly helpful.

The desired elements of a policy management system are:

- Policies can be organized into specific and intuitive sections.
- There is ready access to the system across multiple platforms and document types.
- Security features limit access and revision rights.
- A sign-off feature allows for the documentation of receipt of the directive and an electronic signature acknowledges understanding.
- Easily update directives and send out updates. There should also be a function to allow specific personnel to have directives reissued for review and signing for discipline and training purposes.
- A function alerts the system administrator when a directive is up for review.
- Groups can be established to review and comment on proposed directives. This can allow for the policy-making process to be more inclusive and streamlined allowing remote users to provide input to policy-making options.
- Automatically schedule regular reviews of directives.

Whatever policy communication process is employed, its key components should be regular expected communications that come from a centralized delivery system. That is, as part of an effective policy system, assessments of policy and revisions become an ongoing open process with as many stakeholders involved as possible and originate from the same source.

COMMUNICATION AND POLICY ASSESSMENT

The final step in the policy process is the evaluation process, which itself also relies on effective communication. The intent of the policy review is to ensure that all of the information contained within the directive is still accurate and relevant. A secondary goal is to determine if the directive is working well for those who regularly deal with it. There may be times when a more effective way has been discovered for the process covered by the directive and the opportunity should be taken to improve efficiency. The evaluation process is performed at predetermined times in the life cycle of a directive. There are several ways that a policy review can be prompted. The first is a time-sensitive standard where the directive is reviewed at specific points in time. This could be an annual review of all directives or a review on the anniversary date of the issuance of the directive. I found that reviewing directives by anniversary date was the most effective for me and it spread the work out over the course of a year. A review could also be triggered by an event occurring before the anniversary or annual review. The review could also be set to a particular time on the organizational calendar when the workload is less. This works well for manufacturing and educational institutions and allows for the review to be performed during nonpeak times. There can be any configuration of these, but the important takeaway here is that the reviews must be done.

The review of the directive will require communications between the reviewer and those who implement the directive on a regular basis. They will be best positioned to inform on the effectiveness of the directive. The dialogue between the evaluator and the worker should identify exactly what is right about the directive and exactly what is wrong. This can be accomplished through a survey or by interviewing key personnel. The honest and forthright exchange of information is critical to the evaluation of the policy, and steps must be taken to consider any input sincerely. The opportunity to have a say in the work processes can be a powerful motivational tool if it is genuine and the opportunity clearly expressed to the worker. If changes are necessary, these must be communicated to the author for revision or if an operational employee has the interest, allow that employee to make the revision. The benefit of open communication in the policy evaluation phase is better efficiency and the potential identification and mitigation of unintended consequences. This process takes a bit of hard work and the courage to deal with constructive criticism, but it is a crucial part of a healthy policy system.

TRAINING

Training is the second essential part of the implementation of a directive. By employing effective training directives, the security manager can impact loss, increase employee efficiency, and improve organizational effectiveness. When these improvements occur, the security manager has tangible data to demonstrate the value of the security system. Aside from the efficiency benefits to the organization, training is essential to protect it from unintended consequences. Failure to train is a common cause of action in lawsuits and one that can be foreseen and can be remedied. The concept is that if an organization can foresee a potential harm, then it must train to mitigate it. Therefore it only follows that for every policy in the organization, there must be at least some degree of training. The liability for failing to train can be significant and courts generally do not wish to hear excuses. In both the private and public sectors, there is an impression that training is somehow a luxury line item in the budget and is frequently the target of cuts. This is a bad idea for organizations engaging in relatively low-risk endeavors, and it can be tortious negligence in the security or protective services fields.

Failing to train staff on operational policy can also set up the likelihood of yielding poor results. Training can be seen as supporting policy in two ways. First, it supports the strategic policy by having capable and well-trained personnel. Second, training is essential to the implementation of the directives themselves. Each directive that is issued will require a degree of training to support it. The most basic level is the discussion of the new directive with the affected personnel by their immediate supervisor. This type of training is used when no specific training is called for in the directive itself. Once again, this is an opportunity for the supervisor to establish the informal importance of the directive. An engaged discussion on the new directive can ensure that all personnel understand what will be required and why it is being done. The written format for directives recommended in this book lends itself well to basic line supervisor training of directives. The training segments using the directive format are done in eight steps:

Step 1. The first part of the training is to identify the directive by name and alphanumeric designator.

Step 2. Read and discuss the policy statement to ensure that personnel understand the strategic policy that the operational policy (directive) is advancing. Allow for any questions and ensure that there is no misunderstanding. This is a critical element in understanding the rest of the directive.

Step 3. Read and discuss the purpose statement to ensure that personnel understand the reason why the directive is necessary and important. Allow for any questions and ensure that there is no misunderstanding and highlight any reasons of importance that may personally affect the employees, such as safety or job ergonomics.

Step 4. Read and discuss each definition, if any, to ensure that personnel understand the meaning of each. Take time to ensure that there is no confusion or conflicting definition. This may be the most time-consuming element, but it is essential to obtain universal understanding of the designated definitions.

Step 5. Read each heading of the procedure section and discuss each on their own merits. Stop frequently to allow for discussion and questions. Repeat for each heading until the procedure section is completed.

Step 6. After completing the review of the directive, allow for any comments or criticisms and solicit suggestions to improve the directive. If any comments are offered, take note and communicate them to the author of the directive.

Step 7. If appropriate or necessary, orally quiz personnel to assure mastery. This step should be reserved for topics of special significance or concern by the supervisor.

Step 8. Document the training and have personnel acknowledge the training on a sign-off sheet.

In some cases, the directive will contain a specific requirement for training and these requirements will be supported by the formal training process using internal subject matter experts and external schools. Notwithstanding formal training, line supervisor training should still be performed on a regular basis and can be less formal. When specific training is called for in a directive, the specifics of training should be spelled out to include the level of requirement, the frequency, and any reporting requirements. All training requirements contained in directives should be noted and documented in a separate training directive. The value of a specific training directive is that it allows for one central reference to keep track of training requirements. The format of the training directive should be a general order and should have several categories of training. According to priority, these training categories are:

- Mandatory
- Core
- Certification
- Monthly
- Discretionary

The first training category will always be *mandatory training* and is the highest priority for training resources. This is training that is mandated by a higher authority or a law and will always be the priority training for the organization.

Second to the mandatory training is *core training*. Core training is a policy-driven training category and consists of minimum training courses designated for each function within the organization. The core training policy should identify each position or function within the organization and designate the minimum training for each. For example, the position of security line supervisor would have as minimum training a basic supervision course, a conflict resolution course, and a team-building course.

The designated training for each category is subject to the needs of the organization, but they should always involve a basic training course for the position or function. In addition to listing the specific training, there should be a designated time frame to accomplish the training. Typically the basic training course would be within 60 days of assignment and the remainder within one year.

The next level of training is designated *certification training* and should list any certifications of employees and the identification of each employee. Certifications are necessary but because they are typically assigned to individual employees, there may be circumstances where the organization no longer wishes to pay for a particular certification.

Monthly training is the next level of training and refers to the ongoing in-service training. This training is provided internally by organizational subject matter experts and is a flexible low-cost way to meet ongoing need-to-know training. Need-to-know training is training that organizational members are required to know without consulting reference materials, covering day-to-day operational activities and critical administrative knowledge. It is highly recommended that each month be designated for specific in-service training. This will allow for a continuity in training and for the effective management of resources. It can also come in handy if sued, for example, making the statement that we do our harassment training every January shows a commitment to train and helps mitigate claims of negligence.

The next category of training is *discretionary training*. This is training that is conducted at the discretion of the organization, above and beyond mandatory or monthly training. By having a dedicated training directive, the confusing collection of training requirements of many directives are merged into a manageable operational policy. It ensures that training needs that support policy are met in an organized and efficient manner and bases the decision-making objective on a predetermined priority.

EQUALITY IN TRAINING

Just as training has many dimensions, the types of liability for failing to train are not simply based on foreseeable injury. Training cannot be provided in a manner that discriminates against any protected groups. That is, everyone must be given equal access to training and there should be a justification for sending one person to training over another. One of the ways to deal with this vulnerability is to have a training request process that contains a justification requirement. Justification can be a very simple notification for mandatory or certification training. In cases of discretionary training, the rationale for sending the particular person should be included. To defend against claims of discriminatory training, there only needs to be a reasonable justification for selecting one person over another. The key to this is to genuinely assess and send the right person to the right school for the right reason. This can be accomplished through a training *needs* assessment, basing this assessment on an examination of the needs of the organization and the needs of the individual. For example, if the security company has a sudden influx of long-term customers requiring armed security, organizational training needs may be to train existing officers to carry firearms. The individual needs are assessed normally at the line supervision level and those needs make the employee more effective in carrying out organizational policy. As I have stated before, training is not intended to be a punishment, nor is intended to be a benefit doled out to friends or those politically connected. It can be used as a reward, but again, it must be a justified reward. Training has been successfully argued as a cause of action for workplace discrimination, so be careful during the selection process.

CASE STUDY: DISCRIMINATION IN TRAINING

Imagine you are the security manager of a person of color working for a major security corporation in your home state of Ohio. As security manager, your subordinate, Charlemagne Stalk, has had years of honorable service to the company going back to 1996. In 1997, he was promoted to Motor Patrol Security Officer 2 and in 2003 was promoted to Motor Patrol Security Officer 3. In the company, the assignment as a motor patrol officer is considered a good job and is only available to 5% of the organization. Most other security officers rotate positions, including that of motor patrol. A dedicated motor patrol officer is a special class of security officer offered by the company to premium accounts and requires certifications in defensive driving, use of fire extinguishers, and first aid. Subsequently, despite meeting the required benchmarks for the position, Stalk does not qualify for promotion.

The company begins to assess the viability of eliminating a number of dedicated motor patrol security officer positions as a cost-cutting measure. On hearing this, Mr. Stalk meets with a human resources representative and makes the claim that you and his team leader have not given him the necessary support to become eligible for promotion. He alleges that some politically connected motor patrol officers and friends of supervisors have been assisted with meeting benchmarks to make them eligible for promotion. He has a particular problem because the team leader has taken steps to remedy shortfalls in other motor officer's promotional requirements while ignoring his. On meeting with you, Stalk admits that he has only accomplished approximately 75% of the required promotional benchmarks. It is at this time that Mr. Stalk alleges that members of the motor patrol unit, specifically the team leader, apparently created a noose out of a telephone cord behind Stalk's back prompting a coworker to ask if someone was going to be hanged. Stalk says that when he turned around, the team leader quickly hid what he was holding. Stalk also complains that some of the adverse comments on his performance evaluations authored by you were fabricated. Stalk further complains that because of the actions of the team leader and the rest of the organization's leadership, he was denied additional financial compensation. He reluctantly admits that those promoted were qualified.

Stalk files a lawsuit in federal court claiming race discrimination and retaliation against the organization, citing among other things, a hostile workplace environment and a discriminatory job action that deprived him of a benefit.

- Based on this fact pattern, do you think that failing to train is a form of discrimination?
- Do you think that if a similarly situated employee filed a lawsuit, it would be successful?

If your answer was no, congratulations because you are partly correct; the trial court also felt this was not discrimination. The trial court disagreed in part because Plaintiff Stalk admitted he was not qualified for promotion, only meeting 75% of the required benchmarks. In addition, the court also ruled that failure to train does not constitute a legal harm that is required to maintain a lawsuit for discrimination. On face value, this makes perfect sense because an organization should be able to train whomever they wish and make personnel assignments in what they consider the best interests of the organization.

At this point I must admit that this case study is based on a real case, and the company setting and the name of the plaintiff have been changed. The plaintiff disagreed and appealed, eventually ending up in the 6th Circuit Court of Appeals. After examining the case, the appellate court upheld the dismissal of the hostile workplace claims and in this case, the discriminatory failure to train based on the fact that the plaintiff did not present the issue on appeal. The court did, however, go on to state what would have happened if the plaintiff had not made a procedural error: The claim for discriminatory failure to train would *not* have been dismissed. The court elaborated that failure to equally train is a viable cause of action. The fact is that when a promotion equates to a material benefit, in this case increased salary, then an adverse employment action has occurred. Therefore the organization's failure to give the plaintiff equal training to achieve the required benchmarks was a form of actionable employment discrimination.

The lesson here is that training policy should be drafted to ensure that in any case where the training can be part of an evaluation for promotion, it is provided equally. In organizations without a fixed promotion policy, there will always be the argument that the best qualified candidate, was only best qualified because the candidate was unequally provided training. Additionally, the training policy should be drafted to weed out any questions of favoritism. Strong training and promotion policies that minimize favoritism or the appearance of favoritism are the best defense against failure to equally train suits.

As a collateral issue, favoritism in supervisors can be addressed through policy and training. Supervisors are tasked with a greater level of discretion than line employees and must routinely interpret directives to carry out the mission. This greater level of discretion requires a regular and detailed training investment in these key individuals.

REMEDIAL TRAINING

In some cases employees will make mistakes or violate directives; this is unavoidable and also part of the human condition. In these cases, training of some type is called for, which is known as *remedial training*. At the heart of every workplace failure is some violation or misapplication of a policy. The training policy should make it clear that remedial training is not a punishment but rather a route to improvement. The policy has to be drafted to encourage training to be provided when needed. In some cases, organizational leaders may feel that engaging in regular remedial training is an indication of failure and could result in liability for taking steps after an incident as proof of fault, but that is untrue. The first concern can only be addressed with the concept of ongoing and continual improvement. Ongoing improvement can only be achieved through regular evaluation and adjustments. If something is not working properly, then it must be corrected. It is no different for people and they require continual feedback and guidance to work at optimal levels. Remedial training is nothing more than a course correction and should be considered routine. It is a misconception that remedial training is indicative of fault in any cases against the organization. It has been long-standing public policy to restrict admissibility of remedial actions as proof of fault. Even without this public policy, the existence of a uniform and regular process of employee correction is an indication of a responsible and well-trained organization. The problem actually comes into play when an organization that rarely engages in correction by training implements it after an incident. The point is that training should be an organic part of an organization and is accomplished by sound policy, which sets out the who's, the when's, and the how's of training.

TRAINING AND THE HUMAN FACTOR

In Chapter 5, we discussed things that are inherent in the human condition. These are things like expectancy, the human factor, and complacency. These inherencies have a real effect on policy making and implementation and can impact and be impacted by training. Because the goal of training is to make humans better workers, the human condition is a central concern of the training function. Training can impact the human condition by teaching and reinforcing desired behaviors. In fact, the condition of complacency can only be addressed through ongoing training. In dealing with complacency, the line supervisor carries a great responsibility of taking ownership of the training to prevent it from happening.

Complacency training should be conducted daily by supervisors and can be something as simple as reading news reports of incidents in related organizations to keep the focus on what is at stake. The training should be conducted at the beginning of the shift if possible and as a group with the supervisor being an active participant. In addition, this kind of training, which for our purposes, I will call *roll call training*, is an excellent time to engage individual employees to provide the training themselves. Aside from inducing participation, it is a great way to train employees to be supervisors.

Training policy should also focus on a mix of training methods and should describe exactly how they should be implemented. This is an important element of training policy as adult learners all take in information in different ways. The goal is to provide a training product that reaches all different types of learners. The training methods should include lecture, multimedia delivery, practical application, and exercises. The key to training adult learners is to ensure that the policy directs that the training be relevant, interactive, social, and directed to knowledge, skills, and attitudes.

Finally, the training policy should incorporate electronic learning tools, these computer-based options can allow for training opportunities that might otherwise be limited by the human factors of space and time. Policy that addresses e-learning should ensure that the training be relevant, achievable, and measurable. The e-training should be broken down into manageable blocks that can be completed on the schedule of the employee and should have a testing component on completion with the ability to record mastery for inclusion in the employee's training file.

PRACTICE POINTERS

- Training is an essential part of meeting the goals of the organization and is everyone's job. Do your best to create a culture of training in the organization by getting everyone involved.
- As an organizational leader, you are responsible for ensuring that the people under your supervision know how to do their jobs and are open to training. The manner in which you communicate support of policies and training can determine the level of informal importance attached to them.
- Training policy should include specific designations of the types of training distinguished by priority and training assignments determined accordingly.
- It is critical to prevent training from becoming punishment or being bestowed a as favor. Training should be provided as a function of needs and should be approached as objectively as possible.
- Training assignments can be coveted by employees and can result in lobbying efforts by the individual employee or others. Assignment of training should be specifically laid out in policy and the policy should be followed. Favoritism can result in a legally pursued discrimination claim.

Chapter Recap

- Training is the lifeblood of any organization and its purpose is to support the policy objectives of the agency.
- Communication is an essential supporting element in the dissemination of policy and serves as a critical pathway for evaluation data ton be shared with policy makers.
- Communication is not just written and verbal, communication is also through actions. An organizational leader may signal that a policy or training are unimportant by their actions and attitudes. This can serve to undermine and render ineffective the policy or training.
- Directives can be disseminated through physical hard copy and filing methods, through emails and computer files, or through a policy management system.
- In the security field, training is a necessary and foundational function; failure to train can result in lawsuits and damage to the organization.
- To ensure that training is completed in an efficient and documented manner, training policies are critical. Training requirements must be clearly described and all training properly documented and documents filed in a central location.
- Training cannot be assigned on the basis of friendship or office politics; training must be assigned on a needs assessment. Failure to assign training in an objective fashion can result in a legal cause of action – failure to equally train.

BIBLIOGRAPHY

Brennan, J., & Mattice, L. (2013). Communicate, communicate, communicate. *Security*, *50*(5), 24.

Bunch, K. J. (2007). Training failure as a consequence of organizational culture. *Human Resource Development Review*, *6*(2), 142–163.

Collins, H. (2010). *Employment Law*. Oxford: Oxford University Press.

Coyne, A. (2008). Spitzer's undoing? Sex and interstate commerce. *Maclean's*, *121*, 13.

Davies, A. (2011). *Workplace law handbook 2012: Employment law and human resources*. London: Kogan Page.

German, E., Herbert, K., Madore, J. T., & Mansfield, M. (2008, March 19). Paterson admits several infidelities day after new governor acknowledged single extramarital affair, he discloses having cheated with several other women during his marriage. *Newsday*, A.2.

Goldstein, I. L. (1980). Training in work organizations. *Annual Review of Psychology*, *31*(1), 229–272.

Govil, S. K., & Usha, K. (2014). The importance of training in an organization. *Advances in Management*, *7*(1), 44–46.

Harcourt, B. E. (1998). Reflecting on the subject: A critique of the social influence conception of deterrence, the broken windows theory, and order-maintenance policing New York style. 97. *Michigan Law Review*, 291–389.

Hayasaki, E., & Simon, S. (2008, March 11). Governor of N.Y. linked to call girl; Eliot Spitzer gives a public apology but no details after he is identified as 'client 9' in a federal wiretap. *Los Angeles Times*, A.1.

Hymowitz, K. S. (2011). The national adultery ritual. *Commentary*, *132*, 40–44.

Kite, N., & Kay, F. (2012). *Understanding NLP: Strategies for better workplace communication—without the jargon* (2nd ed.). London: Kogan Page.

Lamb, P. (2011). Social value and adult learning. *Adults Learning*, *23*(2), 44–47.

Lawsuits could follow failure to train, (2005). *HR Focus*, *82*(9), 2.

Levinson, R. B. (2012). Who will supervise the supervisors? Establishing liability for failure to train, supervise, or discipline subordinates in a post Iqbal/Connick world. *Harvard Civil Rights – Civil Liberties Law Review*, *47*(2), 273.

Lovett, K. (2010, January 29). Gov takes humorous 'view' of adultery. *New York Daily News*, 12.

Longenecker, C., & Abernathy, R. (2013). The eight imperatives of effective adult learning. *Human Resource Management International Digest*, *21*(7), 30–33.

Martin, D. (2006). Chapter 1: Discrimination. *Discrimination law* (pp. 1–21). Thorogood Publishing Ltd.

McCreadie, K. (2008). *Sun Tzu's the art of war: A 52 brilliant ideas interpretation*. Oxford: Infinite Ideas.

Moore, E. (2008, March 13). Spitzer out: Silda still stands by her man as Eliot Spitzer took center stage to announce he's resigning as governor, his wife was again at his side, and some people wondered why. *Newsday*, A.8.

Reed v. Procter & Gamble Mfg. Co., 13-5797, 2014 W.L. 553000 (6th Cir., 2014).

Robson, P. J. A., & Tourish, D. (2005). Managing internal communication: An organizational case study. *Corporate Communications*, *10*(3), 213–222.

Roper, C. A., Grau, J. J., & Fischer, L. F. (2006). *Security education, awareness, and training: From theory to practice*. Burlington, MA: Butterworth-Heinemann.

Train your officers according to your facility's needs, (2011). *Briefings on Hospital Safety*, *19*(2), S3–S4.

Villines, J. C. (2010). Training…asset or risk? *Security*, *47*(10), 44–48.

Watts, J. H. (2010). Exploring prosecutorial discretion in Oklahoma: A case study of non-enforcement of adultery laws. Retrieved from: <https://kucampus.kaplan.edu/DocumentStore/Docs11/pdf/CJ/PICJ/PICJ_V6N3_4_Watts_59_74.pdf>.

Wilson, J. Q., & Kelling, G. L. (2003). Broken windows. *Crime*, 277–295.

Wrench, J. S. (2013). *Workplace communication for the 21st century: Tools and strategies that impact the bottom line*. Santa Barbara, CA: Praeger.

11

Supervision and Policy

"The essence of loyalty is the courage to propose the unpopular, coupled with a determination to obey, no matter how distasteful the ultimate decision. And the essence of leadership is the ability to inspire such behavior."

—Lieutenant General Victor A. Krulak, USMC

Organizational leaders come in three general categories and each plays a part in the implementation of organizational policy. From the C-level executives to the middle managers through to the line supervisors, each organizational leader must live organizational policy. Each must be a living example of organizational policy in action. C-level executives are entrusted with decision making in the policy process and have the greatest effect on policy credibility. If the company has a policy of mandatory identification card display and these leaders do not live it, the policy will lack credibility. The C-level executives must also be open to communication about the impact of policy and quick to assess and make changes when necessary.

Middle managers are the key link between the executives of the organization and the line supervisors. Like all other organizational leaders, middle managers also must live the organizational policy and serve as an example to the line supervisors. The middle managers are often the gatekeepers to organizational resources and are essential to supporting the efforts of line supervisors. The middle managers are the only communication link between the leaders with operational situational awareness and the executives. One of the dangers facing middle managers is the temptation to filter information from operational leaders. This can be driven by a desire to put a positive spin on otherwise negative information or to alter information the manager personally disagrees with. Filtered information can result in faulty decision making and bad policy. With this in mind, it is vital that middle managers do not filter the communication between the ground-level leaders and the C-level policy decision makers. Middle managers play a crucial role in the adaptability of policy.

In any policy system, the line supervisor, otherwise known as an operational leader, is a critical link between the intent of the chief executive and the operational staff. The executive sets the direction of the organization and the operational staff carry it out. The line supervisor has the most dramatic effect on the people who must carry out policy. Line supervisors are the tangible representation of organizational policy and are the ones who direct policy implementation. It has often been said that sometimes generals win battles but wars are won by sergeants and in the world of policy context, this is also true. Without effective line supervisors, the implementation of policy is questionable, regardless of how justifiable or necessary the policy is. Their role is so important that oftentimes these leaders can determine the implementation of policy or the failure of policy simply by how they act. Leaders, particularly operational leaders, have a complicated job that requires the adoption of a unique knowledge, skill, and attitude. The key lesson in this chapter is that how a leader acts is often as important as what a leader says. Leadership and supervision are not management, so remember you can manage cattle, but you have to lead people. In a lot of business texts, the focus is on management. Very few outside of law enforcement and the military focus directly on the line supervisory role. The management of a security endeavor is, of course, critical and worthy of the attention, but the line supervisor plays the most significant role in the policy implementation process. This often means doing what is right rather than what is popular. Accomplishing the mission is the core of leadership, but it is not just that the mission is accomplished, it is how it is accomplished that matters. Leadership is a required attribute in the management of an organization and different leadership positions require different skill sets.

Supervision is the act of overseeing people. It has its greatest impact at the first level of an organization where the operational capacity is directly controlled. A person who is selected by organizational executives and granted formal authority to carry out the strategic policy of the organization by implementing operational policy is considered a supervisor. Organizations depend on operational leaders to ensure that everyone in the group carry out their functions through direct supervision and support and this is the work of the line supervisor. In general, there are varying definitions when it comes to leadership and some of these are:

■ *Autocrat leadership* – An autocratic leader directs activities with minimal input from subordinates and is likely to expect directives to be followed to the letter. The autocratic leader makes decisions alone without input of subordinates. This leader engages in a high degree of employee follow-up and direct supervision without a significant degree of two-way communication. The autocratic style of leadership is necessary during times of crisis or in situations of disorder. It is also appropriate when dealing with inexperienced or untrained staff. This style does not work well with highly trained or experienced employees and is not an effective style in circumstances where creative collaboration is called for.

- *Democratic leadership* – Democratic leaders are consensus builders and effective communicators. There is frequent two-way communication between the supervisor and employee in the decision-making process. The democratic leader, however, retains the responsibility to make the final decisions. The democratic leader is a team builder and can produce good results from the team synergy. This style is not appropriate during crisis or during situations where unpopular but necessary decisions must be made.
- *The free-rein leader* – A free-reign or laissez-faire leader does not directly supervise his or her staff. This kind of leader leaves outcomes up to the employee and does not provide feedback. This style of leadership is often inappropriate unless the employees supervised are highly trained, experienced, and have a proven track record of performance. In all other cases, this style may not be appropriate and often results in inferior work products from employees and can lead to disorder and chaos in a crisis.

My first true experience with close supervision and leadership came with my induction into the United States Marine Corps. When I think of an example of a highly capable line supervisor, I think back to a Marine sergeant, a drill instructor who was flawlessly uniformed, intimidating, and intent in purpose. For obvious reasons, his leadership style was completely authoritarian with few wasted words. To be honest, Drill Instructor Sergeant Upchurch scared the hell out of me. But even though I was intimidated, I definitely got the feeling that he knew what he was doing and would never ask me to do something he would not. The drill instructors were up when we were, trained when we trained, and did everything we did – just better. Even though those first days of boot camp were full of chaos, the drill instructors were very clear on what we needed to accomplish, and we quickly settled into a routine, which led us to the goal of being well-trained, disciplined, rule-following Marines. The routine was the same every day; we were given very clear instructions and expected to perform as directed. When we did not perform, we were sanctioned but even when being punished, we followed a set process. It soon occurred to me that we did everything for a reason, and as I learned much later, we were directed by explicit policies and according to plan. This is, at its most basic, a formula for leadership or supervision: Establish clear expectations, be able to perform any act you ask of a subordinate, ensure that the expectations are fulfilled, and when they are not, then take action. Perhaps you are beginning to notice how closely intertwined the policy process is with supervision.

A policy system cannot exist without a supervisory process staffed with qualified and motivated leaders. This is no easy thing, but nonetheless critical. One of the most basic core operational policies is the one that defines the role and authority of organizational supervisors. Absent this directive, it will be left to the discretion of the employees to determine the authority and role of organizational supervisors. In addition, the supervisory function should be codified in a job description that clearly communicates to subordinates and superiors alike the expectations of the job of supervisor. Being a leader does not come naturally and requires as much, if not more, policy direction as subordinates. Studies have indicated that leadership has an effect on job satisfaction and, ultimately, on performance.

SUPERVISION AND THE HUMAN FACTOR

Getting people to do what you want is not a naturally occurring skill. Leaders are made and not born. Humans can be unpredictable, fickle, bullheaded, and sometimes even destructive. The job of a leader is to get people to do what the leader wants because the subordinates want to do it. In an organization with an effective policy system, what the leader wants is adherence to the organization's strategic policy and implementation of the operational policy. A major part of getting organizational members to go with the program is the manner in which the leader acts. Organizational leaders, line supervisors in particular, are what I informally call *policy mirrors*. I use this term to describe how an organizational leader can impact policy by acting in a manner to mirror the policy. Those leaders who uphold organizational policy and do it in an enthusiastic manner create a mirror that demonstrates how the leader is the physical embodiment of the strategic and operational policy, the *policy-leader mirror*. Do the leader's actions and attitudes mirror the policy? If the leader's actions mirror the policy, they create a second kind of mirror.

The second mirror engaged is the *leader-subordinate mirror*. The leader-subordinate mirror is a communication between the supervisor and the employee focused on how well the employee reflects the example of the supervisor. Does the subordinate mirror the behavior and actions of the leader? When the mirrors are synchronized, the strategic policy and operational policy of the organization are fully adopted and there is an optimal level of buy-in from top to bottom. This represents an opportunity to realize full implementation of organizational policy. Having a total synchronization of the mirrors is unlikely, as there is constant change in any organization and there will be people who may feign their commitment. That said, the goal of the concept of mirroring is to serve as a benchmark for leaders to informally assess the relevance and effectiveness of the policy. If a leader realizes that he or she is out of sync with the policy, either the leader must change or the policy should be reassessed.

The mirror test is flexible and can occur between various levels of leadership in the organization under the leader-subordinate mirror. If leaders at any level mirror organizational policy, then those leaders should sync; if they do not, one of them is not mirroring policy.

SUPERVISION AND LEADERSHIP TRAITS

Organizations depend on leaders to ensure that everyone in the group carry out their functions through direct supervision and support. To accomplish this supervision, the organizational leaders need to have credibility with other members. Credibility is not simply a patch on the arm or a title, it is something that must be earned. The clearest example in my mind to a credible organizational leader is a sergeant in the United States Marine Corps – part nightmare, part nanny, but 100% mission facilitator. The Marine Corps is well aware of the intangibles of leadership and more than 200 years have determined that the best and most effective leaders possess or work to gain a list of attributes known as JJ DID TIE BUCKLE. This cryptic statement is the acronym for leadership traits. These leadership traits speak to the way leaders conduct themselves to gain the trust and confidence of their subordinates in carrying out the policy of the organization. The success of the Marine Corps is well documented, and the Corps owes much of this achievement to its line supervisors – the corporals and sergeants. The following sections look at some of the time-tested leadership traits that have contributed to the success of the Corps.

Justice

Justice is the act of dispensing rewards and punishment in accordance with the facts and merits of the case. It is essential to employ rewards and punishment systematically and uniformly in accordance with due process. The leadership trait of justice is to be fair and impartial, and it is critical to obtain and maintain respect and trust. For example, a security shift supervisor should rotate the most undesirable post throughout the staff without exception.

Judgment

Using sound judgment is the ability to critically assess facts and determine all of the potential options when making decisions. The leadership trait of judgment tempers decision making with a well-rounded and factual basis resulting in informed decisions. This trait is essentially the ability to make decisions after honestly weighing the pros and cons of a decision in a meaningful way, for example, a security shift supervisor deciding to suspend outside foot patrols during an ice storm by considering the threat of injury to staff members against the value of foot patrols.

Dependability

The conviction to properly perform a duty in a manner that is definite is regarded as being dependable. This is a trait that allows for the organization and the staff to rely on the leader to do what is expected. For example, dependability is exhibited even in cases where others might fall short – that individual gets a reputation for reliability. In the security profession, leaders must be particularly dependable, even in the most challenging times. It is a foundational element of the security profession.

Initiative

Initiative is the trait of taking action even in the absence being instructed to do so. An essential element of initiative is that the action must be needed and performed in accordance with the best interests of the organization. For example, the lead security officer ensures that the staff members are all properly equipped even without instruction from the shift supervisor to do so.

Decisiveness

The trait of decisiveness is making well-thought-out decisions on the best information available quickly and firmly. A second element of this trait is the ability to communicate the decision in a clear and forceful manner. In some situations, particularly in crisis, the ability to make quick well-reasoned decisions can allow a leader to make a positive material impact on a situation. This trait is the antidote to the leadership vice of hesitation, which can be disastrous in a crisis situation, for example, a security officer who witnesses a hazardous situation and immediately takes action to prevent death or serious bodily injury.

Tact

Tact is diplomacy and allows the leader to deal with others in a way that prevents unnecessary problems resulting from hurt feelings or perceived slights. A necessary trait in all security staff, it is even more essential with insecure leaders. This trait allows for communications to occur in a constructive manner even in times of stress through courtesy and respect.

Security, as a function, must exist within an organization and requires the support and cooperation of all departments, units, and individuals. This is particularly true when performing enforcement of rules or having to deny stakeholders. Without tact, in these circumstances, the likelihood of frustration occurring is magnified. An essential element of tact is that the leader must be able to maintain this trait at times when stress and confrontation are highest. For example, by using tact, a security officer limiting access to an area that is routinely used by organizational staff can mitigate anger and frustration.

Integrity

Integrity is the trait of having a well-developed internal moral compass. It has also been described as having character. This, in essence, means that you do the right thing, even when no one is watching and that you are honest and truthful in all of your dealings with others. Integrity is a perishable quality and it only takes one incident to lose the reputation for integrity. In the security profession, integrity is a necessity and without it, one cannot perform the duties of a security professional. As a leader, this trait brings an added dimension as each action of a leader is watched and scrutinized by subordinates.

Enthusiasm

This trait is the excitement of performing a duty and can be viewed as contagious, but in a good way. It is more than just empty excitement, but it involves optimism and a belief in the mission. As a leader, enthusiasm for a mission can signal subordinates that the mission is attainable and will produce good results. Enthusiasm within a group can boost morale and can allow a group to be resilient in the accomplishment of a mission even in adverse situations. For example, a security detail commander can motivate staff members to accomplish a difficult task by demonstrating enthusiasm and an expectation of good things from the detail. This can be accomplished by the exhibition of a positive attitude and providing genuine encouragement.

Bearing

Bearing is the trait of being able to carry yourself in a manner to encourage the outward impression of competence, calm, and control. It is an essential element of the projection of a professional image. Bearing involves not only physical appearance but conduct and attitude as well. It is essentially looking the part of a leader and encouraging others to do the same. In law enforcement, it is called *command presence* and is a tool employed to manage situations. If you look the part, the people around you will respond accordingly. An example would be alert security officers, attired in well-maintained uniforms, engaging people in a professional manner.

Unselfishness

This trait is essential to the credibility of a line supervisor. Unselfishness is essentially the trait of taking care of your troops before you take care of yourself. It is never being in a position to take from your subordinates for your own gain. Taking care of those people entrusted to your command is the heart of leadership. This means that you will look out for your staff members' needs in every circumstance that does not conflict with the mission. A leader who accomplishes this will have a more capable group of people to advance the interests of the organization. Given that the security profession is quasi-military, this style of leadership lends itself well to accomplishing the mission. An example of unselfishness is a security supervisor directing traffic in the rain alongside his staff or making sure everyone has had a lunch break before they do. These are not formally required parts of a supervisory job description, but it is an essential part of being an effective leader and goes a long way toward boosting staff morale.

Courage

Courage as a trait is *not* the absence of fear but instead is the trait of understanding the nature of the situation, accepting the fear, and carrying on while dealing with the fear. Fear can come about because of literal physical danger or from threats of danger. It can also be a product of nonphysical dangers, such as threats to career status or threats of embarrassment. It can also materialize as a fear of criticism. Courage is a mental quality that allows a leader to work through these fears and still do the right thing. In the security profession, all of these fears can be very real, but from a policy perspective, the fear of criticism is the most significant. A leader cannot be afraid to ensure that an unpopular policy is followed out of fear of criticism. For example, a shift supervisor can show courage by prohibiting the day shift from coming off post early while the afternoon shift is in engaged in pass-down.

Knowledge

The trait of knowledge is actually a thirst for understanding. It is the trait of always trying to better oneself through the intake and retention of new information. A critical part of being a leader is to be able to advise staff in the processes of their jobs. A supervisor is looked on as the person to go to get an answer. But it is more than that, engaging in the pursuit of knowledge can support other traits, such as judgment by giving the leader a broader base of information to make decisions. It can also assist in decisiveness and bearing because strong knowledge can bring about confidence. As a leader, the trait of knowledge should be shared with subordinates in that a leader should always be encouraging them to gain knowledge. Providing staff members with the opportunity to engage in knowledge expansion is essential to their job satisfaction through growth of skills and personal development. For example, each security officer should have the knowledge of how to perform each job at the site and be provided all of the related equipment even if not routinely assigned.

Loyalty

The trait of loyalty is the belief and demonstration of allegiance and support to someone or something. Loyalty is an essential trait for security professionals to be faithful to their organization. It must be more than just an internal belief it must be demonstrated daily. Loyalty is related to the sense of duty and ethics in that the allegiance to doing what is right cannot be questioned. To protect, security professionals must invest support in what or who they are protecting. Loyalty can also be to the staff that a security leader supervises. The leader will make sure that his or her staff members are the best trained and supervised as they can be and that the staff members are held accountable and protected when appropriate. An example of loyalty is the security supervisor professionally carrying out a mission that he or she privately disagrees with.

Endurance

Anyone who has ever exercised can understand the concept of endurance. It is the level of stamina that a person has to deal with in physical, mental, psychological, or professional challenges. It is the ability to weather hardship and still carry on the mission. Endurance is an essential trait for security personnel because they must face a daily grind of protecting people and things. This protection requires vigilance at all times, security cannot ever take a day off, and thus the nature of the profession requires a sufficient level of endurance. The supervisor plays a critical part in developing the endurance of their staff members in preparing for the physical, mental, or psychological drains of the job. This is accomplished through training and leading by example. An important factor in building endurance is to build up the bearing and dependability of staff.

Each of the traits just described are focused on leading by example. This is a concept that is fairly easy to understand, yet it is much more difficult to do in practice. A leader must live up to policy at all times; a leader must be a cheerleader for policy and when the policy is not working, a leader has to be courageous and forthright in making a change. Every action by an organizational leader is magnified and can have drastic consequences, particularly if the act violates a policy that the leader enforces on others but fails to live up to him- or herself.

To end this chapter, I present a case study on a situation where a policy against workplace harassment was violated, creating very adverse impacts, which were the result of failing to lead by example.

CASE STUDY: HOW MUCH DOES A JOKE COST?

On March 3, 2005, the chief of a midsized urban New Jersey police department told a joke at departmental training. The joke became the central theme of a public scandal and a discrimination trial. The leader in question was a well-respected chief of police with a solid track record within the community. The community has a concentration of Hispanic citizens and a large representation of Mexican Americans.

The plaintiff was a Mexican American officer on the police force. The plaintiff was reportedly a marginal employee and allegedly had some discipline issues. On March 3, 2005, the chief attended a patrol shift muster and provided an update on the construction of the new public administration building. Approximately 67 officers were present. The department had been instructed to check the steel on the building site. The chief said that officers "have to keep an eye on the steel to make sure that it doesn't go away... some Mexicans were going to come by and pick up the steel" (Munoz v. City of Perth Amboy, 2009).

It was reported that the plaintiff heard the remarks firsthand when he attended the second training session on March 8, 2005, where the chief repeated that Mexicans may pilfer the steel. The plaintiff testified that the chief also talked "about Mexicans being a bunch of gangbangers" (Munoz v. City of Perth Amboy, 2009).

After the chief made this statement, the plaintiff claimed he was the subject of likeminded jokes by others in the agency. One such joke pointed out that the flatware should be hidden from the plaintiff as the forks were made of steel. At the trial, the plaintiff also testified about prior and ongoing discriminatory incidents. He testified of hearing jokes told by other staff members about Mexicans and being hurt by them. He described additional incidents about the permissive nature of the workplace in tolerating these types of statements. He described another incident where he was sent to a call in order to translate and a lieutenant at the scene dangled his handcuffs over the subject and taunted, "Ha ha, you are going back to Mexico" (Munoz v. City of Perth Amboy, 2009). The lieutenant then ordered the plaintiff to tell the person he was going back to Mexico. The plaintiff alleged that he was humiliated and embarrassed over the incident. A third incident testified to at trial involved a fellow officer making the statement at a public event that it was embarrassing and humiliating that a mariachi band was playing the national anthem. This also hurt and embarrassed the plaintiff.

At the trial, the plaintiff made claims that he had symptoms related to the incidents. These included upset stomach and diarrhea, sleeplessness, and chest pressure. The plaintiff testified that these symptoms were aggravated because of the joke made by the chief at a departmental training (Haydon, 2009). In response to all of these issues, the plaintiff testified that he met with the police director and deputy chief and made complaints about these incidents. The response to the meeting was allegedly being told that the department had some rotten apples and that the only way to get rid of them was retirement or for those staff members to leave the department. No other action was taken.

The defendants deny that the plaintiff ever reported any harassment or discrimination and that the meeting was about the plaintiff's job performance and he made no mention of problems with other officers or discrimination. The trial testimony of the plaintiff did not match testimony under oath from his deposition. At the deposition, the plaintiff stated he did not recall any jokes or being ostracized at work because of his ethnicity. He also testified he had no physical symptoms related to these incidents. At the trial the chief admitted making the comment, but said it was not intended to offend nor was it intended to be a slur. The chief pointed to the fact that he apologized to the department, to interest groups, and at a press conference.

The defense tried to dismiss at the summary level and at the end of the evidence, based on the testimony at the deposition, which was that none of the claims presented at trial occurred. Despite the conflicting sworn testimony, the judge ruled that the case should go to a jury. After a trial, the jury ruled that plaintiff had proven, by the preponderance of the evidence that he had been subjected to harassment solely because of his country of origin; that the harassment was severe or pervasive enough to alter his workplace; and that a reasonable person of the plaintiff's background would find that conduct created working conditions that were offensive. The jury found both the city and codefendant chief liable for the harassment. In particular, the jury found that the city was vicariously responsible for the chief's wrongful conduct and that the city had not exercised reasonable care to prevent or correct promptly. The result was an award of $1.9 million against the city. This was later reduced to $379,000 in a remittitur action.

The lesson here is that even though the chief was trying to make a joke, it was a violation of the harassment policy. And although it was a minor breach, it still had an impact.

The court found that an environment existed that was hostile, despite evidence from a deposition that contradicted this claim. The fact that a jury found a hostile workplace environment and that the organization did not take the steps necessary to enforce its antiharassment policy, speaks for itself.

The issue of whether the chief intended to harass is not the point. The chief lost his bearing for a moment and breached the commonly accepted prohibitions of antiharassment policy.

There were other leadership traits, besides bearing, that were compromised by telling the joke – first and foremost was judgment. It would not be an understatement to say that the comment by the chief lacked judgment. All of the potential ramifications were not considered and it cost the city hundreds of thousands of dollars. In addition, knowing that he had a subordinate that was Mexican American and tell that kind of joke was contrary to the trait of justice – he singled out a group for humor. The trait of tact was also noticeably missing in this incident and had tact been employed, the joke would not likely have been told.

The truth is that in the military, law enforcement, and security professions, good-natured teasing is common. The trick is to know the difference between humor that is not directed at an individual's traits and what is considered harassing behavior. This case clearly shows that avoiding teasing altogether may be the best approach. On the other side of the situation, the chief did exhibit the trait of courage by apologizing publicly. Despite the fact that it was most likely a joke, it set the tone in the organization and the jury recognized this fact. Leaders must always live the policy, and every time they fail in this, the potential for policy failure follows.

PRACTICE POINTERS
- An organizational leader must be the embodiment of policy and must ensure that those around him or her live it as well.
- Executive leaders must have the courage to allow unfiltered communications to flow through the middle managers and to make changes to policy when appropriate.
- Middle managers must work hard to support line supervisors by providing the necessary resources and by facilitating a free flow of communication between all leaders.
- The line supervisor or the operational leader is the most critical link in the successful implementation of policy. Without effective and committed leadership at this level, policy will not be implemented. This will result in harm to the organization.

- Line supervisors should embrace this critical role with a solemn pride and be resolute in their performance.
- Leaders do not get to take a day off from being enthusiastic about policy or ensuring that others carry out the policy.
- Hold yourself accountable and hold your people accountable. If there is a failure to follow policy and it is the result of you or your people's actions, take the necessary steps to correct this. If the policy is not working despite honest and determined efforts of your people, then get it changed.

Chapter Recap

- There are three different levels of leaders each with their own roles in an organization.
- The C-level leaders are the policy makers and must be open to communication from the lowest levels of the organization to facilitate policy implementation and necessary change.
- The middle managers are the communication link between operational leaders and the executives and must ensure that communications are not filtered. They are also the gatekeepers for resources and must work to support line supervisors.
- Line supervisors, otherwise known as operational leaders, are the most critical element in the effective implementation of policy. They are the leaders with the best sense of situational awareness and must communicate information to the executive decision makers.
- Leaders in an organization act as policy mirrors. These mirrors reflect the effectiveness of policy through demonstrated behavior. If a leader embodies the policy, the subordinate will know if they are doing the same by how well their performance "reflection" appears.
- Leadership is an almost entirely human-based endeavor that requires the winning of trust and confidence.
- To win trust and confidence, a leader must adopt or have a number of leadership traits. These traits will help advance the policy of the organization.
- At the end of the day, a leader must lead by example. When a leader fails to provide the example of living the organizational policy, it can create an environment that produces similar mirror results in subordinates.

BIBLIOGRAPHY

Bennett, D. A. (1985). Supervision. *Marine Corps Gazette (Pre-1994)*, *69*(11), 60–61.

Bhatti, N., Maitlo, G. M., Shaikh, N., Hashmi, M. A., & Shaikh, F. M. (2012). The impact of autocratic and democratic leadership style on job satisfaction. *International Business Research*, *5*(2), 192–201.

Brennan, J., & Mattice, L. (2013). Start with an introspective analysis. *Security*, *50*(1), 20–21.

Carrison, D., & Walsh, R. (1999). *Semper Fi: Business leadership the Marine Corps way*. New York: AMACOM.

Colangelo, A. J. (2000). *Followership: Leadership styles*. Retrieved from: <https://shareok.org/bitstream/handle/11244/5979/9972517.PDF?sequence=1>.

G4S. (2015, April 7). *Our group values*. Retrieved from: <http://www.g4s.com/en/Who we are/Our Group Values/>.

De Haan, E. (2012). *Supervision in action: A relational approach to coaching and consulting supervision*. Maidenhead: McGraw-Hill Education.

Haydon, T. (2009, May 10). Perth Amboy police chief to retire after 32 years on force. *The Star Ledger*. Retrieved from: <http://www.nj.com/news/index.ssf/2009/05/perth_amboy_police_chief_to_re.html>.

Krulak, V. A. (1986, November). A soldier's dilemma. *Marine Corps Gazette*, *70*, 24–31.

Levinson, R. B. (2012). Who will supervise the supervisors? Establishing liability for failure to train, supervise, or discipline subordinates in a post Iqbal/Connick world. *Harvard Civil Rights – Civil Liberties Law Review*, *47*(2), 273.

Munoz v. City of Perth Amboy Police Department, No. A-6254-06T1 (N.J. Super. Ct. App. Div. July 29, 2009).

Munoz v. City of Perth Amboy Police Department, No. A-3415-09T4 (N.J. Super. Ct. App. Div. Nov. 22, 2010).

Shusko, J. (2013). Leadership 101. *Marine Corps Gazette*, *97*(9), 42–44.

Simi, R. F., Jr. (1996). Fourteen traits, eleven principles, but only one belief. *Marine Corps Gazette*, *80*(2), 50–52.

Sterrett, E. A. (2002). *The manager's pocket guide to emotional intelligence: From management to leadership*. Amherst, MA: HRD Press.

Tracy, B. (2014). *Leadership*. New York: AMACOM.

U.S. Marine guidebook. (2010). New York: Skyhorse.

Zalud, B. (2013). Security officer success: Define expectations up front. *Security*, *50*(2), 14–21.

Selected Core Directives

This chapter is dedicated to providing some examples of strategic and operational policies that I feel are essential or typically unaddressed and should be a part of any policy system. The policies selected here will supplement the chapters on leadership and training as essential facets of an effective policy system. My decision-making process is based on the typical causes of action in a lawsuit. The main culprits are failure to train, failure to supervise, and negligent hiring and retention. Training and supervision are covered in Chapters 10 and 11 respectively, and negligent hiring is covered here along with other sources of suits such as harassment, workplace violence, the application of discipline, and damages as a result of negligent responses to emergencies.

There is no shortage of directives that could be in this chapter but because of space constraints, I will address only a few. When it comes to non-lawsuit-related directives, this list is certainly not broad or inclusive, and there are many other directives that play a part in liability mitigation. At the end of the chapter, I will provide a list of policies that are common for security organizations (see Appendix C). This too is not a full listing as policies are driven by the circumstances of the organization.

STRATEGIC POLICY
Core Values

Values are beliefs and attitudes held by individuals or groups. Values also are principles that guide behavior. The values held within an organization are the values shared by the organization's members. These organizational values go beyond individual values. Core values are timeless, guiding principles that require no external justification. Such principles have intrinsic value and importance to those inside the organization. An organization's culture is made up of core values that unify the social dimensions of organizations. Core values become the foundation and conscience of the organization, which distinguish successful organizations from the unsuccessful.

Core values influence organizational perceptions and decisions (English, 2006). Core values cannot be canned, they cannot be purchased, and they require some organizational souls searching to identify them. The way to establish organizational core values it to get all of the stakeholders in the organization to participate in the process and to start making lists. Have them list what is important to the organization and answer the question, "Why do people want to work here?"

Once a list is compiled, the next step is to distill similar priorities then reorder the list according to importance. Once this is done, it is time to determine which ones really relate to the organization and are either already being done or are actually viable. For example, it would be unreasonable for a police department to have customer satisfaction as a core value because a large function of the job is enforcing the laws on people they come into contact with. The final step of the process is to publish the final product to the organization at large to solicit comments or suggestions. Any suggestions or comments should be thoughtfully assessed and considered and if appropriate, incorporated.

The goal of stating core values is to say succinctly what the organization stands for. The statement of core values serves to notify the members of the organization of any contradictions between the organizational values and the personal values of the individual. For example, a very religiously devout person may have core values that are entirely opposed to abortion. This may not be an issue, except that the organization may have a core value that supports abortion. A public declaration of values puts people on notice and allows for honest decision making. The ultimate test of the core values is for all those involved to readily accept that the organization really does stand for the stated values. It is essential to understand that this is not merely a perfunctory exercise; the organization actually has to live what is in the core values or it will lose credibility.

Vision Statement

The vision statement lays out the image for the future. It intended to be longer range than a strategic policy, yet be compatible. A good vision statement should be a description of the future and the big picture as it pertains to the organization. It should also be grounded and specific. There is a fine line between being visionary and fantasizing. Contrast the present and the future and lay out the exact end. Engage a sense of exploration and be convincing. State a compelling reason why the organization wants to go there. An organization, like a person, works more effectively if everyone involved understands the goal. On September 12, 1962,

President John F. Kennedy gave a speech to 35,000 people at Rice Stadium in Houston, Texas. The following is an excerpt of President Kennedy's speech:

> *We choose to go to the Moon. We choose to go to the Moon in this decade and do the other things, not because they are easy, but because they are hard, because that goal will serve to organize and measure the best of our energies and skills, because that challenge is one that we are willing to accept, one we are unwilling to postpone, and one which we intend to win, and the others, too.*

The purpose of the speech was to gain support for the United States to complete a crewed space mission to the surface of the Moon before the end of that decade. Kennedy was, in effect, asking Congress through the American people to expand the National Aeronautics and Space Administration (NASA) and take on a massive task. This was no minor goal. The apparatus for space travel and exploration did not exist then as it does now. Through his speech, Kennedy was able to focus the nation on the mission to the Moon and energize the American people by painting the big picture and leveraging the American pioneer history.

As we all know, the United States did place a man on the Moon on July 20, 1969, with Apollo 11, the first crewed mission to the Moon. A vision statement should be clear in purpose, bold, be inspiring, leverage core competencies, forecast the future, and motivate organizational members.

President Kennedy's Moon speech did all of these:

- The purpose, which was to go to the Moon before the end of the decade was clear.
- Going to the Moon was very bold, but within the outer limits of existing technology.
- Going to the Moon was inspiring and tapped into the national competition with the Soviet Union.
- The goal of a crewed Moon landing was well within the industrial and technological core competencies of the nation.
- A lunar landing forecast the dominance of the United States and a positive futuristic world.
- The idea of the United States putting a person on the Moon motivated the nation and in particular, it motivated Congress to support the endeavor.

When creating a vision statement, it is important to build on the core values of the organization, and it should provide a general context for strategic policy making. The vision statement serves as a guidance tool assisting the policy decision maker when determining strategic policy options.

A vision is created by first performing a strengths, weaknesses, opportunities, and threats (SWOT) analysis. And then, similar to the core values process, bring stakeholders together to produce a short list of options that best meets the values and mission of the organization. These options start with preliminary statements and continue to be refined through the process. Keep in mind that the process for determining a vision is like painting a picture, with each successive revision or layer bringing the picture into closer focus. Once the final option is chosen, it should be presented to the organization at large for comment. These comments should be considered and if appropriate, the statement revised until the most accurate product is obtained.

For a security organization, a vision statement is essential because of the nature of the work and the significance of adverse outcomes. Clarity of mission and the commitment of personnel to accomplish the security mission have a direct effect on the outcomes of security. Having a clear vison also helps combat complacency and keeps morale high. Much like the core values statement, if the vision statement is perfunctory and not lived by organizational leaders, its effectiveness will be significantly reduced.

When it comes to statements of core values and vision statements, there are any number of theories on how these should be implemented and no universally accepted manner. The fact is that these documents should be as simple as possible and viewed not as laws but as tools to guide the policy system. The process can be confusing and there will be any number of conflicting sources available when drafting them. The takeaway is that the organization should clearly communicate what its values are, the vision of where the organization wants to be in the future, and a statement of the mission involved in getting there. The exercise of producing these documents serves a purpose as well, it uncovers any contradictions and facilitates engagement between stakeholders. The process should be tailored to fit the individual organization. The only real rule is that the production of these documents is not perfunctory. That is, having a vision or core values statement is not done only because it *should* be done. If it is discovered that the organization or its personnel are not living up to the core values or vision, there are only two appropriate responses: Change the vision or core values or change the behavior of the organization or personnel to conform to them.

OPERATIONAL POLICY
Job Descriptions

Job descriptions are foundational documents that lay out the core requirements for the assigned job. Job descriptions are the product of an organizational job analysis that identifies key skills and abilities specific to the job. The description itself should include duties and responsibilities and the level of responsibility. A job description should also contain information regarding the level of performance required for the position in a brief descriptive paragraph. The description should also contain qualifying knowledge, skills, and abilities. These are typically the minimum education, experience, and/or certifications required. Also included are salary information and other administrative information such as probation period and job range. The job description should also indicate who the employee will report to and where the job falls in the organizational chart (see Appendix A).

Organizational Hierarchy

Organizational hierarchy is a foundational directive as it lays out the chain of command in the organization. This directive should be the first directive. This directive is important because it describes the makeup of the organization and where the employee fits in the grand scheme. It is also important because it sets the formal authority and the chain of command. This chain of command establishes a designated communication channel as well as the structure for supervisory responsibility.

Rulemaking

The rulemaking directive is the "policy" policy. In this directive, the process for formulating operational policy is expressed in great detail. This is an essential part of an effective policy system, as it is the tool used to ensure uniformity and accessibility of the policy process. The first element of this directive is to establish the one person who is the issuing authority. The issuing authority is typically the chief executive of the organization. The issuing authority allows for the chief executive officer to ensure that the operational policy supports the strategic policy. The other key elements of this directive are workplace harassment, workplace violence, security response to calls for service, background checks and selection, and crisis communications.

Workplace Harassment

Workplace harassment and discrimination are a leading cause for lawsuits against an organization. The laws pertaining to sexual harassment provide for specific policy requirements for organizations to combat workplace harassment. In exchange for these policy conditions, those organizations that comply are afforded an affirmative defense against legal claims. This is a no-brainer, and every organization should have a directive that contains and follows these policy elements.

The seven elements are:

1. A zero-tolerance policy statement and the actual enforcement of zero tolerance of workplace harassment. The statement should leave no question as to the intent to investigate all incidents and punish if sustained. Leave nothing to guess and foster a culture that even if it is just a joke, it should not be made at the workplace.

2. Provide concrete examples of what is expected – what harassment is and what the consequences are.

3. Provide very clear reporting instructions to include how and who to report incidents. Have multiple avenues of reporting to include after hours. State clearly that chains of command are not relevant in reporting harassment; *any* member of organizational leadership must accept and act on complaints.

4. Provide a clear statement on the prohibition on retaliation for filing a complaint. Retaliation cases can be successfully brought against an organization even if the underlying harassment complaint was without merit. As a matter of organizational survival, retaliation cannot be tolerated.

5. Provide clear instruction that victims of harassment have a duty to report the incident as soon as practical. In addition, provide a clear mandate to supervisors that once they are made aware of a harassment incident, they are obliged to take immediate formal action. Supervisors who do not take formal action may be held legally liable for their actions or inactions.

6. The harassment complaint and investigation process shall be exactly described to include any due process or issues related to victims, witnesses, or targets of investigation. The policy should also include a confidentiality requirement for anyone involved with the incident or investigation. The prohibition shall allow for disclosure of information only to authorized investigators or arbiters. The confidentiality of the victim or complaining party must be clearly communicated. It is essential to the process that victims and witnesses feel safe about participating in the process.

7. The harassment policy must contain a thorough training direction that designates the specific elements of the training, the schedule of training, whether annual, biannual, or other, and the documentation of training.

In some cases of harassment, adhering to the preceding requirements can insulate the organization from liability. A workplace harassment policy is only effective if its contents are carried out. The bottom line is that providing a safe workplace is not only a moral imperative, it is also a necessary part of an efficient workplace. A sample workplace harassment directive can be found at the end of the chapter (see Appendix B).

Workplace Violence

A workplace violence directive is essential to the multidisciplinary approach to responding to warning signals of an impending incident. The goal of a workplace violence directive is to first clearly state that violence of any type is prohibited in the workplace. The directive should clearly spell out exactly what constitutes violence and may include verbal threats or threatening behavior. These should include the objective actions of physical violence and verbal abuse and threats, and should also include the subjective actions of threatening behavior and harassment. The directive should identify the typical offenders of workplace violence: outsiders (strangers, customers, the mailman, etc.), clients, employees, and family members of employees. The key elements of a directive are to prevent, respond, and then investigate.

The directive should call for a multidisciplinary team to deal with the hazards, threats, and occurrences of workplace violence. The primary goal of the workplace violence preparedness team is to mitigate the hazards of workplace violence. This is accomplished through identification of hazards, threats, and conditions that lead to workplace violence and a risk assessment. Other mitigation strategies include education programs and training, physical security measures, employee support through employee assistance programs, and regular preparedness audits. Another goal is to intervene when required through disciplinary actions, mandated counseling, and other actions to prevent threats from reaching fruition. The final goal is to take action when the threat of violence has occurred. These actions include returning the situation to a safe condition through the intervention of law enforcement or security, supporting the victim, gathering evidence for an internal investigation into the matter, and evaluating the effectiveness of the policy. One of the most significant ways to impact workplace violence incidents is through the screening and selection process. Psychological screening can weed out people with violent tendencies.

Security Response to Calls for Service

For a security organization, a directive that clearly spells out the method of responding to incidents can protect the security personnel and the organization from unintended consequences of unguided responses. This directive pertains to the manner of response whether on foot or in a vehicle. The point is to establish that security personnel are not first responders and are not expected to respond to a call the same way as police, fire, or emergency medical services (EMS). This policy is grounded in protecting the officers and others from injuries as a result of running or driving at a high rate of speed to a call. In addition, this directive should describe exactly the manner of response expected of security personnel. For example, in the event of an emergency, security personnel on foot posts are expected to respond at a controlled rapid walking pace. When in a vehicle, the response shall be in accordance with all traffic laws to include speed limits and traffic control signals. This directive seeks to ensure that personnel with limited training, such as security officers, do not create more problems when responding. The dangers of driving in a rush are obvious, but this can also apply to running on foot. A security officer running will have an oxygen debt on arriving and decision making may be compromised. A security officer who inadvertently runs into someone and injures them may cause more injury than the emergency he or she was responding to does. There is a saying in firearms training: "Slow is smooth, smooth is fast." The same applied here. Responding quickly in a controlled manner will still get you there rapidly.

Background Checks and Selection

Much in the way failure to train is a common claim against security organizations, so is negligent hiring and negligent retention. The legal basis is that because of a negligent background and selection process, harm resulted. That is, the organization hired someone who should have never been a security officer and a reasonable background check and selection process would have discovered this.

The elements of a good background policy should include a thorough list of definitions as they are applied to the background investigation process. There should also be a provision for waiver forms to be signed before any background actions begin. And there should be a list of expected areas of investigation with a provision that the investigation is not limited to those areas. At a minimum, the following are areas to be investigated:

- Criminal records, including state, national, and federal
- Court records, including civil, chancery, and bankruptcy
- Pending criminal cases or charges
- Sex or domestic violence offenses
- Credit
- Driving records (Department of Motor Vehicles)
- Employment history
- Education
- References
- Professional licenses and/or certifications
- Social Security number
- Form I-9

- Military credentials
- Social media and Internet

With the advent of Internet-based searches, many of these areas of investigation can be efficiently searched. The need for investing work hours to ensure that you are not negligently hiring a person with a disqualification has been cut dramatically. Any organization that does not screen for these background areas is encouraging unintended consequences.

Crisis Communications Plan

The contemporary world is a place where information is itself a commodity. Social media is a technology that all but guarantees that any incident involving your organization stands a good chance of being communicated, regardless of organizational desire. The only way to effectively deal with this release of information is to have a communication plan. In some cases, the plan will be a stand-alone document, while others will have a plan supported by operational policy. The stakes are high and a botched initial response to a crisis can set an organization back and can sometimes even be a threat to its very existence. A crisis communication plan is the blueprint to protect the reputation of your organization. A blueprint for a crisis communication plan should contain the following eight elements:

1. A designated spokesperson who is properly trained and is included as a key member of the management structure. The spokesperson should have personal contacts with local media sources.
2. A dedicated crisis communications team. All key stakeholders should be a part of the crisis communications team and should include executive management, security, information technology (IT), operations, human resources, and any other key organizational players. The goal of the crisis communication team is to work the problem at hand and ensure that information is free flowing internally and managed effectively externally.
3. A support team for the spokesperson, who are trained in the aspects of communications and are well versed in the practical applications of crisis communications. These members should regularly be involved in all aspects of organizational communications to ensure that they are indoctrinated in organizational strategic policy, values, and visions. The availability of physical resources to facilitate communications should be outlined in the operational policy.
4. A process to develop and screen communications quickly and efficiently to ensure that the messages are on point and factual.
5. A defined process for dealing with the media to include identifying contacts and the maintenance of regular relations with these contacts.

6. An operational policy for dealing with the media applicable to all organization members. The essential element is a directive to have all communications come from the spokesperson only.

7. A breakdown of foreseeable crisis situations and an appendix in the directive designating resources, personnel, and other relevant information for dealing with individual events.

8. Training assessment and evaluation of the plan and the personnel tasked with the communications function. Exercises should be conducted regularly to test the policy and the capabilities of the personnel involved in communicating.

A crisis communication plan should provide information to the organizational stakeholders in a clear and honest manner. The communications policy or plan should have the following attributes:

■ Well timed: Information release should be geared to balance out the needs of the stakeholders and the needs of the organization. The timing should be such that the organization maintains positive control of the message.

■ Relevant: Communications should be relevant to the issue at hand. The balance here is to provide the right amount of information not too much or too little.

■ Accurate: The communication should be truthful and should not be "spun." Stakeholders can see through information manipulation and it can damage organizational credibility. This does not mean that the organization cannot present their side of an issue, just that any undisputed facts should be presented as such.

■ Reliable: Any communication must be based on the facts as they are actually known. Communications should not be rumor or innuendo, stay with the facts. If the organization does not have the information, just say so.

■ Compassionate: Any information should be released with the needs and circumstances of those involved considered. This is particularly true if victims are involved. The truth is the truth but it can be communicated in a factual yet diplomatic manner (Walker, 2012).

These attributes will advance the credibility of the organization in other communications and will keep stakeholders informed. A key element to the crisis communication plan is the identification of the target audience. The policy or plan should contain a list of key stakeholders and this list should be broad and inclusive. As with any policy or plan, the process will include an analysis and attempt to identify and mitigate any unintended consequences. The crisis communications plan and its supporting directives are living documents and are subject to changes driven by external and external forces. This means that should be an ongoing assessment process to ensure that the plan and directives remain relevant.

PRACTICE POINTERS

- A statement of core values and an organizational vision can be a good compass to ensure that the strategic policies are in line with what the organization is all about.
- Determining and publishing values and a vision is not simply something for show. It requires significant investment and a very real organizational look in the mirror. It should not be undertaken if the only intent is to check off a box on a list of things that *should* be done. This requires a real buy-in from top executives and key stakeholders.
- Once a vision is determined it will be expected that the organization will follow it. Once core values are determined and published, the organization and those who are part of it will be held accountable to them.
- It is critical that the core values and vison statement be lived. If you find they are not, there are only two choices: Change them or change the behavior of the organization to conform to them.

BIBLIOGRAPHY

Azaddin, S. K. (2011). Three fs for the mission statement: What's next? *Journal of Strategy and Management, 4*(1), 25–43.

Badzmierowski, W. F. (2007). Critical decisions, critical actions. *Security, 44*(6), 66.

Ballard, S. D. (2012). To the moon!. *Knowledge Quest, 41*(1), 4–5.

Bruce, M. D., & Nowlin, W. A. (2011, winter). Workplace violence: Awareness, prevention, and response. *Public Personnel Management, 40*(4), 293–308.

English, F. W. (2006). *Encyclopedia of educational leadership and administration.* Thousand Oaks, CA: Sage.

Gilley, A. M., & Praeger, P. (2009). *The Praeger handbook of human resource management.* Westport, CT: Praeger.

Hidden liability: Understand the risks of negligent hiring. (2013). HR Specialist: *Texas Employment Law, 8*(7), 4. Retrieved from: <http://www.businessmanagementdaily.com/35921/hidden-liability-understand-the-risks-of-negligent-hiring>.

Lashier, R. (2005). 6 big mistakes & how to avoid them. *Security, 42*(7) 26N–26P.

Matthews, S. A., & Matthews, K. D. (2013). *Crash course in strategic planning.* Santa Barbara, CA: Libraries Unlimited.

McCrie, R. D. (2007). *Security operations management* (pp. 62–67). Amsterdam: Butterworth-Heinemann.

Nater, F., & Ahrens, S. A. (2011). A risk mitigation strategy in preventing workplace violence. *Security, 48*(10), 22–24. 26, 28, 30–31.

Notaroberta, A. S. (2012). Workplace violence prevention: Team collaboration is the key. *Security, 49*(3), 100.

Scott, C. D., Jaffe, D. T., & Tobe, G. R. (1993). *Organizational vision, values and mission.* Menlo Park, CA: Crisp.

Vellani, K. H. (2007). *Strategic security management: A risk assessment guide for decision makers* (pp. 265–283). Amsterdam: Butterworth-Heinemann.

Walker, D. C. (2012, January 18). *Mass notification and crisis communications: Planning, preparedness, and systems.* Florida: CRC Press. pp. 379–398.

Winnett, N. C. (2014). Workplace violence. *Rock Products, 117*(3), 37–38.

APPENDIX A: A DOMINGO SECURITY SERVICE

Job/Title: Payroll Management Clerk
Branch Supervisor: District Manager, Region 3
Location: Greentown regional office
Job Classification: Administrator I
Hiring Range: $29,999–$50,500
FLSA Status: Nonexempt
Probation Period: 12 Months
Pay grade: Level A3

JOB OVERVIEW

The Payroll Management Clerk is responsible for performing duties under the direction of the District Manager. The Payroll Management Clerk works independently as well as with others to ensure that payroll is completed on time and accurately. The Payroll Management Clerk Performs payroll data entry, maintains files, generates reports, and other duties as assigned by the District Manager.

DUTIES AND RESPONSIBILITIES

- Assumes all duties, responsibilities, and special assignments as assigned by the District Manager
- Maintains and coordinates daily payroll submissions, as well as maintains paper files
- Checks all pay sheets for accuracy and completeness
- Enters pay sheets into the central payroll system in a timely fashion
- Coordinates with account managers in the submission of managed accounts payroll sheets
- Generates daily "payroll report" and checks it for accuracy
- Follows up on missing payroll sheets and reports deficiencies on the daily deficiency report
- Responds to incoming telephone calls to the office when necessary
- Performs the payroll function reliably and with minimal defects
- Performs other duties as required by the District Manager

MINIMUM QUALIFICATIONS

Associates Degree from an accredited college in finance, accounting, or a related degree. Training and experience in payroll and accounting procedures. The ability to maintain the confidentiality of payroll records. Maturity and strong organizational skills are also essential. The job requires excellent analytical and communication skills. Financial reporting and accounting activities are an essential element to this position. Employment subject to a successful background screening and clean drug test.

KNOWLEDGE SKILLS AND ABILITIES

- Knowledge of payroll manual data entry and accounting skills.
- Knowledge of budgeting processes and electronic payroll systems.
- General clerical skills.
- Ability to work accurately with numbers is essential.
- Ability to adhere to company policy and best practices for payroll operations.
- Ability to maintain complex records and files.
- Ability to work with minimal supervision.

APPENDIX B

A DOMINGO SECURITY SERVICE

General Order		Workplace Harassment G.1.01	
DATE(s)	**AUTHOR ID NUMBER**	**AUTHORITY**	
Effective: **11/01/2007**	Computer # **833**	Daniel V. Morghulis, CEO	
Revised: **09/21/2012**	Computer # **833/1081**	Daniel V. Morghulis, CEO	
Revised: **03/27/2014**	Computer # **1081**	Daniel V. Morghulis, CEO	
Revised:	Computer #		
Revised:	Computer #		
Source(s): **NJ Common Law, New Jersey Law Against Discrimination; N.J.S.A. 10:5–12, Federal Law and regulation**			
Old Number: **N/A**	Appendix: **None**		Pages: **4**

G.1.01.1 POLICY

The A Domingo Security Service is committed to creating and maintaining a positive, productive work environment in which all employees are free to put forth their best effort and have an opportunity to succeed as a result. Therefore, this organization will not tolerate workplace harassment of any person, either by fellow employees or nonemployees, or others based on race, sex, religion, color, national origin, age, disability, the exercise of a protected activity (such as filing a complaint), or any other reason deemed impermissible under the law.

G.1.01.2 PURPOSE

The purpose of this procedure is to prohibit any form of harassment directed at an employee or group of employees. The harassment prohibited is in any form, through any conduct or communication.

G.1.01.3 DEFINITIONS

Harassment can include offensive verbal conduct, such as foul or obscene language, epithets, suggestive statements or innuendo, derogatory comments, or "jokes." Harassment may further include touching, gestures, or other offensive physical conduct, or creating, displaying, or reading offensive graphic or written materials in the workplace that relate to the *sex, race, religion, color, national origin, age, veteran status, or disability* of an employee. Any of these behaviors may be considered harassment if it would make a reasonable person experiencing the conduct uncomfortable in the workplace, or if it could hinder the person's job performance.

Harassment occurs when:

1. Submission to such conduct is made, either explicitly or implicitly, a term or condition of an individual's employment; or
2. Submission to or rejection of such conduct by an individual is used as the basis for tangible job decisions affecting such individual; or
3. Such conduct unreasonably interferes or is intended to interfere with an individual's work performance or creates an intimidating, hostile, or offensive working environment.

Supervisor: anyone having the authority to either direct another employee's day-to-day work activities, or undertake or recommend tangible job decisions.

Tangible job decision: includes, but is not limited to, hiring, firing, demoting, disciplining, assignment of work-related benefits and reassigning employees.

Personnel: includes all employees, volunteers, contractors, interns, consultants, or other persons having affiliation with the A Domingo Security Services.

Applicable Law

a. United States Constitution
b. Constitution of the State of New Jersey
c. 42 U.S.C.A. § 2000e–2000e-15, Title VII Civil Rights Act of 1964 (as amended by the Civil Rights Act of 1991)
d. 29 U.S.C.A. §§ 621-633a, Age Discrimination in Employment Act
e. 42 U.S.C.A. § 12112, The Americans With Disabilities Act
f. 38 U.S.C.A. § 4311-23, Veterans Benefits
g. 42 U.S.C.A. § 1981
h. 42 U.S.C.A. § 1983
i. 29 U.S.C.A. §§ 2601-2619 Family Medical Leave Act
j. 29 U.S.C.A. § 206(d) Equal Pay Act
k. N.J.S.A. 10:5-1 et seq, New Jersey Law Against Discrimination

G.1.01.4 PROCEDURE

A. PERSONNEL
1. This Anti-Harassment Policy applies to all Security employees at every level and every function. Violation of the policy will result in an investigation and if sustained, disciplinary action, up to and including discharge.
2. It is important that you ask any questions you may have about the policy, the definition of harassment, or the application of the policy. Questions may be directed to your immediate supervisor or to the human resources department at any time.
3. Any questions regarding this policy may be directed to your Supervisor, Account Manager, District Office Manager, or the Human Resources Manager, freely and without fear of reprisal.
4. All personnel are strictly and explicitly prohibited from engaging in any form of harassment as designated by this directive.
5. In the event there is a question of whether a potential act or behavior may be harassment, the employee shall refrain from the act or behavior.
B. SUPERVISORS
1. All personnel are covered by and subject to this directive. However, supervisors should be aware that their unique role in directing and managing others places them in a position in which their behavior is particularly critical.
2. You are considered an employee's supervisor at any time you have this authority, even on a temporary basis.

3. Occasionally, while you may not actually be a particular employee's supervisor under the chain of command, an employee may nonetheless reasonably believe that you have supervisory authority over him or her.
   a. This could happen when the employee is not aware of the chain of command, or if you are a relatively high-ranking company official that employees may perceive as having authority over them.
   b. You should never assume that employees know the limits of your authority in your interactions with them, nor should you say or do anything that tends to exaggerate or underrepresent the scope of your authority in those interactions.

C. REPORTING
   1. Report harassment targeting yourself or of another employee immediately, even if you believe that the conduct was reported by someone else.
   2. Do not wait until the behavior becomes severe or is repeated.
   3. Similarly, do not assume that your supervisor is aware of harassment or that if you were to report the offense, that no corrective action would be taken.
   4. This organization will not tolerate improper behavior from any employee, regardless of rank or position, and will investigate each report of harassment.
   5. In every case, this organization will identify and take any and all appropriate remedial steps to prevent further harassment, including disciplinary action. All reports will be kept as confidential and all practical steps will be taken to protect the identity of victims and witnesses.
   6. Moreover, because this organization expects you to avail yourself of the protection the Anti-Harassment Policy offers, steps will be taken to ensure that no retaliatory action is taken against you, or other reporting personnel.
   7. Harassment complaints can be made to:
      a. Your direct supervisor
      b. Another supervisor
      c. Company executives
      d. Human Resources
      e. *Complaints can also be called in to (7854) 687-1212 ext. 9999 at any time 24 hours a day.*

D. INVESTIGATION AND ADJUDICATION

  1. This organization takes all complaints very seriously and will promptly investigate all allegations of harassment. The investigation process will include:

    a. A review of the complaint

    b. Notification of the target of the investigation

    c. Temporary reassignment of the target if necessary

    d. The investigation to include interview of witnesses and gathering of evidence

    e. Presentation of the evidence to legal counsel for a legal opinion

    f. Organizational disciplinary hearing

    g. Finding of fact by the Executive Vice President

    h. Appeal process if exercised

    i. Imposition of discipline

  2. In conducting the investigation, the Agency will disclose information relating to the complaint only on a limited, need-to-know basis.

  3. Due process will be afforded to the target of the investigation.

  4. Complaints will be followed up to help ensure that personnel are not subjected to any form of retaliation.

  5. Retaliation, like harassment, violates organizational policy and the law, and will not be tolerated. Complaints of harassment shall be vigorously investigated as an internal affairs investigation as guided by General Order G.1.12.

E. TRAINING

  1. Workplace harassment training shall take place once a year each in the month of March. All personnel are required to attend the training and must sign an acknowledgment of participation.

  2. The training shall be instructor led and shall include a question and answer period.

  3. All personnel shall receive training on this directive at least once each year and this training shall be documented.

APPENDIX C: ADMINISTRATIVE DIRECTIVES

Equal Employment Opportunity

Reasonable Accommodation

Anti-harassment, Anti-discrimination, and Retaliation

Sexual Harassment

Pregnancy

At-Will Employment
Terms and Conditions of employment
Site Assignments
Chain of Command
Infractions and Disciplinary Action
Employee Recognition Program
Workers Compensation
Attendance
Jury Duty
Sick time
Vacations/Paid time off
Tuition Reimbursement
401(k)
Family and Medical Leave Act (FMLA)
Medical Insurance
Life Insurance
Drugs and Alcohol Free workplace
Prescription and Over-the-Counter Medications
Drug Testing
Personnel Records and Privacy
Confidential Files
Medical Files
Annual verification of credentials
Collective Bargaining Agreements (CBA)
Employee Code of Conduct
Fraternization/office dating
Non-disclosure
Conflict of Interest
Outside Work/moonlighting
Termination
Return of Issued Equipment
Attendance
Timekeeping/Timesheets
Overtime
Leaves of Absence
Military Time
Evaluations and Pay Raises
Social Media
Computer Use
E-Mail Use
Computer Network Security and Use
Uniform and Dress Code
Required Workplace Notices

OPERATIONAL DIRECTIVES

Expectations of Security Officers
Expectations of Security Supervisors
Objectives of Security Officers
Objectives of Security Supervisors
Limitations of Security Officers
Limitations of Security Supervisors
Field Supervisors
Fire
Medical Emergency
Infectious Disease Control
Backup and Assistance
Decision-making Authority
Timely Reporting for Duty
Post scheduling
Required Equipment
Post orders
Pass-down
Key control
Responsibility for Post Equipment
Post Sign-In Sheet
Post Check-In
Distractions on Post
Personal Telephone Calls
Meals and Breaks
Tobacco in the Workplace
Appearance on Posts While Off Duty
Foot Patrols
Emergency Response
Use of Force
Incident Reports/Report writing
Reporting Injuries and Accidents
Conduct While in Uniform
Contact with the Public
Contact with the Client
Contact with Law Enforcement
Contact with Company Management and Staff
Problem Solving/Conflict Resolution
Reporting Workplace Misconduct
Insubordination
On-site Disciplinary Action
Vehicle Operations

Vehicle Sign-out and Maintenance
Preventable Driving Accidents
Rental Vehicles or Other-Owned Vehicles
Personal Use of Company Vehicles
Passengers
Defensive Driving
Personally Owned Vehicles
Reporting Damage
Accident/Incident Reporting
Patches, Badges, Insignias: Authorized Use
Grooming
Body Markings, Piercing, and Jewelry
Employees' Statements to Media Representatives
Company Media Spokesperson

Budget as Policy

The goal of this chapter is to examine how the budget impacts the implementation of policy choices and outcomes. Budget policy affects all facets of the organizational operation including training, supervision, and strategic and operational policy options. By employing effective policy, the security manager can impact loss, increase employee efficiency, and improve organizational effectiveness. When these improvements occur, the security manager has the opportunity to produce tangible data to demonstrate the value of the security function to the well-being of the organization. Budgets impact organizations as policy implements in their own right and are subject to the same types of organizational sensing, sensemaking, and outcome analysis as other organizational policies. Conversely, the budget can affect other policy decisions and how they come about, because every organizational action is dependent on available funding.

To function, an organization requires cash on hand to pay for expenses. This is known as *operating capital*. Operating capital is the lifeblood of an organization, and an organization can only achieve its objectives if supported by adequate funding. As we have seen, organizations are made up of humans, and human labor must be compensated. Even organizations that are entirely made up of volunteers, it must have money to support the activities of the volunteers. Revenue and expenses must be managed, and organizations that do not have budgets policies are highly inefficient and cannot survive. There are also occasions where budgets fail because of emergencies or unexpected circumstances. In these cases, budget allotments will be redistributed from other areas. It is important to follow operational budget policy and expend budget allotments proactively and anticipate budget problems through sensing and sensemaking and adjust accordingly. Simply put, be alert to budget shortfalls and ensure that all of your budget has been expended in the advancement of the security function.

Budgets are a unique type of policy and are considered the fiscal roadmap for the organization and have strategic and operational policy aspects of their own. Budgets are operational policies; they are limited to one year and are designed to carry out the strategic policy of the organization. It might be helpful to restate the definition of a strategic policy and an operational policy. *Strategic policy* is the setting of organizational goals or desired outcomes. *Operational policy* is the process of producing formal materials to support and accomplish the strategic policy.

BUDGET AND POLICY

As part of operational policy, budgeting tends to have precise rules, including those from the Internal Revenue Service (IRS) and specific industry rules. These industry rules are from the accounting discipline and can be exceptionally thorough and well thought out. People who deal with this tend to be highly skilled, typically having at least an undergraduate degree in accounting. More often than not, the accountant has an accreditation or outside credential of some type above and beyond the college degree. This is normally the certified public accountant credential. Most organizations are very serious about the policies and directives of accounting and budgeting because it deals with profit and loss. Failing to pay attention to the accounting and budget process normally results in the demise of the company. The fundamental fiscal strategic policy of any organization, even if unwritten, is to live within the budget to maximize profit or to ensure the delivery of goods and services. The budget process has its very own policy-making process that occurs in a regular cycle. It is essential that security leaders take part in this process and communicate the value of the security function to the overall profit and advancement of the organization as a whole. Decisions made during the policy-making process of the budget cycle can have an effect on future policy options in all other areas. The reality of budgeting is that there will always be limited resources and policy choices will be made sometimes abruptly to ensure that the resources last the entire budget period.

It is universally understood that to run out of money is a very bad thing. The cost of fighting on two fronts during World War II cost the United States almost $250 million a day. At the start of 1945, the U.S. government was running out of money to prosecute the war and the nation had endured six war bond drives already. The government's salvation was a photo of the Marines raising a flag on Mount Suribachi during the battle of Iwo Jima. The photo resonated with the public and President Franklin D. Roosevelt tapped into this and ordered the surviving members home immediately to headline the seventh war bond drive, which was a resounding success. It seems very odd to think that something as simple as a budget problem could cause problems in the closing months of the war, but it was a real concern. The simple message is that everything an organization, any organization, does relies completely on having a way to pay for operations.

Where the strategic policy on budgeting is almost intuitive, that is spend only what you bring in, the operational policies of budget and accounting tend to be complex, strict, and allowing minimal discretion. These operational policies governing the financial aspects are normally common and accepted among all organizations and driven by law and business realities. These policies fall under the domain of the chief financial officer or treasurer and are proven and conservative. Thus the issue with budgeting itself is not the lack of directives but the failure to follow them.

There are few cases where budgets are more spelled out than in government. Budgeting in governmental organizations is not only a critical part of the duties of its organizational leaders, but it is also a sacred trust. Like any policy-making process, there are stakeholders involved, and the process can often bring visceral responses showing that the stakes are real and immediately identifiable. Budget decisions are rarely easy, and the political maneuvering for a share of the finite budget resources can be intense. The winners and losers in a budget process see a material gain or loss. These have tangible effects on people and the political aspects of policy making are of significant concern.

The budget process provides a fine example of the multiple streams theory that we discussed in Chapter 1. As a quick recap, the multiple streams theory of policy making says that in order for a policy to be made, there must be a problem stream, a solution stream (also known as a policy stream), and a political stream. The political stream refers to the political will to employ the solution stream. The multiple streams theory came about as a result of the struggle to explain why clearly poor policy decisions were being made. Simple policy theory posits that when a problem occurs, solutions would be considered, and the most rational choice would be made. The most rational choice means the one that has the best outcome for the organization as the goal. In a budget-related multiple stream analysis, the problem is almost always not enough money. The probable solution streams usually involve either reductions in staff or service or other ways to economize or locate other revenue streams. But as with any analysis of policy options, there will be those options that are possible though not probable. Possibility and probability in this case is related to the most reasonable.

The problem in budget policy making occurs in the political stream of the process. Often the probable and most reasonable solution to budget issues are the most distasteful in a political sense. In this situation, stakeholders with the most influence will leverage this to protect themselves from adverse budget decisions that may not be in the best interest of the organization. For example, sometimes policy decisions are made that are unmistakably contrary to the strategic policy of the organization. It would make sense for the chief executive to address a budget shortfall by selecting a solution stream action that would balance out the shortfall. In reality, organizational chief executives are under enormous pressure to avoid policy decisions that impact the most influential stakeholders. This can lead to questionable policy options being viewed as viable choices. The following case study is an example of how a bad solution can also get political support and become policy.

CASE STUDY: BUDGET? WHAT BUDGET?

The State of New Jersey operates on a July 1 through June 30 fiscal year. The budget must be balanced at both the beginning and end of the process. The budget process is started when the departments of the state assemble their budget requests after being provided data and instructions from the office of management and budget. These budget requests go to the governor, who makes budget determinations and then forwards the recommendations, some of which may have been amended, to the legislature. The legislature then vets these budget requests in committees and, if necessary, makes changes and then returns them to the legislature. The legislature then votes on them and submits these final products as an appropriations act back to the governor. The governor then has the option to sign or exercise veto powers. Once signed, the act becomes law (Office of Management and Budget, 2014). This process assures that the policy goals of the state are supported by the means to pay for them. Yet, despite this well-thought-out process, the New Jersey has faced significant budget shortfall on a routine basis. These budget shortfalls constitute a problem, and the activation of our first stream in the multiple streams theory.

The budget problem is nothing new. It results from the tradition of failing to make honest budget choices during the formal budget process. The State of New Jersey routinely faces dire annual financial situations. This problem is mostly complicated by policy choices, known as *gimmicks*, to balance the state budget. The choice of a gimmick would seem to be irrational but these gimmicks were used, and continue to be used, for the sake of political expediency. The reason, of course, is that austerity policy choices are very unpopular with voters. Therefore politicians, when given the policy option of reducing the budget or working some budget magic, have almost without exception chosen the less politically painful alternative. It illustrates the impact political considerations have when picking a policy solution to a problem. What is more surprising is that the political concerns have outweighed well-known and well-established best practices of budgeting.

The political factor in public budgeting policy in New Jersey is particularly troubling. It has become rampant and has resulted in the failure of effective budgetary rules to constrain policy decisions that are against the best interest of the state. The New Jersey state budget process is straightforward. The state uses the budget process to further the accomplishment of goals (strategic policy). These goals may be required by law or they may come as a result of public demand translated to legislative action or political influence.

The process begins when the budgetary ends are established. In budgetary terminology, *ends* are the public policy goals of the state. To meet these ends, the means are provided though budgeting. *Means* are the budgetary term for the money to pay for the ends. The budget process relies on information streams to identify resources (means) and to set priorities (ends). In New Jersey, the designated ends must match the means precisely. If this process is out of balance, then the ends or the means must be adjusted. This is a legal obligation based in the New Jersey Constitution. This simple requirement (balanced budget) and simple process (ends and means) is sadly vulnerable to manipulation. Manipulation occurs when an overdeveloped political power exercises too much influence. In New Jersey, this has resulted in the evolution of tactics to avoid the consequences of failing to keep the process in balance.

Data obtained from the State of New Jersey, from New Jersey public employee unions, from the New Jersey League of Municipalities, other advocacy and professional groups, from media sources, and legal filings provide evidence that elected officials purposely engaged in practices to circumvent the requirement to balance the state budget. That is, everyone in the state knows that when it comes to budget policy choices, the leaders of the state are not making decisions that follow the strategic policy. The State of New Jersey, as directed by successive legislators and governors, has repeatedly abandoned budgeting best practices and has used financial gimmicks to avoid making budget choices in both good and bad economic environments. These actions are in stark contrast to commonly accepted best policy practices in government budgeting where actually balancing the budget is required, that is, only spending as much as the organization brings in. The practice is so commonplace that budget gimmicks, including misrepresentation of revenue streams, have become a de facto structural part of New Jersey budgeting policy for at least the past 24 years, contrary to established balanced budget laws.

In discussing the budget policy decisions of the state government, I must first define the legal background that has created the environment that has led to the institutionalized practice of budgetary gimmickry. There are various groups that have all contributed to the political dominance in the policy-making process and their role and impact are described.

The State of New Jersey is one of the states that have a strict balanced budget requirement, with all other states having a requirement for balanced budgets of varying degrees. The intent of a balanced budget law is noble, and there is data indicating the stricter the balanced budget requirement, the more likely that a state will weather up-and-down business cycles (Mitchell & Tuszynski, 2012). New Jersey is constitutionally required to have a balanced budget and according to the United States Advisory Commission on Intergovernmental Relations, New Jersey is among the strictest in the nation in this requirement. But New Jersey is an outlier. It has been less able to weather the financial cycles as evidenced by the ongoing financial ratings downgrades by the major financial firms (Schwarz, 2014). Although research data and common sense indicate that having a requirement to only spend as much as you take in is a good thing, in practice, it has created a situation where politicians get very creative in skirting the requirement (Eucalitto, 2013).

The New Jersey budget history is rife with the use of budget policy employing gimmicks. The responsibility for this policy decision falls on the branches of government and on the special interests of the state and to a degree, the very citizens themselves, who remain partisan in their election of officials.

Special Interests

Organized public employee labor unions have been complicit in the use of gimmicks, which have resulted in the undermining of their pensions. The public sector in New Jersey is dominated by powerful unions that have been successful in gaining favorable benefits packages from political allies. Political influence is not always limited to overt politicians. In every organization, influence can be exerted indirectly to hijack the political stream. Benefits have been largely out of view, yet have grown to a significant portion of the state's budget (Osband, 2012). Costs of benefits were hidden from the public through creative accounting that set the return on pension investments at more than 8%.

A fallacy that has allowed not just the public employees to delude themselves as to the sustainability of the pension but encouraged raiding of the funds by politicians. It is important to take a moment to realize that the budget policy choice in this case was to lie. This is never an acceptable policy choice, particularly in the protective services!

Governor

The power of the governor can have an effect on the influence of budgetary policy. The impact correlates to the executive authority vested in a particular governor (Barrilleaux & Berkman, 2003). The governor of the Garden State is one of the most powerful in the nation. The governor is the sole appointment maker and he or she has veto power, including line item veto. The governorship is the only position of power directly elected by all of the citizens of the state. Direct election provides sufficient incentive to take actions that appeal to the populist notions of the citizenry, notwithstanding future consequences. This incentive, combined with the power of the office along with the constitutional mandate to balance the budget, creates a significant tension – a tension that has resulted in a long line of governors closing budget gaps with one shot deals and other gimmicks (Luppino-Esposito, 2014).

In 1991, the New Jersey Turnpike purchased 4.4 miles of property from the state allowing then Governor Jim Florio to plug a $400 million gap in the state budget. In 1997, the genesis of the public pension crisis began when Governor Christine Todd Whitman took $2.8 billion from the public employees' pension system to fund tax cuts. In 2002, Governor Jim McGreevey raised taxes on corporations and doubled the cigarette tax. McGreevey also skipped paying back the $2.9 billion *borrowed* from the public employees' pension system. In 2004, Governor McGreevey issued $1.9 billion in bonds to close the budget gap. This measure was declared unconstitutional by the New Jersey Supreme Court, yet inexplicably, it is permitted to stand. Each succeeding administration has engaged in similar gimmicks, each time edging New Jersey closer to financial ruin. These examples all demonstrate the conflicting outcomes in contrast to the well-defined organizational strategic policy of fiscal responsibility. In every case, the strategic policy was overridden by the operational policy adopted and implemented.

Sometimes budget policy decisions were made that did actually live up to the strategic policy. Governor Chris Christie made a platform of dealing with the abuses of the budget and decried gimmick use. Governor Christie called out not only politicians, but interest groups, such as public employee labor unions, for their contribution to the fiscal situation brought on by decades of poor budget policy decisions. His platform asserted that the underlying budget problem that necessitated budget gimmicks was, in Governor Christie's estimation, public employee pensions and benefits. This resonated with the citizens of the state, appealing to populist notions, and helped create a wave of legislation designed to overhaul the pension system and reign in benefits. Appearing to finally be a reformer dead set on living up to the constitutional balanced budget requirement, legislation was passed to fix the problem and to force the state to live up to its obligations to deal with budget issues now. The policy solution was that in return for concessions on pension and benefits for public employees, the state would guarantee payment into the pension funds. But follow-on budgets presented the same problem stream – a shortfall. When faced with a budget deficit himself, the governor simply used a legal maneuver to avoid paying (Ein, 2014). The solution stream was different this time around – simply not pay into the pensions as promised by the previous policy and to fight it out in court. In this case, the obvious solution streams would have included paying some of the promised money, paying all of it, and cutting somewhere else, or any combination of these. Instead, the political stream drove the solution stream, resulting in a policy decision that not only went against the strategic policy of the state but against the governor's own platform.

Aside from this pension sleight of hand, the governor also engaged in the misrepresentation of revenue projections and creative accounting practices, such as delaying the property tax rebates disbursement from May until August, effectively adopting a policy of pushing the deficit to the next budget (Zernike, 2013). At the end of the day, the executive branch has the best chance of preventing budget deficits through the line item veto. One of the reasons for vesting such strong power in the executive branch regarding vetoes is to ensure that the budget is executed according to constitutional requirements. The power vested is implicitly linked to serving the constitution and acting in good faith ("About NJ Government," 2015). It is troubling that the last opportunity to live up to the constitutional balanced budget requirement is lost because of motivations that are political. The governor could simply veto line items to force a balanced budget. This has yet to happen. Much like the legislature, the political motivations trump both fiscal and constitutional policies. No one wants to say no and risk the ire of the voters.

Courts

People have sued the state to prevent the use of budgetary gimmicks in the past and have succeeded. Yet the court failed to provide remedy. For example, when the state issued bond prospectus materials between 2001 and 2007, they misrepresented their contributions to the state retirement system. This fraud was caught in 2007, and the state was prosecuted by the Securities and Exchange Commission (SEC). The state could have been required to properly fund the system as laws prohibit the comingling of retirement funds and general funds. Yet the outcome was that the state merely reached a settlement with the SEC and paid a fine. The opportunity to remove the incentive to be creative with the budget was missed.

In another case, the state attempted to securitize a settlement with the four major cigarette producers. This settlement provided a large monetary windfall for New Jersey, which was one of 46 states to receive billions of dollars more than 25 years. Members of the legislature objected to issuing bonds secured by this settlement to balance the budget and won in the New Jersey Supreme Court. Yet the courts, despite acknowledging the unconstitutional nature of the action, chose to prospectively outlaw the act. By choosing sunbursting instead of holding the governor accountable, they also became complicit and missed another opportunity to remove the incentive to use budget gimmicks. In fact, the use of gimmicks that serve to saddle future generations with debt in order to balance a budget have been soundly rejected by the courts. In *N.J. Sports & Exposition Auth. v. McCrane*, the court held: "one Legislature from incurring debts which subsequent Legislatures would be obliged to pay, without prior approval by public referendum." This defining of the constitutional debt limitation clause details in explicit language the prohibition against mortgaging the future to pay for the present.

Legislature

The New Jersey legislature has the typical power of the purse that is common in the United States. Along with this power, comes the responsibility to ensure a balanced budget each year as required by the state constitution. This requirement of a balanced budget in a single year has been upheld by the New Jersey courts in such cases as *City of Camden v. Byrne*. In *City of Camden*, Camden, along with others, challenged the constitutional requirement for a single balanced budget. The court refuted any interpretation that would allow for flexibility in application of the article. This underscores the rigidity of the balanced budget requirement, yet highlights the supremacy of the legislature to allocate any funds that fall within the budget as it sees fit.

This interpretation places authority and responsibility with the legislature to control the purse strings. Yet the legislature has been complicit in allowing the circumventing of the balanced budget requirement. It has played a major part in the previous gimmicks and most recently, allowed the governor to pass a $32.5 billion budget that includes skipped pension payments and raiding of funds (Ein, 2014). At the end of the day, the public policy for balancing the state budget is quite simply to live up to the intent of New Jersey state law.[1]

Barring action to enforce the strategic policy or operational policy directive, it is unrealistic to believe that the governor and other elected officials would live up to the law of the state. The body of past practice has shown this to be unlikely. If desired, the governor could unilaterally live up to the strategic policy and simply use the power of the veto to bring the budget into balance and negate the need for gimmicks. To date, this has not happened.

In light of the effect of disproportionately represented stakeholders and the pervasive and damaging influence of politics, New Jersey's strategic policy solution to this situation should be to amend the constitutional provision to specifically reject gimmicks that are used to circumvent the state constitution. This remedy would run into a significant challenge on political grounds. Getting support is unlikely, as it would place limits on the executive and the legislative branches of state government. As sad as this situation is, it is a clear lesson on how even a very simple and understood budget policy can fall victim to creative operational budget policy making.

---

[1] New Jersey Constitution, Article 8, § 2, par. 2 and par. 3: "No money shall be drawn from the State treasury but for appropriations made by law. All moneys for the support of the State government and for all other State purposes as far as can be ascertained or reasonably foreseen, shall be provided for in one general appropriation law covering one and the same fiscal year; except that when a change in the fiscal year is made, necessary provision may be made to effect the transition. No general appropriation law or other law appropriating money for any State purpose shall be enacted if the appropriation contained therein, together with all prior appropriations made for the same fiscal period, shall exceed the total amount of revenue on hand and anticipated which will be available to meet such appropriations during such fiscal period, as certified by the Governor."

This case study is a good example of how pervasive the political factor is in budget policy. It is not uncommon to also see these types of creative budgeting policy choices occurring in the private sector in much smaller organizations. One only has to look at the corporate financial scandals involving WorldCom, Enron, or the mortgage industry and the housing "bubble" in the early part of the century.

One of the key takeaways from the case study is that even in an organization where the strategic policy carries the weight of constitutional law, the temptation to make bad choices because of political reasons is just too much to ignore. When it comes to private sector organizations, the temptation is no less. This is a bit disturbing when you consider that the consequences for making poor policy choices for political reasons does not break any laws. The watch word for our purposes is "caution." Policy making that deals with budgets can be a land mine for organizational leaders. It is critical to recognize that when analyzing policy options in these situations, there may be forces at play to encourage policies that go against the interests of the organization. The tendency in a budget process is to focus on the short term, which is to be expected, as budgets are short-term plans. This policy decision, however, may go against the long-term interests or the strategic policy of the organization. As a leader and a policy professional, it is expected that you will not allow the analysis to be stunted to a narrow focus on short-term outcomes. At the very minimum, the long-term effects and alternative policy solutions must be introduced. From a functional perspective, the goal is to get all of the facts on the table to provide as full a situational awareness as possible. The decision maker of the organization will pick a solution and it will become policy. It is your job to give the decision maker as much reliable information as possible, even if it unpopular.

BUDGET BATTLES, TACTICS, AND SOLUTIONS

Aside from your part in providing information in the policy-making process, you may find yourself having to advocate for your part of the organization. This can be particularly problematic in the private security field. There has always been a tension between the security department and the accounting department during the budget policy-making process. The reason is simple math. Accounting essentially is the study of plus and minus. Some departments or units are in the plus category, meaning that they bring in profit. Others, such as the security department, are in the minus column. The security function is a cost center not a profit center, so accountants naturally want to limit costs and maximize profits. At budget time, security managers are always searching for ways to justify their cost. But how? Security is always an attractive target and will always be unless the value of its contribution to the bottom line can be fully demonstrated.

This reminds me of a story that happened during a particularly lean budget year. Thinking that the accountants would be swayed by the impact the security officers had on loss, the security manager proudly reported that thefts were down a certain percentage, which equated to a dollar amount. The reduction resulted from the introduction of a program of giving security staff members stickers that could be placed on unsecured property inside the building. While on patrol, officers would affix bright orange "Gotcha" stickers to unattended valuables, which was a tangible reminder to be more conscious. This coincided with an employee education program regarding theft prevention and personal accountability. As I said, it worked well because it raised awareness and the security manager was proud to make it a part of the budget proposal. The only response received back from the budget committee was if thefts are down, why do we need the same amount of security funding? The point of the story is that when it comes to cost centers and times are lean, security departments will always be the target for cuts.

So how can policy help in a lean budget time? It can help in two ways. The first, as we have discussed, is to provide information that supports the premise that cutting the security budget will go against the strategic policy of the organization. The second, which is likely to have more impact, is to employ operational policy so as to diversify the security department and to make its role invaluable. This concept is known as *providing a value-added service*, and this type of tactic is within the operational policy-making authority. To illustrate a value-added service, the following section uses an example from the fire service.

Value-Added Service

Most fire departments are reactionary organizations in that although they are true necessities, they are only employed for fire-related incidents. Unlike police or security forces, they have no ongoing proactive patrol function; they respond to calls for service. I am certainly not downplaying the importance of the fire service. They are a critical part of homeland security and essential to community resiliency. For the purposes of this analysis, I am looking at them strictly as cost centers.

From a cost-benefit position, fire departments needed to provide enhanced justification for their budgets because they recognized that they are a cost center. As early as the 1960s, fire departments determined they could provide a value-added service through assumption of emergency medical services (EMS). Fire departments were quick to recognize that they were positioned to take on the mission, as they were staffed 24/7 and were located throughout the community, allowing for a more rapid response than contracted services or volunteers. In fact, in the contemporary budget environment, nearly all U.S. firefighters have some medical training, and virtually all of the 200 largest cities in the United States have the fire service providing EMS. This is an example of a value-added success story and can be replicated by security departments with a little creativity. By engaging in value-added services the security leader should focus on performing functions that can be done with minimal impact to the operations and can be effected with a minor policy change. For example, if the security department has a motorized patrol, they can also provide value-added functions, such as jumpstarting dead batteries, assisting with lockouts, and courtesy transports. These value-added actions should be communicated as supporting and improving employee efficiency, morale, and safety. The idea is to clearly and persuasively describe the return on investment that the organization receives from every penny spent on the security budget. Because the security department helps employees with their car issues, employees are returned to productive work quicker, resulting in better performance to the company. Also, because an employee knows that a courtesy transport may be available in inclement weather, the employee may stay later to finish a project rather than trying to get out ahead of the weather.

In addition, when dealing with budget issues, it is critical that the security leader learn how to be a nonpartisan politician. It is important to increase the security function to the status of critical stakeholder in the organization. During budget times, other departments will be exercising as much influence as possible, and security professionals must be prepared to follow suit. It is essential that a security leader understand exactly which security functions are essential and which ones are less essential. This security capability and responsibility audit should be systematic and honest and should detail if the function is critical, essential, or discretionary. Having this level of detail will allow the security leader to negotiate at the budget table. For example, security patrols and staffing key posts is a critical function. Providing courtesy transports or responding to employee locations to take reports is discretionary. When faced with losing these discretionary services the budget policy decision maker might be convinced to cut in other places. This is nothing more than using a communications strategy to convey accurately the impact of cuts to the security budget to decision makers. The goal is not to protect security at all costs but to ensure that the department gets the resources necessary to perform its job effectively. To this end, the security leader can break security policies into best practices, acceptable practices, and minimally acceptable practices. In essence, prior to the budget process, the security leader should identify which polices can be enforced or acted on relative to the budget allocation. The best practices level allows for the implementation of all policies, whereas the minimally acceptable level will allow for only the most critical policies to be implemented. This is a management tool used to provide a realistic view of what can be accomplished in relation to funding and can trigger policy adjustments. Caution should be used in publication of this information for security and reputational reasons. The point is to ensure that the security leader knows exactly the effect on policy implementation the budget will have. For example, let us say an organization has a strategic policy that states that no unauthorized personnel will be permitted to enter the building and an operational policy that accomplishes this through identification checks at all public entrances. If the budget no longer provides for the assigned post to perform checks, then it cannot be accomplished. This is information that can be made available to the decision maker and if still unfunded, the policy must be altered, perhaps to a random inspection.

Policy and budget are intimate and mutually supporting and as such, policy makers must recognize the ever-changing landscape and be aware that changes in one have the potential to impact the other.

PRACTICE POINTERS

- As an organizational leader, it is essential to recognize the duality of a budget as both a policy in its own right and how it affects every other policy choice through funding.
- A budget is nothing more than a plan to provide the means to advance the goals of an organization. It is important to ensure that policy makers, especially during budget policy-making season, understand the value of the security function to overall success of the organization.
- Understanding the strategic policy of budgeting is almost intuitive. Spend only what you bring in. Problems occur when there are budget shortfalls and resources must be shifted. It is critical that funding be expended when needed and for its intended purpose. The tactic of holding back money in the budget can result in redistribution.
- Do not rely on organizational executives or budget professionals to always act in the best interests of the organization, regardless of how clear and compelling the strategic policy. Ensure that you do not enable counterproductive policy decisions.
- Do not be afraid to take on additional traditionally nonsecurity-related functions. These functions, if not a drain on core security functions, can be salvation during tough budget cycles. Focus on services that are low impact on operation effectiveness but popular with stakeholders. This is known as value-added service and is an effective way to insulate the security budget from cuts.

Chapter Recap

- Budget policy affects all facets of the organizational operation including training, supervision, and strategic and operational policy options.
- Revenue and expenses must be managed, and organizations that do not have budgets policies are highly inefficient and cannot survive.
- Budgets are considered the fiscal road map for the organization and have strategic and operational policy aspects of their own.
- Budget shortfalls bring out the worst in organizational leaders, and the political stream has a disproportionate effect on policy making.
- The pressure during times of budget shortfalls can cause organizational policy makers to abandon the strategic policy for a quick fix or a budget gimmick. This occurs even in organizations with extremely clear strategic policy.
- Security is a cost center and not a profit center; as such, security will always be vulnerable to cuts during budget season.
- To counter the issue of security being a cost center, the organization can engage in operational policy changes that allow for value-added activities to be performed by the organization. These value-added programs can be very popular and discourage budget cuts.

BIBLIOGRPHY

About NJ Government. (2015, December 10). Retrieved from the official website of the state of New Jersey. <http://www.state.nj.us/nj/gov/understand/>.

Advisory Commission on Intergovernmental Relations, & Anderson, G. (1987). *Fiscal discipline in the federal system: National reform and the experience of the states* (A-107). Retrieved from: <http://digital.library.unt.edu/ark:/67531/metadc1449/>.

Aydlott, J. A. (2007). *The quick guide to small business budgeting*. Lakeside, CA: San Diego Business Accounting Solutions.

Barrilleaux, C., & Berkman, M. (2003). Do governors matter? Budgeting rules and the politics of state policymaking. *Political Research Quarterly, 56*(4), 409–417.

Brennan, J., & Mattice, L. (2013). Communicate, communicate, communicate. *Security, 50*(5), 24.

Campbell, A. L., & Sances, M. W. (2013, November 1). State fiscal policy during the great recession: Budgetary impacts and policy responses. *Annals of the American Academy of Political and Social Science, 650*(1), 252–273.

Chiaramonte, M. (2003). Learn to be a politician without partisanship. *Fire Chief, 47*(11) 26–26, 28.

City of Camden v. Byrne, 82 N.J.L. 133, 151 (1980).

Dean, A., & Messoline, M. (2011, February). Fire-based EMS: The solution for an ailing system? *Fire Engineering, 164*, 32–38.

Ein, M. (2014, June 30). *Christie signs $32.5b New Jersey budget with vetoes.* Press of Atlantic City. Retrieved from: <http://www.pressofatlanticcity.com/news/ap/christie-signs-b-new-jersey-budget-with-vetoes/article_c5882168-0042-11e4-a25c-001a4bcf887a.html>.

Eucalitto, C. (2013, April 4). Unbalanced: Why state balanced budget requirements are not enough. Retrieved from: <http://www.statebudgetsolutions.org/publications/detail/unbalanced-why-state-balanced-budget-requirements-are-not-enough>.

Evans, B. (2003). It's time to embrace 360 degrees customer service. *Fire Chief, 47*(7), 18.

Fay, J. (2011). *Contemporary security management.* Amsterdam: Butterworth-Heinemann.

Gates, S. (2008). IT budget relief strategies. *Information Today, 25*, 21.

Hairman, R., & Lucaites, J. L. (2002). Performing civic identity: The iconic photograph of the flag raising on Iwo Jima. *Quarterly Journal of Speech, 88*(4), 363–392.

International Association of Fire Fighters (IAFF). (1997). *Emergency medical services.* Washington, DC: IAFF.

Johnson, J. (2010, May 1). Offer value-added services to your customers: The Ginsu phenomenon & the fire service. *Firefighter Nation* Retrieved from <http://www.firefighternation.com/article/command-leadership/offer-value-added-services-your-customers>.

Krupnikov, Y., & Shipan, C. (2012, December 1). Measuring gubernatorial budgetary power: A new approach. *State Politics and Policy Quarterly, 12*(4), 438–455.

Luppino-Esposito, J. (2014, January 3). The worst state budget gimmicks of 2013. Retrieved from: <http://www.statebudgetsolutions.org/publications/detail/the-worst-state-budget-gimmicks-of-2013>.

Matejka, K., & Murphy, A. (2005). *Making change happen on time, on target, on budget.* Mountain View, CA: Davies-Black.

McCrie, R. D. (2007). *Security operations management.* Amsterdam: Butterworth-Heinemann.

Mitchell, M., & Tuszynski, N. (2012). Institutions and state spending an overview. *Independent Review, 17*(1), 35–49.

N.J. Sports & Exposition Auth. v. McCrane, 61 N.J. 1, 13–14 (1972).

Office of Management and Budget. (2014, December 9). The state budget process. Retrieved from: <http://www.state.nj.us/treasury/omb/ReadersGuide/budgetprocess.shtml>.

Osband, K. (2012, August 3). Failing fiscal federalism. *The European Financial Review*, 30–33. Retrieved from: <http://www.europeanfinancialreview.com/?p=1467>.

Russ, H. (2014, September 4). Fitch downgrades New Jersey credit rating on fiscal concerns. *Reuters New Service* Retrieved from: <http://www.reuters.com/article/2014/09/05/newjersey-ratings-fitch-idUSL1N0R62JO20140905>.

Schwarz, H. (2014, September 8). New Jersey's credit rating has been downgraded more under Chris Christie than any other governor. *The Washington Post* Retrieved from: <http://www.washingtonpost.com/blogs/govbeat/wp/2014/09/08/new-jerseys-credit-rating-has-been-downgraded-more-under-chris-christie-than-any-other-governor/>.

State Budget Crisis Task Force. (2012). Report of the State Budget Crisis Task Force: New Jersey Report. Retrieved from: <http://www.statebudgetcrisis.org/wpcms/wp-content/images/2012-10-22-New-Jersey-Report-Final.pdf.

Varlotta, L. E., Jones, B. C., & Schuh, J. H. (2010). Developing budget models, communication strategies, and relationships to mitigate the pain of tough economic times. *New Directions for Student Services, 129,* 81–87.

Villines, J. C. (2010). Training…asset or risk? *Security, 47*(10), 44–48, 50.

Zernike, K. (2013, October 30). Christie embraces budget strategies he scorned as a candidate. *The New York Times* Retrieved from: <http://www.nytimes.com/2013/10/30/nyregion/christie-embraces-budget-strategies-he-scorned-as-a-candidate.html?pagewanted=all&_r=0>.

Index